CHERO EXTRANJERO

FOREIGN FRIEND

Ninety-one days
in Central America

DARREN HOWMAN

Chero Extranjero (Foreign Friend) copyright © Darren Howman
First published as a book June 2024 by Everytime Press

ISBN: 978-1-923000-31-5

BP#00128

All rights reserved by the author and publisher. Except for brief excerpts used for review or scholarly purposes, no part of this book may be reproduced in any manner whatsoever without express written consent of the publisher or the author.
Any historical inaccuracies are made in error.

Everytime Press
32 Meredith Street
Sefton Park SA 5083
Australia

Email: everytimepress@outlook.com
Website: https://everytimepress.com/
Everytime Press catalogue: https://everytimepress.com/everytime-press-catalogue/

Front cover original photo – Terminal de Oriente, San Salvador – taken by the author using an Agfa disposable film camera
Front cover design by Matt Potter
All photos copyright © Darren Howman
Original author portrait by Rob Conibear, oil on canvas, used by permission

Also available as an ePub eBook
ISBN: 978-1-923000-33-9
Also available as a Kindle eBook
ISBN: 978-1-923000-35-3

Everytime Press is a member of the
Bequem Publishing collective
https://www.bequempublishing.com/

for

Conchi, the Teachers

and the Pupils of

Margarita Duran School, 2013

In no particular order I would like to thank the following for making this book possible:

My wife Varsha for always supporting and believing in me.

My publisher Matt Potter and editor Michelle Elvy for their painstaking work to make this a reality and to everyone mentioned in this book for ultimately making the story what it is.

A special heartfelt thanks goes to Conchi Castro for everything she did to make my stay in El Salvador an unforgettable one.

Travel Warning
to inform U.S. citizens about the security situation in El Salvador:

Crime and violence are serious problems throughout the country. In 2011, El Salvador had the second highest murder rate in the world: In 2012, a truce between El Salvador's two principal street gangs: Marasalvatrucha13 and 18th Street, contributed to a decline in the homicide rate. However, the sustainability of the decline is unclear, and the truce had little impact on robbery, assaults, and other violent crimes. In March 2012, as a result of an administrative review of the security situation, Peace Corps El Salvador substantially reduced the number of its volunteers in the country.

22 U.S. citizens have been murdered in El Salvador since January 2010. During the same time period, 230 U.S. citizens reported having their passports stolen. Armed robberies of climbers and hikers in El Salvador's national parks are common, and the Embassy strongly recommends engaging the services of a local guide certified by the national or local tourist authority when hiking in back country areas, even within the national parks.

The Government of El Salvador lacks sufficient resources to properly investigate and prosecute cases and to deter violent crime. Crimes such as arms trafficking, murder-for-hire, carjacking, extortion, armed robbery, rapes, and other aggravated assaults. El Salvador, a country of roughly six million people, has hundreds of known street gangs totalling more than 20,000 members. Gangs and other criminal elements roam freely day and night, targeting affluent areas for burglaries, and gang members are quick to engage in violence if resisted.

Extortion is a particularly serious and common crime in El Salvador. For example, in 2011, a 2 year old U.S. citizen was kidnapped from the home of his grandparents in El Salvador by 8 to 10 armed men. Ransom demands made to family members in both El Salvador and the United States were traced back to a local prison used exclusively to incarcerate gang members.

U.S. citizens should be vigilant of their surroundings at all times. Whenever possible, travel in groups of two or more people. Avoid wearing jewellery, and do not carry large sums of money or display cash, ATM/credit cards, or other valuables. Avoid walking at night in most areas of El Salvador, and do not walk alone near beaches, historic ruins, or trails. Incidents of crime along roads, including carjacking, are common in El Salvador. Motorists should avoid travelling at night and always drive with their doors locked to deter potential robberies at traffic lights and on congested downtown streets. Travel on public transportation, especially buses, both within and outside the capital, is risky and not recommended.

PREFACE

It started with an old *National Geographic* in the back of a charity shop. 'El Mirador' — a place buried deep in the Petén jungle in northern Guatemala and mysteriously deserted 500 years ago. The article described this lost city as 'The cradle of Mayan civilisation'.

The few hours I had spent exploring San Salvador in 2009 left me unsatisfied. Mainly frequented by the flotsam of news reporters, missionaries and drug traffickers, it was an often-avoided part of Central America.

By now, my Spanish was growing rusty. The sporadic lessons I had been trying to keep on top of in New Zealand were not really helping. My semi-fluent tongue was forgetting the feel of the words.

El Mirador, then?

If I could hike to this city and find a volunteer programme to help brush up on my Spanish, the trip would have at least two purposes.

A few days before setting off, I read the U.S government travel warning on El Salvador.

I wished I hadn't.

But I stuck with the plan and zipped the last zip on my pack. Perhaps to prove the warnings wrong. Perhaps to prove myself wrong.

CONTENTS

1. OUTWARD BOUND 7
2. THE JUNGLE HIKE 33
3. CROSS COUNTRY 75
4. EL SALVADOR BEGINNINGS 93
5. EL GOLFO DE FONSECA 129
6. BACK TO SCHOOL 145
7. HIGH COUNTRY 183
8. TECLEÑO 209
9. NICARAGUA 233

EPILOGUE 285

1
OUTWARD BOUND

DEPARTURES AND ARRIVALS

When I made the decision to return to Latin America in 2013 after my 2009 extended stay, I booked the best set of flights I could find. 'Best' meaning 'cheapest'. I was filled with excitement and ready to go. This was well before I'd met the German girls or the Brit couple, well before I'd plunged into the jungles of Guatemala. And well before I knew just how much of my Spanish I'd lost.

*

The cut price airfare to get me to the small town of Flores in northern Guatemala involves five flights, six airports and a total duration of approximately fifty-six flying hours, the last of which is in a light aircraft. Customs and airport transfers would add to that huge hour count, but by how many, I wasn't sure.

The first flight, handled by Air Tahiti Nui, departs Auckland, New Zealand and touches down to refuel on the small group of Tahitian islands halfway across the Pacific.

Newlywed honeymooners fill the majority of the seats, eager to begin the romantic package deals under their straw roofed, stilt prop houses that hover above a turquoise ocean. They excitedly push and shove to exit the confines of the aircraft. I wait at the gate with a fresh crop of newlyweds while the plane is cleaned and topped up with fuel.

Re-boarding the flight, now bound for Los Angeles, I discover my new flying companions are not so excited as the previous bunch.

The next set of passengers are far from Tahitian honeymooners. They are replaced with a new – and tired – group when I board the L.A. to Mexico City flight.

"Good evening, sir, please take your seat," two women repeat robotically to each passenger in a condescending tone while hurriedly herding us to our seats for a safety speech.

I am flying with Alaska Air. The grey-haired, has-been flight attendants are dressed in gaudy brown cardigans, tweed skirts and cream collared shirts. They stare at us unwelcomely as we board the aircraft. It's clear they hate their jobs and look forward to their impending retirement.

My row receives the undivided attention of one of these women. "OK!" she barks at us while two hard nipples poke through her sweater like gun barrels. "Those who are sitting in the emergency aisle – I need your FULL attention! You'll be in charge of opening the door in an emergency!" She commands respect, showing us how to unlock the door if the plane goes down.

"Do you understand me?" she barks.

Fucking hell, I think to myself as we all nod like naughty school children.

"I need a verbal affirmation!" she barks again, turning her focus to the guy in front of me reading a paper.

"Please put the newspaper down, sir! … Sir!"

The woman is infuriated that he's not listening to her and pushes the top of the paper down with a long witchy finger. I'm reminded simultaneously of Roald Dahl's nasty headmistress Miss Trunchbull from his book *Matilda* and the film *Robocop*'s 'You have twenty seconds to comply' scene.

We all give a synchronised 'yes' to 'Robogran', avoiding 'six of the best' or, worse, being machine-gunned to pieces by her fake 1980s semi-automatic titties.

It's a night flight, and I reach for the buttons that will ease me into a slight recline for a bit of sleep. But no, it appears they have no such mechanism and I'm to stay bolt upright for the entire 3hr 40min flight. Still scared of being gunned down by Robogran for disobedience, I quietly shuffle into the most comfortable position I can muster. I've managed to sleep with shoulders and head on fold out trays a few times already.

No sooner am I drifting off, Robogran's leaning over me. "Sir … Sir! You must sit up," she snaps, adjusting her brown cardigan.

"For fuck's sake," I mutter as I slowly raise my head.

To confirm this being the shittiest airline in the world, we are fed a mismatched snack of puffed potato chips and ketchup. The packet contains four-and-a-half two-centimetre-long potato puffs the diameter of a chubby child's finger and the ketchup spits on my top as I tear it open.

This is what she got me up for?

The fold-out food tray is better used for sleeping on, in my opinion. I depart the plane with an empty stomach, a crooked neck and ketchup dribbles on my sweatshirt. I'm not entirely confident I'll ever see my bag again after the 'Alaska Air Experience'. I wonder if Guatemala City airport even has a luggage carousel. I decide not to worry, knowing I have no other choice than to forget about it until that point in the future.

Mexico City airport is a welcome surprise. Big shiny glass windows stretch from floor to ceiling and a plethora of food choices are a far cry from the images I remember of Mexico. It's a surprise they even let those Alaska Air jokers land here. Sports channels play on massive TV screens hanging above clean carpeted open lounges while well-dressed families sit slurping bright coloured smoothies.

I sit in the terminal and wait, and wait, and wait. The departures flicker on the digital board above me but my flight never appears. With only an hour until my plane leaves, I feel panic set in and I ask an airport staff member. She informs me I'm reading the wrong number on my ticket and should be in the other terminal. Panic washes over me and frantic, I rush there in a state, relieved to find the flight to Guatemala is delayed. I rub my sore eyes, exhausted from being awake for twenty-five hours.

The click of my seat belt is the last thing I remember, and I wake five hours later very appreciative that the Aeromexico flight attendants have left me alone. I think if they'd even tried to wake me up, their efforts would've been futile. From the window, the lush green jungle of Northern Guatemala floats by below. If I could just parachute out now, maybe I'd save a whole lot of time reaching my destination. I smile to myself, thinking of how quickly I'd die down there on my own.

The wheels hitting the runway in Guatemala City wake me. I'm not sure what to expect and, although excited, am far too tired to be navigating another busy airport. My previous experience in this city involved being locked inside a bus with a couple of annoying Peace Corps girls at a gas station due to it being too dangerous to get out.

The terminal seems much like any other: clean, tidy and relatively modern. I haven't spoken Spanish regularly in over two years and silently wait at the carousel, anxious to see my bag appear.

I watch as other passengers collect their belongings but my heart sinks as the conveyor slowly empties and shuts down. A group of armed security guards chat over by a pile of luggage lying against a wall. My nerves kick in as they all stare in my direction when I approach.

"No tengo mi equipaje."

I point at the carousel, nervously telling them my luggage is not there. They ignore me.

"¿Ustedes tiene algo mas?" I ask them if there is any more luggage.

"Si hombre, aqui," one begrudgingly answers me, lazily pointing with the barrel of his AR-15 to a pile that never made it to the conveyor belt.

Peeling back the pile of bags, I'm elated when I find mine at the bottom. Signs direct me down a shiny grey corridor to a money change desk and a pretty Guatemalan girl behind its bulletproof glass. Her makeup and black eyeliner cannot hide her nervous disposition as her boss stoops over her making sure she seals the deal. I'm tired, I need money and I'm not thinking straight. I remember the money changer at the Costa Rican border in 2009 who ripped me off, but surely this is as legit as it gets. Glass booths, a reputable exchange company and a man in a tie standing behind a woman in a uniform. Her quick-fire Spanish instantly tangles my brain in knots. My receptors are at low-battery level. Her mouth is moving in fast-forward and so are the words coming out of it, none of which I understand.

"Mas lento por favor," I say. I need her to speak slower.

She looks offended but I don't want to be ripped off. She slows her speech, but I'm still finding it hard to work out what's happening. She hands me a stack of quetzal notes while the guy in the tie puts his hand on her shoulder and smiles like a shifty car salesman. He directs me to the main concourse with his other hand, shooing me away as if I'm now loitering at his establishment.

The main waiting area masquerades as a cargo holding bay. The floor of the lofty aircraft hangar is covered in worn, red carpet tiles and has next to no seating. I sit down on the floor to count my notes and curse myself when I work out it's cost me twenty dollars to change seventy. Four plastic seats are positioned against a wall near the front sliding doors of the hangar. Two are occupied by security guards eating sandwiches who eyeball me as I approach. I change tack towards the exit doors that slide open automatically and am hit with an unnerving but familiar culture shock.

Round, short women in striped dresses sit kerbside selling cheese-crusted corn and hot tamales while a guy flicks a stack of money in my face.

"¡Cambio, amigo! Cambio, amigo!" he beckons to me in a husky voice, asking if I need money changed.

"No gracias, señor, pero. ¿Cuanto commission para 50?" I decline but ask his commission rate.

"Tres dolares." He confirms the $17 robbery I've just been subjected to inside the terminal.

Back in the hangar lounge, apart from the lack of seats, I really could be anywhere in the world.

In the last god-knows-how-many hours, I've transferred through five countries. The street scene just outside has been the only culture shock I've felt. I approach the Avianca desk to check in for my flight.

"¿Santa Elena?" The clerk asks.

"No, Flores," I reply.

"Si, Santa Elena," she repeats, handing me my ticket. "Es lo mismo." *It's the same.*

I leave confused and check the boarding time. It reads 6pm. I check my watch. I have seven hours to kill in the world's emptiest airport. Back at the boarding gate level, it's completely empty of life albeit for two unloved fast-food restaurants. It's a stark contrast to the brightly illuminated choices of Mexico City airport. The suspiciously KFC-looking 'Pollo Campero' has a large lit-up menu board above the head of a girl sitting impassively at the counter. With eyes glued to the screen of her little Motorola phone, I startle her.

"Pure de papas por favor." I ask for the mashed potato pot.

13

"¿Solo esto?" Is that it? she asks, looking confused.

"Si, gracias," I confirm.

She slowly lifts herself from her chair and hands me a thimble-sized pot with a miniature spoon stuck in it.

Staring at the tiny receptacle pinched between my thumb and forefinger, I can't help but chuckle at the situation: this could easily be a 'Lego' figure food accessory. The girl's confused look when I ordered now makes sense. I scoop out the contents with one scrape of the tiny spoon, and eat it with my confidence bruised. I order a taco from the other restaurant, embarrassed by the potato transaction.

I'm no longer under the illusion that my Spanish is still 'fine'.

The décor of the airport seems positively modern in contrast to what I'm looking at when I enter the bathrooms. Not one of the cubicles is equipped with a toilet seat and I squat uncomfortably, taking solace in the doors at least having a lock.

The next few hours pass slowly. Apart from the restaurant workers, I'm alone in this airport. I read my book and occasionally stare out across the neglected tarmac runway. Black tar has been carelessly dragged through the cracks in the surface and a few rusty old planes sprout grass, lying forgotten at its edges. As the afternoon drags on, more passengers join me. Two-beige clad nuns and an American man in dad jeans and sweaty shirt read religious magazines. A young curvaceous woman sits down opposite me. The waist band of her tight black jeans floats loosely around her tiny waist like a hula hoop and are solely held up by her voluptuous ass and hips. She holds a cosmetics bag and looks like she's just been through the works in a makeup salon. Her blushed cheeks and bright red lips match her red heeled shoes. I walk behind her across the tarmac, mesmerised by her peach buttocks as the small, twenty-seater jet is towed into position by an old tractor.

The little plane shakes nervously as it rattles down the runway and continues to lose any loose bolts as we bump through turbulence, flying north. Touching down an hour later, it is now approximately seventy hours since I left Auckland.

We walk across the narrow strip of tarmac as a sweltering jungle heat wraps itself around us like a hot wet blanket. Filing into a low-pitched wooden building, the nuns, American man and Miss Hula Hoop disappear into the night while I wait alone for my backpack.

The little baggage carousel hasn't even been turned on and a man in a dirty denim shirt simply appears with my bag on his shoulder.

"Tuya." He passes it to me.

Dim orange lights illuminate a lay-by outside that quickly empties of vehicles the moment I exit the building. Only one van is left. A grubby man in an open Guayabera shirt rubs his hairy belly and swiftly ushers me into the vehicle.

"¡Flores, amigo! Amigo, si, si!"

He pulls the squeaky sliding door shut behind me as I step in. The interior panel falls off as it slams, revealing frayed wires and the handle mechanism. He jumps in the front and pulls away with a jerk, but stops before we even leave the lay-by.

"Esperame, hombre," he says, holding up his palms, asking me to wait.

As I await his return, I notice a hole where the ignition used to be that sprouts a tangled bunch of wires hanging from it.

FLORES

Mr Hairy belly finally returns to the dilapidated taxi van and within minutes, swerves onto the causeway that links Flores Island to the mainland. The area has undergone huge changes since I was last here four years ago. It is quite a shock being here again after a few years. What once was a paddock on the corner where mangy horses roamed is now a two-storey mall and a McDonalds drive thru. In spite of this, it feels familiar.

"¿Es Nuevo?" I ask the driver.

"Hace tres años estaba," he replies. Three years old.

The interior panels of the van chatter and clang as it bumps its way through the cobbled lanes of Flores. We pull up under a familiar wooden sign that hangs over the street.

'Los Tres Amigos.'

A wave of nostalgia from 2009 washes over me. The iron gate and buzzer are just as I remember and entering, nothing else has changed either. Gap-year students shout over tables full of beer bottles and half-eaten nachos.

I check in, noting my pre-booked room. They tell me only dorms are available. I wonder why I wasted my time booking one on their website. My worst fears become reality as I step into the dorm: it too has not changed. Soggy towels hang on anything that dares to stick out from a wall and a broken shower head in the bathroom drip feeds the floor puddles.

Famished and foggy headed, I sit at the bar with a rum and a bowl of overpriced nachos. A conversation sparks up with a couple of Israeli actors who have been performing in plays in San Salvador. They mention a cheap taco shop in the plaza when I grumble about the price of the nachos.

"¡DARRRRENNNN, tu cuarto esta lista!" the lady from the desk calls out.

My room is ready? She explains that a room has freed up and that it's mine if I want it. Without even finishing my food, I grab my bag, farewell the Israelis and follow her outside and down the narrow street to another building.

It's quiet and cosy and a very different atmosphere to the hostel I've just come from. The two floors have four or five rooms on each with a communal but clean bathroom. It's almost as if they keep it a secret from the younger crowd. Lying down, I'm swallowed by the spongy mattress and immediately sink into a deep sleep.

I wake in a cold sweat. I spring forward, sitting bolt-upright, unsure of where I am for a good ten seconds. I'm bewildered, petrified and confused all at the same time. My heart is beating fast as I look around the room, still unaware of my surroundings.

Seeing my backpack on the floor snaps me from my shock. I check my watch. It's just after midnight. I've only been asleep for forty minutes.

I crash out again and the next time I wake, the sun is shining through the wispy yellow curtains.

I check my watch again. I've slept for thirteen hours. The last seventy-odd hours since I left New Zealand have taken their toll.

The building is quiet except for a cleaning woman outside the bathroom.

"Buenas tardes." She bids me a good afternoon and wrings out her mop before swishing it across the floor. I re-tread my steps up to the main hostel for food.

The guests in the common area are all transfixed by their devices, shut off from the outside world.

I walk around the courtyard, pulling their earbuds out one by one and introducing myself and lecture them about socialising becoming a thing of the past.

I don't do that, of course – I stop the impulse to set them all straight. Instead, I eat my expensive eggs and tortillas alone, determined to find cheaper food while I stay here and figure out my next move.

I meet with a guide, Juan, a gold-toothed, mid-30s Guatemalan who comes to the hostel every morning with a sales pitch for the various treks in the area. He talks in a very confident manner while dragging a comb through his slicked hair.

"Vamos a las cinco el lunes." He surprises me saying we can depart for El Mirador in two days' time.

"Es doscientos cinquenta, pero, necesito tres personas minimo," he adds. $250US each, but three people minimum.

"Maybe you can help me find the others?" He throws in the curve ball that will really decide whether or not we leave so soon.

"Flores is nice place to wait, amigo. Always easy to find compañeros, amigo."

His gold tooth glints as he beams an unconvincing smile.

THE WAITING GAME

The Guatemalan jungle hike I'd researched before the trip seemed so magical in theory. What I hadn't thought about was the game of roulette I was in for to find willing companions. I search out the taco stand the Israeli actors I'd had a drink with at the hostel bar had mentioned last night.

I can almost touch the rough walls of the narrow lane I climb with outstretched arms. Little open doorways give a glimpse of Guatemalan life where villagers hide from the beating sun. An old, crooked lady sweeps a living room floor with a broom made of leaves in one house, while in another a fat man in only his boxers lays in a hammock watching a small TV set.

The plaza at the summit is shaded by several large trees that crack the walls of their concrete planters. Bright red flowers bloom out of control and attract hummingbirds that buzz in and out of the branches draining the nectar. I spy the taco stand, tucked in a corner and perched precariously on the edge of a small cliff. At any moment it could slip backwards into the street below. The grey wooden shed has a shelf that runs along its frontage below two opening hatches where a young boy fries up strips of gristly grey meat on a huge hot plate. The sign above the hatch offers tacos for 3 quetzals each. However the tacos taste, the $7 nachos at the hostel don't stand a chance.

On one side of the plaza and down a level stands a white church and a concrete basketball court where a family bounce a ball between each other. I sit down on the bleachers to eat my tacos. The mother runs rings around her husband and the two daughters, dribbling the ball between them before shooting at the hoop and scoring. Next to me, an old lady in a woven shawl claps as the mother scores. I bite into my first taco. It's not bad, but it's not good either. The meat is chewy and tastes of something I haven't eaten before. I'm not sure of the animal it's from but the salsa is so fiery hot, it's sure to wipe out any bacteria living in it.

Voices on the other side of the plaza turn my head. I'm met with stares from two camouflaged soldiers holding M16 rifles. On one side of me a family laugh and play basketball; on the other, an armed patrol stand guard, ready to kill. I ask the old lady about the soldiers. She explains the problems with criminals and muggers targeting tourists in the village. She adds the town folk have realised tourism fuels their livelihoods and that's why it's regularly patrolled and now has a gated sentry post halfway across the causeway.

A giant, burnt-orange sun sets over the lake as I stroll around the island's perimeter road. Women young and old sit piled on motorbikes that rasp past, competing with the grind of tuk tuk engines that carry families on circular joyrides. Couples on the sidewalk stroll holding hands. The orange glow of Lake Petén's surface silhouettes brim-hatted men in their wooden boats.

This warming scene shouldn't make me feel lonely, but it does.

Juan's minimal efforts to find companions for the hike are worrying. I need to sell it to people at the hostel in order to escape the creeping solitude.

My morning coffee at the hostel is accompanied by a stream of yellow wastewater being brushed out of the toilet bathroom stalls and across the tiles in the common area. While it swirls down a drain in the middle of the floor, I get talking to a guy called Gus from Colorado.

"Yeah, I'm just taking a break from studying Spanish in Xela. My bus back there leaves this afternoon."

In that single sentence he crushes my hopes of talking him into the Mirador trip. We head down to the jetty and take a swim in the cool lake. It's a refreshing respite from the baking hot sun and a surreal experience as tiny fish surround our feet and nibble the dry skin from them.

We tread water a while in the shade of the jetty above us.

Gus leaves mid-afternoon and the rest of the day crawls by slowly. I visit the taco stand again and read my book in the common area of the hostel. I'm still having no luck with the few people I ask about the trek.

The morning begins with torrential rain streaming through the gaps in the courtyard's roof and the sheet metal overhead flapping in the high winds.

"Cuidado." The maid tells us it's a cyclone.

The storm temporarily takes the power out, the daily crowd leave for Tikal and another quiet day ensues. I read my book, take a few solo walks around the town between rain showers and eat at the taco stand again. The meat is tougher and greyer today but the sauce just as hot. I buy extra to kill more time. The hummingbirds suck the red flowers of the trees.

Juan arrives and picks up my spirits, telling me he's found two keen people that we'll meet at 6pm.

At 6, I ask the reception if they've seen him.

"No, hombre. No he visto."

I retire to the bar and brood.

"We have to wait, my brother." I'm startled by Juan's voice as I sip my glass of rum. He leans over my shoulder.

I look for the other two keen to take the trip. He grins his gold smile and grabs my shoulder.

"Still we have no people. Todo bien, amigo." He disappears.

Contrary to what he's just said, everything is not OK. I can't just hang around hoping that two keen companions will miraculously show up before I'm due to leave for San Salvador. It may not have been the wisest idea to travel across the world on a whim without already having companions for the hike. I go to bed early in a miserable mood.

An upset stomach and the mild shits get me up early. The cheap tacos are starting to take their toll. I'm losing the motivation to keep asking people about the trek. I need to withdraw more quetzals from the ATM in the new mall and head out on foot across the causeway, passing the sentry point and its armed soldiers.

Do they know where I'm going?

It's the only ATM in the area where foreigners can get money. Their wages are probably way smaller than what I'll have in my pocket returning. I pass them, trying not to look rattled.

I look around to check I've not been followed. To my relief, the card works fine and I nervously walk back with my wad of cash, still wary of my surroundings.

Old men in canoes slice the glassy surface of the morning lake with their outboard motors. The soldiers at the sentry gate eye me.

"¡Buenas!" I chirp to them happily, trying to act normal.

They stare and merely nod in my direction.

Dispersing the cash through the various slips and pockets in my backpack, I stuff it under my bed and meet two Irish guys back at the hostel bar and ask them the obvious.

"No mate! Haha! We're going to Tikal tamarra."

I'm confused at their laughter to my question.

"We just heard 'bout chu! Yerr da Mirador fella!" I cringe that I'm now known as 'The Mirador guy'.

I know that I'm never going to find anyone coming through this place who has a week up their sleeve to hike to a lost city they've never heard of. I'm gutted that the place I so desperately wanted to go to has slipped out of reach. The chances of ever coming back to undertake such an adventure are next to none.

I regrettably have to change tack and make different plans for the time I have allocated here before heading down to San Salvador. I figure a boat trip on the lake will be a good way to clear my head and figure out just what that new plan is.

POTENTIAL CANDIDATES

"Hey man, how's it goin'?" Two young American guys with loaded packs arrive as I leave the hostel for a morning stroll.

It's the shorter one who speaks – as if we've met before. He adjusts his round glasses perched on his nose and ruffles his fingers in his fuzzy hair.

"Good, man," I reply. My mind races, trying to remember if we have met. I tell him I'm going for a boat ride across the lake.

"Really? Can we come?" His tall friend appears behind him.

"Yeah, sure – the more the merrier."

"Cool, man! Just hold up a second and I'll get my camera."

His friend shakes my hand, his fluff of hair, chino shorts and Hawaiian shirt reminds me of Ted Danson from the 1980s sitcom *Cheers*.

"I'm James," he says.

"Where have you guys come from?" I ask curiously.

"We met in Xela at Spanish school and wanted to do something fun before we head back to the States," he replies.

He has the air of a fraternity college boy about him. I'm waiting for him to say they are going to Tikal tomorrow but we're interrupted when the shorter guy returns with his camera.

"I'm Keelan," he says, pushing his spectacles up the bridge of his nose again.

"So you've been in Xela, huh?" I ask him.

"Yeah, really needed to see some of Guatemala though before we jet," he replies.

"Yeah, James was saying that."

I bite my lip in an effort to not push Mirador on them. I know if anyone is going to say yes it's probably these two. I hold my tongue and continue with less pressured conversation.

"So what do you guys do back in the States?"

We follow the cobbled street's pastel walls.

"James is at college, but I captain freight liners around the Gulf of Mexico." He pulls his old camera from its leather case.

"You what?" I'm surprised by his answer. He seems far too young to captain one of those behemoths.

"Yeah, man, it's a great way of traveling because I'm on a shift contract two months on and a month off. My last vacation was up in Alaska living in an igloo."

Keelan's sentence reminds me of why I love travelling. It's not often back home that you talk to someone who's been living in an igloo.

Reaching the shoreline, we ignore a guy in a boat who calls out an overpriced offer. "¿A donde va?"

"¡Ida a vuelta!" he says.

"¿Cuanto para media hora?" I ask how much for a half-hour, not caring where we go in his vessel.

He calls back a price that I haggle down to 25 quetzals.

"Dude, this is awesome! Where did you learn Spanish?" Keelan is impressed with my negotiating skills.

"Nicaragua," I answer.

"Man, I'm interested!" he says. "Tell me more!"

This guy has zest. His energy is infectious, but still I hold my sales pitch for the lost city trip. The boat putters across the lake encircled by low lying hillsides. The driver receives a phone call that promptly results in us U-turning.

"¿Que paso?" I ask.

"Recojer mi Papa," he says.

"It seems we are going to pick up his dad," I relay to the boys, who are now both hanging over the side dragging their hands in the water and not really too bothered where we go.

The boat slows as we approach a muddy shoreline. A boat ramp made of concrete slab climbs up through the sludge, turning into a road that cuts through rows of shanty structures lining it on either side. Faded Coke and Fanta posters flap in the breeze outside a little dilapidated shop.

We wait for the father to arrive. Keelan and James, now unable to drag their hands through the rushing water, have shifted their attention to a trail of leaf cutter ants that form a dark line across the boat ramp. It's like they've never seen ants before. Keelan takes photos while James stares at them with his mouth open.

HIJACK

Back at Los Tres Amigos hostel, I gently pitch the El Mirador hike to Keelan.

Within a few sentences he's frantically Google searching it.

"Dude, I'm in!" he squeals, scrolling through the images on the screen. I buy us another round of beers.

James has a few more questions, curious to the types of stores they have in the jungle and if the toilets are clean. One thing is for certain — he's either going to sit in Flores for a week or come with us.

Juan is in the middle of packing away his desk for the day when we enter the office. With eyes lit up and gold tooth glinting, he explains the trip to the boys before making the necessary arrangements for our departure in two days' time. I buy another round of drinks for us back at Los Tres Amigos.

I'm over the moon that I've found willing companions.

Two German guys join us and grin when I tell them how much we've paid. "Vee hef found zee tour for $50 less zan zat." they say, gloating.

After experiencing just two beers with them, I'm glad they've not chosen Juan's company. I've also read that the cheaper tours provide a very poor service. I change the subject and discuss the supplies we'll need to buy for the hike. Juan has stressed we'll need soft bags because they are placed directly on the mules' backs.

"No pokey parts and a basic first aid kit, toilet roll and some plastic bags to keep your gear dry if it rains." James repeats what he's remembered. Keelan and I nod.

When I meet up with the guys the following day, they've already been supply shopping. James has his essentials in the form of whiskey, wellington boots, tissues, socks, chocolate, granola bars and a few Gatorades. I don't think he's really grasped the idea of where we're going. We have a beer with an old guy at the hostel who tells us of a good place to eat.

"Huge chicken plates!" he says, wiping his lips in an American accent.

"A ton of fries and a beer too! Can't beat that for five bucks!" he smiles, contentedly rubbing his belly.

A thick blanket of drizzle sets in as we arrive at his recommendation. Two collapsed sagging tent canopies are supported by buckled frames and shelter a cluster of plastic chairs and tables at the lake's edge. The place is full. Locals crowd around all the tables, tearing up hunks of chicken, stuffing fries in their mouths and tapping their feet to the salsa music that plays from inside the kitchen. A round man with slicked black hair and a moustache sizzles chickens on a BBQ spit.

"¡Bienvenidos gringos!" he cries, causing a few patrons to look up from their food as a waitress seats us.

While the broken tents drip water, the moustachioed man flame grills food that his daughters and wife ferry to the tables.

The place is buzzing.

We wait patiently, taking in the delicious aromas that waft from the BBQ. Suddenly every head in the place turns when an almighty bang comes from the street. A moped loses control and slips onto its side, skidding down the road spitting a spray of sparks and ending up under the back of a parked bus. Picking himself up quickly, the rider wrenches the bike from the clutches of the bus while his passenger dusts herself off. They jump back on and disappear into the traffic that circles the island. The restaurant patrons return to their eating like it happens all the time.

Donna and Alicia, two Australian girls join me, Keelan and James at our table. The place is packed and their company is welcome. It's nice to have some cheery and, more importantly, female company.

Waiting for my food with my new friends, I reflect on how close I was to giving up on finding such companions for the trip.

"What are you smiling about?" Keelan asks me, laughing.

I don't have to say anything. He knows exactly why I'm smiling.

The cheery mood shifts when the girls recount the bus ride that brought them here. I've had some dicey rides, but this story sticks with me.

"About two hours in, once we were out of the city, these guys all jump up, pull out guns and rob everyone," Donna tells us like it was nothing.

"But that's not the worst bit," Alicia butts in. "The bastards cavity searched all the women."

We're all glued to their story, waiting to hear what happens next.

"Guatemalan women keep their money up their cooches," Alicia says.

We all gasp at the same time. James can't believe what he's hearing. His face says it all.

"We've still got our credit cards and passports as they didn't want anything traceable. Just cash, phones, jewellery and laptops," she adds.

"Did the police get them?" Keelan asks.

Donna looks at him. "No, they made the bus keep moving so the GPS stayed on track. Whoever was monitoring it would've been none the wiser. They got it to slow down so they could jump off in the middle of nowhere where a car was waiting for them."

"That fucking asshole," Donna says, remembering the hijacker who put his hand over her mouth and the other down her knickers in search of money. "One of the other guys calmed him down. I thought he was going to rape me."

I sit stunned, thinking about the different bus rides I'll be taking in the next few months.

"¡Aqui esta! ¡Buen aprovecho!" The round man appears with six paper plates piled high with grilled chicken, fries, salad and tortillas. Accompanied with a rum, it costs less than $4 each and breaks the atmosphere left by the girls story.

"Damn, this could be our last good meal for a week," Keelan says.

"Tomorrow we go to the jungle!"

I fear he may be right. I'm curious about the food we will eat over the next few days, and how we'll be looked after. Keelan, now gnawing on a chicken leg, is far from worried about such things.

I doubt he'll sleep a wink.

LUCKY

As dawn breaks, the only remnants of the busy fried chicken restaurant we sat at the night before are the tatty tents and a few napkins blowing around in little whirlwinds on the floor. Our bus to the jungle is collecting us here. I check my watch. It's 04:45. From the shadows appear the group of German guys who had mocked us for choosing the more expensive jungle hike with Juan's company.

We all wait in silence together.

Before long, the faint sound of a bus grows louder. Two headlights swing into the opposite end of the causeway of our island on the lake. The engine sounds pained as it pulls up. I prepare for the worst. Bolivian transport springs to mind.

The windscreen of the small silver bus is graced with a blue sticker strip across the top reading 'Dios es amor'. The doors creak open and a skinny Guatemalan guy jumps out.

"Hola! I am Alex!" he greets us. "Mayan tours?"

"Yep," I reply.

"Good, good. OK, give me your bags." He dumps them next to a pile of provisions.

Sacks of dried beans, rice, a chilly bin of poultry, four 20-litre water drums and some other assorted bags are what we'll be taking with us into the jungle. In contrast to our guide Alex, the Germans are greeted by a grumpy, overweight man who seems none too pleased to see us on the same bus. He insists his group stay in the front seats as if to make sure we don't mingle with them. They strangely load less than half the gear that Alex has brought. I can't help but smirk, remembering their bragging of getting the cheaper deal.

"OK, amigos," Alex says. "My brother Eric will meet you in Carmelita. Adios!" And with that, he jumps back off the tiny bus.

"What?" I say to Keelan. "That's it? But how will we know where to get off?"

Frantically, I slide open the side window and call out.

"Don't worry, my friend," he says, sensing my panic. "In only three hours Eric will meet you. It's the last stop! Breakfast waiting!"

He disappears into the darkness before I can answer.

The bus grinds into gear and takes off into the dark morning. I look over sheepishly to the Germans who still have their guide with them. The driver is large, quiet and hairy. His 'co-driver' is a deranged teenager who hangs from the door and shouts our destination to people on the side of the road. Whenever potential customers are sighted, the driver slows the vehicle for the boy to jump off and push the passengers into the bus while manhandling their baggage and throwing it up onto the roof. He then sprints after us and heaves himself back on board like a pro. It's a job for a young and fit hustler.

On the outskirts of Santa Elena, the death trap starts to make a strange clicking sound. The driver swerves erratically into a grease-splattered gas station and rises from his seat, showing the whole bus an arse crack that sprouts clumps of brown hair. We watch as he pulls his saggy jeans up and then slips out of the bus. We see his silhouette move across the oily forecourt underneath a flickering light to a barefooted attendant in stained jeans and a grubby t-shirt. The driver, still clutching his belt, starts to talk with the attendant while he fills our diesel tank.

He boards the vehicle once more, turns the key in the ignition. A painful grating sound comes from the engine.

"Hurrummph," he grunts and drops to his knees in the aisle, giving us another look at his arse crack, just in case we missed it the first time.

The man lifts open a centre hatch in the floor just behind the gear stick. Keelan and I smirk at what we're witnessing. James is already out cold, mouth open with his head pressed on the window. Scrabbling around in the glove box, the man produces a roll of gaffer tape and tears a few strips off before wrapping them around something in the hole.

Gaffer tape, I think to myself. *This is a great start.*

After a few more rips of the tape, he exhausts the roll and throws the cardboard inner reel out of the door. It rolls across the forecourt before settling by the base of the pump. Now shoulders-deep in the hole, he's totally committed and continues to groan and clink away. When he emerges, his face is bright red after being upside down for five minutes.

He pulls up his jeans, grabs a hammer and starts to bash something in the hole. Keelan and I are no longer smirking. We're wondering whether we'll get started again. We're wondering about breakfast.

Back upright, the driver slumps into his seat and pumps the gas, turning the key. Insanely, the bus fires into life first go and everyone cheers as we slowly pull out of the station. The engine sounds like he's left the hammer in there.

The further we travel, the denser the jungle grows, bringing with it a humidity and heat that could fry an egg on the vinyl seats. More people fill the little vehicle from the tin- and straw-hut villages we pass through as we drive deeper into the wilderness on a rough, unloved dirt road.

Two hours in and the bus is stuffed to bursting with a strong smell of styling gel that slicks back the majority of the heads now riding with us. An endless trip and a torturous road, the potholes and uneven tracks grooved by other vehicles and torrential rains twist the route into a rollercoaster ride that throws us around in our seats. I'm certain my bum will be bruised for weeks. I had never thought it could get worse than the pink Bolivian bus ride back in 2009 but I'm now having my doubts.

The driver blows his horn as he approaches each settlement where signs of rural life are at their most basic. Pigs squeal, tied to fences with rope; children kick deflated footballs through makeshift stick goalposts. The bus slows at a fork in the road where a thick morning mist envelopes a triangular configuration of posts supporting a pitched tiled roof. Wispy smoke plumes twirl from several fire pits under it. A short lady in a pink shawl pats out tortillas on a hot plate. Next to her is a young woman who catches my eye. With streaked blonde hair and a pink-and-white-striped shirt, she stands out among the more traditionally dressed people milling around the lean-tos. A few younger kids beckon her to play with them but she declines, picking up a couple of large striped laundry bags and swinging them up onto the bus. I offer to put her bags on my lap as she reaches me, which she gladly accepts, sitting down by my side.

"¿A donde va?" She flicks her hair from her round face and smiles a grin of teeth decorated with gold hearts and stars.

"Carmelita," I reply. "Vamos a hacer un trek a Mirador."

"Ahh, que bonito, nunca hago." She tells me she hasn't been.

"¿Y tu nombre?" I ask her name.

"Lucky."

"¿Y eres Maya?" I ask of her Mayan ancestry.

"Si, pero hace anos, hay mucha mezclando." She explains the 'watering down' of the race over the years.

I ask her about her teeth and how the gold is done.

"Pega," she replies. 'Glue.'

I continue the conversation, interested in the stripy bags on my lap. She tells me they're full of lipsticks, nail polish, bottles and plastic containers.

"Yo vende a los pueblitos." She purses her lips in the direction of the bags.

She's a Tupperware saleswomen and beautician specialising in nails and facials. I revel in this interaction we're having, each of us sharing photos from our phones as we rumble deeper into the middle of the jungle. The bus stops and Lucky gets up and grabs her wares. My watch tells me we should have already arrived.

"¿Que mas a Carmelita?" I ask her, knowing we must be close now.

"Como dos o tres horas mas," she says.

"Fuck, two or three hours more?!" Keelan says, understanding from across the aisle. "Oh my god," he moans.

I feel bad I've roped him into this trip.

"¿Enserio?" I ask Lucky.

"Si, es lejos. El ultimo paro." The last stop.

She kisses me on the cheek, laughs at how far we still have to go and barges herself and her bags along the aisle to the front before disappearing into the undergrowth. The bus grinds into gear with a jolt and the Tupperware Princess disappears out of sight forever.

James, still fast asleep against the window with his mouth open, is clearly undisturbed by the giant potholes throwing us around and Keelan, who earlier was writing intently in his notebook, has now given up due to his pencil bouncing around on the page. I think about Lucky for a while, imagining where she lives and what types of plastic tubs she'll sell at the end of the track she disappeared down. I suppose even remote jungle villages need Tupperware.

2
THE JUNGLE HIKE

On the summit of 'La Danta'
with Keelan, James and Eric.
Mirador Basin, Guatemala.

CARMELITA

Lucky, the Tupperware salesgirl is now all but a memory, as we continue to bounce and bang along the carved-up jungle road for another two hours. Just when I think I can't take any more, the driver blasts the horn and we enter a clearing.

A large wooden sign reads 'Carmelita'. The gruelling five-hour journey is over.

The horn wakes James, who now has a line of dribble connecting his bottom lip to his sweatshirt. He has achieved the impossible and slept most of the way.

A few mules chew grass outside straw and tin-roofed bamboo houses that surround a village green. Goalposts made from branches stick out of the grass at either end. I've been on film sets that look like they've been modelled on this. This is the real deal. Dogs chase our bus, excited for new visitors as it skirts the field avoiding free range pigs before coming to a stop next to an alleyway. The other guide hurries the German group we met in Flores off the bus and ushers them down the alley.

"See you out there!" Keelan calls out to the bunch.

They look tired after the terrible bus ride. The guide looks back suspiciously as if to check we are still on board. His manner is strange, making it feel there could be some rivalry between the guide companies. The bus drives across the green, pulling up outside a house surrounded by bananas that hang heavy in their trees. The doors squeak open and we're greeted by a guy who looks exactly like Alex, the guy that had loaded us onto the bus in Flores.

"¡Hola, amigos!" he greets us. "¿Como estamos?" He grabs the gear through the now open back doors of the vehicle and sets it down by the garden fence.

"They must be twins!" Keelan whispers to me.

"Either that or he flew here," I joke.

"Soy Eric, hermano de Alex." Ah! Alex's brother.

He leads us through the banana trees and into the cool interior of the house. The floor is dirt, the decor simple and a few hammocks hang in each room. At the rear, huge bunches of plantain hang from a row of trees along the fence line of the kitchen. A short Mayan woman cradling a baby appears. She's no more than 18 years old.

"Mi esposa y mi hija," Eric says, introducing his wife and baby.

She nods shyly while bouncing the little girl in her arms and heads to the kitchen area.

Sitting around a large wooden bench, Eric tells us about his family being the first to offer tours to Mirador and that they have been doing so for close to thirteen years.

I translate some info he tells me to the boys. "They are good friends with the explorer Richard Hansen, the archaeologist who has excavated El Mirador annually since he first discovered it back in the early 1980s."

Keelan's excited. James looks confused, perhaps wondering what he's got himself into.

Eric's wife places plates of beans and an egg each in front of us. A stack of tortillas and a plastic pitcher of red juice follows. We make light work of the food and drink after such a long drive.

A thin-framed old lady appears from an adjacent room. She has a weathered but kind face and a few remaining teeth poke from her gums.

"Hola, soy Maria," she introduces herself. "¿Habla Espanol?"

"Si." Keelan and I reply simultaneously.

She tells us to put anything we don't need into the large sacks that Eric is packing.

"Mi hijo siempre esta circa, aunque no te visto."

She tells us that Eric will always be close by even though we won't see him a lot and they don't want to be stripping the gear off the mules if they don't have to. Eric begins skilfully stacking and strapping the gear to the animals, maintaining a balanced pile on each and waterproofing it all up neatly in blue tarpaulins. The mules, familiar with the weight, don't flinch.

"¿Tenemos botas y chaqeutas para llueve?" Maria checks we have rain gear. It seems a strange question as the baking hot sun beats down on us.

"¡OK, listos!" She kisses her granddaughter goodbye before grabbing a small backpack that contains only a first aid kit.

"Espero que no necesitamos," she says with a cackle through her few remaining teeth.

"I hope we don't need it either," I translate to the boys.

Adding a few bananas to her flimsy bag, she leads us to the front gate and along the edge of the village green moving like a woman half her age.

"Keep up, guys!" Keelan calls back to us, scurrying along behind her.

Maria's English is limited, and Keelan's Spanish is limited, so I agree to translate when needed. She begins to feed us information as we begin our adventure. This is something I enjoy, knowing how beneficial the Spanish practice is going to be for teaching the kids in El Salvador. We reach a stone track where three teenagers are climbing the outer frame of a water tower and howling like monkeys.

"¡Los monos!" 'Monkeys!' Maria shouts up to them, laughing.

"Oooo! Oooo!" they call back, scratching their armpits.

We are quickly absorbed by the nature around us. The hum of birds and insects grow louder the further from the village we walk. We have entered a new world.

Maria speaks fondly of this Richard Hansen guy that her son had mentioned. I vaguely remember reading something about him in an old *National Geographic* magazine.

Eric catches up and passes us, swaying along with the two mules behind him and disappears into the undergrowth up ahead. The remnants of rain are still apparent underfoot, blocked by the canopy above that prevents the sun from drying the earth. Maria picks flowers and leaves, telling us their names and what animals or birds feed off them. I ask her questions as we tread the mulch path, marvelling at her knowledge of the flora and fauna and their medicinal properties. I notice she stuffs a few of the leaves into her pocket. It's obvious she's at home here, basking in the tranquillity of the jungle. As we walk, I translate anything to the boys that I feel is worth sharing, always trying to keep them included. I'm finding it so beneficial in regaining the language. Occasionally she breaks into song, singing old love ballads in Spanish. I decide not to translate these parts and serenade the boys. Her voice blends with the sounds of the nature around us. I feel safe with her. I can tell this trip is going to be a good one. She keeps up a formidable pace as the temperature begins to rise.

"Estes son muy altos." Maria points at a group of tall trees with a stick. "Ramón y Sapodilla," she says.

The trees must be nearly 150 feet in height and bare scars up their trunks where crusted white sap has hardened. She tells us the trunks are slashed by skilled labourers known as 'Chicleros' who collect the sap that is then used to make chewing gum.

"Para Chicles."

I look down at my watch and notice the glass has steamed up. The heat is rising. We've been on the trail for two hours now, a trail that is quickly becoming more vine tangled. It's as if we've travelled back in time. James is swatting flying insects while the rustling of howler monkeys among the upper branches of the canopy becomes louder. We can't see them but it's obvious they are following us. When we catch up to Eric, he's busy chopping down branches of dark green leaves with his huge machete. The mules drink from a trickle of water nearby that Maria tells us would be a rushing river in the wet season. Keelan wants to know why Eric's cutting the tree.

"Hojas para las mulas," Maria says.

"Ellos necesita comer tambien." The mules need to eat too.

"Eric, agua por fa." Eric unties a barrel of water from a mule and refills our bottles.

"¿Quieres comer o no? Almuerzo en una hora." She asks if we want to eat, saying lunch will be in an hour.

With thirsts quenched, I tell her we'll wait, not wanting Eric to dismantle the packed mule.

"Esta bien," she says. Then she speaks in English for Keelan and James: "Feet OK? No bleesters?"

James and I are good so far and Keelan has opted to walk barefoot, much to Maria's disagreement.

Slinging her limp backpack on her shoulder, she sets off again with us in tow. A little further down the track, James ducks when he hears a swishing sound. Keelan points his camera into the canopy. Three howler monkeys give us our first glimpse of them swinging through the branches. They are so close I can see the glint in their eyes. They continue to follow from above until we reach a dried-up riverbed.

"Whoa, check it out!" James gasps at the sight in front of us.

A bridge of logs and twine, standing six feet above the ground, crosses what once was a raging river. James's voice startles the monkeys who start violently shaking branches. Their growls are aggressive.

"They're angry." James states the obvious.

Maria casually assures us they are merely curious.

Keelan, being the keen explorer, takes the bridge while the rest of us stay on the ground and walk through the dried trench and up a gradual incline on the other side. The fauna thins out to either side of the trodden path and becomes a clearing. Off to the left I hear what sounds like a jackhammer.

"Parajo carpintero." Maria points at a giant woodpecker ferociously tap-tap-tapping the trunk of a tree in the distance.

I translate to the boys. The hollow sound echoes out across the forest while the bird continues to rapidly headbutt the tree. I've never heard anything like it.

We stop and Maria pulls a flask from her backpack. She pours us a cup each of the sweet herb tea, telling us Richard Hansen is trying to save all of the sites in the forest but the authorities just don't have the resources or money to do so. Out of the fifty-one recorded sites, only four are protected.

Keelan and I stare at each other. "Fifty-one sites?!" We are shocked.

Something from above bounces off my head. I continue drinking from my cup. Then James gets hit with a stick and Keelan with a piece of fruit.

"The little bastards are throwing things at us!" Keelan laughs.

"¡Oye!" Maria screams at them, shooing them with her stick. "¡Vayase!"

"What are these?" James picks up one of the little green balls of fruit that the monkeys have thrown at us.

"Zacote. Muy buenas." She picks more of the leaves I saw her stuff into her pocket earlier.

I pick a fruit up and try it, washing it down with a mouthful of tea. It tastes sweet and has a furry skin.

Eric passes us with the mules, who have by now picked up a trail of giant horseflies. Maria tells us to stand back but James is too close.

"Fuck! It bit me! Damn that hurt!"

"OK, vamos, y no tocar el morde." Maria tells James not to scratch the bite, prompting him to change into sweatpants. He tucks his sweats into a pair of cheap wellington boots. His top half is adorned with a white button-down dress shirt. He looks a little ridiculous.

Keelan, walking barefoot, is more of a problem – and now bugging Maria. She says there are many insects that will bite your feet, and tells him to stick to the path. I translate for him but he doesn't seem bothered. She stops dead up ahead and tells us to be quiet while crouching us down with a lowered hand.

"Mira, mira," she whispers, pointing into the trees.

A giant red orchid sprouts in the undergrowth.

"No, no," she whispers again. "Mas lejos, mira." We look up past the flower, and our focus is drawn to something else.

Between two large trunks, a small deer stands frozen, staring back at us.

"Ooo, Venado, un joven. Muy bonito." She whispers, excited she's spotted the fawn.

Keelan quietly peels off a few photos with his old camera.

"Dude! What the fuck is that?" James breaks the silence, sending the baby deer into the forest.

Maria scowls at him for ruining the moment but he's now staring at something on the jungle floor. Amongst the rotting brown leaves, a yellow-and-black-striped centipede, fatter than a finger and as long as a pencil, is crawling between his wellington boots. It slowly crawls across the decaying forest floor, oblivious to the four giants standing above it.

"Can we eat it?" he asks.

"No. Es toxico," Maria says flatly.

FIRST BASE

Not a word is spoken between us for a good hour. We soak in the sounds and smells of the jungle. Eric has stopped in a clearing of log stumps; he's already preparing our food. The mules munch leaves from a pile of branches he's cut with his machete.

"No va cerca." He tells us to stay away from the mules and their flies.

Maria asks James about his bite. He rubs it and shrugs. She turns her focus to opening a tin of tuna.

"Tenemos Atún, piňa, frijoles y tortilla. ¿Esta bien?" she asks.

Tuna, beans, tortilla and pineapple. I translate but James gives me a weird look.

"This is going to keep us energised for longer than a sandwich and a Coke." Keelan says what I'm thinking.

"Menos que tres horas caminando." Maria takes my knife, slicing the pineapple with it, telling us we've got less than three hours to go.

We continue on. The jungle is dense and dark. Thick vines hang from ancient tree trunks and large roots riddle the path that we walk. We are miles from civilisation now. We catch up with Eric, who refills our bottles again before moving on ahead. Back on the trail, James is now limping and whining from a blister developing on his foot. The cumbersome and no doubt boiling hot rubber boots are making it hard for him to keep up.

"¿Tienes otra zapatos?" Maria asks me to translate.

"Yeah, I do have sneakers but they are strapped on the mule," he replies.

"Just go barefoot, dude." Keelan is surprisingly unaffected from walking without shoes most of the day.

"I got too many fucking bites already, man. I'm keeping them on." James is not keen.

The mud under foot turns to a sticky red clay as we pass through drained swamps that sprout small sapling trees. We stop to pluck the clods of clay from our boots. Maria confirms these patches are inaccessible in the rainy season.

"Los mosquitos tambien, muy fuerte." She tells us the mosquitos in the wet season are ferocious.

For the next hour, the sticky clay slows us dramatically. We are unable to take more than five or six steps before having to peel thick clods of it from our boots. The sheer weight of the stuff is like concrete. The forest becomes ever thicker, and we arrive at an area where two giant gnarled trees disappear upwards into the canopy.

"Es arbol de ama. Dee lovers' tree." Maria says.

The astoundingly enormous trunks of the two trees, entwine each other and twist up, disappearing into the canopy.

"Scoot over a little." Keelan flicks me out of his frame.

Maria says a small prayer while we stand under the ancient giants.

Pushing on, James surprises me when he asks what exactly we're walking all this way to see.

The timing is weird, the question is weird. Has he not listened to anything? I'm dumbstruck and decide not to answer.

"James!" Keelan growls, tapping himself on the side of the head with his fingers.

"We are going to a city of temples lost in this jungle!"

"Oh, like Indiana Jones shit?" he replies.

"Fuck me," I think out loud.

Maria tells us the reserve has 300 species of trees and 200 different types of animals, many of them endangered or threatened.

"Jaguars?" I ask.

She hasn't seen one in a while but goes on to say we may see other types, as there are five different wild cats here, all indigenous to Guatemala.

The trail under our feet begins to firm up from the soft mulch and raises itself to a six-metre-wide strip that drops a metre either side to the forest floor. Through the leaves underfoot I can see a chalky white layer.

I ask Maria if this is a Mayan road beneath us.

"Si, es Sacbe, ahora estamos cerca a Tintal."

"No shit!" Both Keelan and I drop to the floor and dust the leaves away with our hands, revealing the white bricks of an ancient Mayan 'Sacbe' road.

"She says we're on the outskirts of the city of Tintal!"

For the next twenty minutes we catch each other staring off into the bush, imagining the hidden temples and where they might be.

Before long Maria confirms our searching.

"A ver." She points left. "Unos templitos."

"Holy fucking shit!" We can't believe what we're seeing.

No more than ten metres from the edge of the trail are two pyramid-shaped mounds of partially buried stone that sprout curly thick vines from their tops. These grand structures that Maria merely regards as 'little temples' give me shivers as to what is in store for us when we reach the main city.

"Casas de seguro. Maya ancianas."

I translate Maria's words to the boys. "We are at the edge of the city of Tintal. These two structures would have been sort of guard huts where horns would've been blown to alert the city of approaching visitors."

The path begins to snake through the forest as we grow nearer the complex. More temples appear in the dense green forest, and moss-covered rock walls lead to small plazas flanked by structures that were once lived and worked in by the Maya, they are now at the mercy of the vines, creepers and roots that strangle and distort them. Not a word is spoken as we stare at the buildings, swallowed by years of jungle growth. Maria sternly tells us not to wander; she says we'll have plenty of time later to explore.

Either side of the path, the temples show their scars in the form of holes where giant stones have been pulled out. Maria tells us that this city has been heavily ransacked by looters searching for jewels and treasures. Explorers throughout history have carelessly and ruthlessly tunnelled into these majestic structures in hope of finding gold.

She cups her hands around her mouth and makes a weird hooting sound. We stare at each other grinning. Moments later, the call is returned and then again.

"Who or what is that?" Keelan squeaks excitedly.

"Los hombres que vivir aqui."

"The men that live here?" I translate confused, imagining savages in grass skirts wielding poisoned tipped arrows.

She explains they are a group of men acting as security guards to ward off any looters and that they alternate between Tintal and Mirador. I am still anxious about who we are going to meet. We keep moving along a trail, flanked by rock structures, as it curves and descends down further into the dense green foliage until the sounds of voices are upon us.

"Es Henequen. Va," Maria says, pointing at a giant dirt staircase that disappears up into the canopy.

She tells us to go up to its summit and to follow the path left on our return where we'll find her cooking our dinner. I look up at the stairs and wince. James too. Keelan on the other hand is already scrambling up the incline with his camera swinging from his neck. After the day's walking, the 100 steps are a quad-burning chore but we emerge from the undergrowth onto a flat, sandstone rock platform. Centuries of fallen leaves, now composted into mulch, have hidden this giant pyramid. We are on top now, and the view stretches into the distance, to what we've walked today and more. Other temples of Tintal poke from the top of the green jungle canopy as far as the eye can see.

"And this is just the small city on the way to Mirador," Keelan says, still snapping pictures.

A lone tree sticks out from the top and we sit with our backs against it, staring out, each with a differing view. We sit in comfortable silence for what seems like ages — even James. A 360-degree carpet of dense green forest stretches off the horizon.

I breathe deep. I'm truly a very long way from modern day civilisation.

Back at ground level and under the canopy of forest, the temperature has dropped and the late afternoon sun casts eerie shadows over the stone ruins. This mystical place is not of an earth that I've known before. The sound of voices becomes nearer and we spot Maria chopping vegetables under a roof of black plastic tarp supported by four log posts.

"¡Hola, muchachos! ¿Como fue?" She greets us, asking of the Henequen temple climb.

"¡Magico!" I say.

Eric sits with two camp guards who stare at us suspiciously, each smoking a cigarette. Maria points at another two clambering around on the hut replacing giant leaves that act as roof tiles. They are in stark contrast to the images I had of grass-skirt-wearing tribesmen. Potbellied, short and dressed in ill-fitting slacks and button shirts, each has a machete hanging from his belt.

We light up the fire pit in the middle of the bench. Everyone, including the guards, is excited to taste Maria's food as the delicious smells begin wafting from her pots. Placing a lid on the largest pot she's stirring, Maria leaves the kitchen area and tends to James's foot wound with some crushed bark. Back at the fire pit, she pours steaming leaf water from a blackened pot into tin mugs. The smell is incredible. They are the leaves she's been picking and stuffing in her pocket all day. The sweet clove aroma of the tea is like nothing I've ever tasted and I can feel my body rejuvenating with every sip of the delicious hot drink. The chicken that's been roped on the mule's back all day is served up with a salad of cucumbers, tomatoes, rice and tortillas. We eat silently and slowly, relishing every mouthful while illuminated by a few candles. After we prepare our sleeping areas situated behind the kitchen, one of the guards, José, is instructed by Maria to show us Tintal.

He leads us through piles of dark grey stone in the undergrowth. In the evening light shaded by the canopy, it has an eerie feel. The rubbled city of temples and doorways ends in a clearing where patches of short fine grass and saplings sprout from it. Flanked on either side of the clearing are raised mounds. José asks if we know what we are standing in.

The energy feels strong here. As if a thousand people once congregated at this very spot.

"Es stadium de pelota." He says it was once Tintal's sports arena, or what their version of one was.

I tell James and Keelan, pointing at the rocky mounds along each side that would have once been grandstands where crowds watched and cheered as half-naked Mayans tossed a ball around.

"Maybe they used cut-off heads," James says, imagining a macabre scene.

Returning to camp, we find the German group who were on the bus now cooking their own dinner while the guide smokes a cigarette with the security guards. I notice they have only one mule. They stand wearily over a different fire pit and warm up some tinned food. They look exhausted and don't attempt to come to our end of the camp.

I feel a moment of sadness for them but also glad we are experiencing this with Maria and Eric and getting looked after properly. I pour another cup of the clove tea before bedding down inside mosquito nets under a woven roof of giant green leaves.

I drift off to sleep miles from civilisation. A symphonic rhythm of rain sprinkles through the giant canopy above.

BOAT SHOES

Maria's wooden spoon clunks around a blackened fry pan, stirring refried beans and tomatoes over the log stove. She tells us to pack our bags first before eating.

We do as she says.

The remainder of last night's rain drips from above as a guard shuffles around shirtless. Another sits in a broken plastic garden chair and rubs the sleep from his eyes. Maria serves us a piping hot breakfast and more of the clove tea.

The German group slowly appear one by one down at the other end and are fed cold cereal. A girl still wrapped in a blanket timidly approaches us. James finishes his last mouthful and washes it down with the clove tea.

"Toma toma, niña," Maria says, passing the girl a cup of tea, rubbing her back.

Maria says something to one of the guards. I sense her angry tone and that she's directing it at the guide of the other group, who's now puffing away on another cigarette.

We leave Tintal behind and begin another day of walking, passing the base of Henequen once more before turning off down a track I would not have noticed if Maria wasn't leading the way. I close my eyes every now and again, listening to the constant hum of biological activity all around. It's an almost disorienting sound that's been here every second of every day for ever and ever. Surrounded by a thousand shades of green and an infinite mass of forms and textures, getting lost in this jungle would be easy. Maria picks out more deer, bright luminous insects and another woodpecker as we move through the trees. I notice that James, still wearing the sweatpants, has now switched up his footwear for a pair of baby blue boat shoes.

"MATE! WHAT. THE. FUCK. ARE. THOSE?!"

Keelan laughs out loud at my comment.

"Man, it's all I got. I can't wear those boots anymore, dude."

Although there were no shower facilities last night, I made sure I put clean socks on and dried my feet. I fear for James having not done the same. The boat shoes and no socks can only mean trouble.

Maria tells us more about Sir Richard Hansen and how he hired her family to help carry his expedition gear and show him the way to the lost city. At first he just wanted to study the rocks and carvings, if there were any that could be studied without disturbing the site too much.

I translate what I can to the boys as we walk and talk.

Since his plane crashed here in 1983, he has returned annually to continue carefully excavating the site. He always uses Maria's family and the wages he pays them have gone towards their archaeology studies. After a few years, it was decided that they should offer up a guide service for visitors as this would help pay for the guards to protect the settlements from looters. But things turned sour once the other families in the village saw that Maria and her family were making a little money out of it. This prompted a Carmelita cooperative so that they could get in on the act. She tells us it wasn't a problem, but the fact that they aren't looking after their clients well tarnishes the reputations of the others providing tours.

"No bebidas calientes, y siempre fumando poro."

'No hot drinks and they're always smoking weed.' She's not happy about the other guide groups.

I translate to the boys, now kind of wishing I hadn't brought the subject up with her. She tells us that because Eric has worked alongside Richard for so long, he's gained a rich knowledge about the carvings that we wouldn't be told with the other guides. I ask about the plane crash.

In 1983, Richard, his wife Jody and daughter Micalena began to have engine problems while flying over this area in their Cessna airplane. She tells us of the terrible crash, and how they could see the smoke from Carmelita.

James butts in, ruining the story. "I'm allergic to this whole jungle."

He slumps down on the ground and swats the flies off him before slipping off a boat shoe. He has another blister the size of an egg on his heel.

"It's so fucking painful." He scratches his horsefly bite.

"¡No tocar!" Don't touch! Maria scolds him like a mother, slapping his arm.

Keelan and I laugh.

"Ok, vamos a comer." She decides now's a good time for a food break.

Putting her fingers in her mouth, she lets out a high-pitched whistle through the forest and we wait in silence until a similar sound comes back from somewhere in the distance.

"Eric," she says, "Se viene." He's coming.

A few minutes later he appears, ties the mules up and takes a black plastic bag from the tied down cargo. Refilling our water bottles, Maria shares out boiled eggs, rice, raw carrots, apples and nuts from a black plastic bag. Her ears prick up as rustling and voices grow nearer.

The Germans appear from the bush, looking exhausted. They gaze longingly at our food, but their guide keeps them moving through the clearing where we rest. He stinks of marijuana and a couple of the Germans have dopey grins on their faces. I'm guessing he's passing those joints around.

Maria tells us the guide doesn't want us to compare stories with them. She pours some 'Tang' powder into our bottles.

"Energia de azucar," she says. Sugar energy.

Applying a blob of cream to James's blister, she sticks a giant-sized plaster over it. As Eric tightens the last strap over the mule, he puts his finger to his mouth.

"Shhhhhh," he whispers, pointing to a fallen log on the floor.

A giant cricket is perched on the trunk. As long as my hand, it remains motionless, showing off its iridescent yellow stripes laid over a gloss black body. Despite the pattern, it is camouflaged against the log. I look away for a second and find it hard to spot again when I look back. James, in true form, ruins the moment, when he sneezes, making the cricket leap with a head-high spring into the undergrowth.

Back on the trail, Maria slows up and tiptoes forward, pointing at a bush. She's spotted a green toad the size of a small dinner plate. Its giant eyes look backward at us without moving the rest of its head. We are all silent as we study it. Even James. Before Keelan can capture it on camera, it leaps off into the undergrowth never to be seen again. New gangs of monkeys follow from above and throw twigs at us. Every so often, there are breaks in the bombardment that Maria tells us are gaps between the primates' territories. New groups pick up our trail where the last ones left off. Giant ocellated turkeys shimmering feathers of pink and purple gobble in the undergrowth pecking around for insects.

Maria stops us on a long stretch of path.

"Aqui yo vi un jaguar."

I translate: She saw a jaguar here, once. The boys listen. She goes on to say she heard the growl and looked up, spotting it in the distance ahead. It was feeding on something it had just killed and froze as soon as it saw her and just stared. I'm having trouble keeping up the translation but muddle through for the boys as best I can.

"¿Que paso?" I ask her what happened.

She tells me she kept walking and it disappeared. "Como fantasma," she says. Like a ghost. "Mas al Mirador. Es su ciudad. Se vagan aca."

There's more at El Mirador. It's their city now. I translate her chilling words to the boys as the pungent smell of weed hits my nostrils. Sure enough, up ahead we overtake the Germans, now plodding very slowly in the heat.

"Cuidarse su niños." Maria tells the guard to look after his 'children'.

He doesn't reply as we pass them. I notice that one of the girls is covered in red bites.

SECOND BASE

"Estamos cerca." Maria scrapes her foot from side to side through the leaves, revealing white stone.

It can only mean one thing.

Mirador is getting close, and civilisation is about as far away as it's ever been. We've no connection to the outside world and Carmelita is two days' walk. In any other direction we'd most certainly meet our doom. The green canopy thickens and harnesses a small rain shower above us in its interlocking branches, leaking in a few weak spots. The pull of Mayan history is palpable as we walk the road made by those very people centuries ago. It starts to rise up a small hill. Maria tells us we are climbing up the side of Mirador's 60-foot-high perimeter wall. I can only imagine how vast its circumference is. Reaching the top, we are still shaded by the canopy and standing on a level area approximately six metres across in width. Maria asks us to stand in a circle and hold hands. We do as she says. She begins to chant in a Maya dialect, blessing the ground and paying our respects to be guided safely. It's a special moment and another little personal touch she's added. Her respect for this ancient civilisation is strong as she shares her ritual. We traverse down the hill on the other side of the wall through thick foliage. We are now inside the city's perimeter wall.

She tells us we've walked twenty and now have no more than two kilometres to go. I tell the boys.

Keelan spots something on the ground.

"Gold!" he yells, grabbing his camera from behind his back that swings from the leather strap.

On closer inspection, we discover it's a bug that looks like a blob of gold paint.

"La Mariquita," Maria says. A ladybug.

"Why does everything sound so much prettier in Spanish?" Keelan asks.

Before he has a chance to take a photo, James leans in to grab the gold speck but two tiny wings open and propel the insect into the air and away from danger. How pretty it escapes, flitting away in a glittery sparkle. Keelan scolds James for being an idiot while we continue on but his lecture soon turns to silence, and all four of us once again become lost in our thoughts among the trees.

And then out of nowhere a most marvellous sight suddenly hits us like a freight train.

Hundreds of butterflies fill the air all around us in a clearing. The spectrum of colours temporarily blinds us and we cannot see what Maria is walking towards.

Two magnificent temples rise from the earth. They sprout blotchy green tufts of moss from their sandstone bricks.

We stand in silence, numbed by the view.

Keelan runs towards the first one and climbs up to its lower platform.

"Dude!" he shouts in a deranged frenzy.

Before he can climb higher, a heavy shower of rain falls from the sky.

"¡Vamos Adentro!" Maria runs around the side of the second temple.

We follow her and enter a vertical opening between the stones.

"In! In!" she beckons us through the tiny doorway.

We have to crouch down to fit inside; we crawl into a cold, silent and chalky tunnel.

Keelan is now at the point of bursting. "Holy shit! We're inside the fucking temple!" he shrieks, stating the obvious.

Leaning against a wall, I rummage in my bag for my head torch. The interior is musty and deathly silent. The bowels of the temple have silenced the torrential rain outside.

"Templos de grupo del Muerta."

"These are the tombs of the dead!" I translate.

"This is fucking weird." James pushes his wet hair back over his head.

Looted a long time ago, the narrow passageways leading to a series of small tomb rooms are approximately three metres in length and a metre wide. Within the silence we hear a faint squeaking sound.

"What the fuck is that?" James howls, making for the entrance.

"Calmate." Maria tells him to calm down.

"Es solo hogar de Murcielagos." It's where bats live.

As I slowly look up, my head torch illuminates a thousand glimmering red eyes.

"Fuuuuuuck thiiiiis maaan, I'm out!" James's voice sends a hail of flapping wings that slap against us as the bats make a dash for the door.

Cowering, hands on heads, we let James, and the flurry of bats, escape out into the jungle. The sight of him being slapped by a thousand wings as he scrabbles his way out of the thin vertical opening is hilarious.

"Hey, it's not raining anymore!" he calls from outside, desperate to not be alone out there.

The sun is now beaming light directly onto the outer walls of both temples.

"This woman is good energy, man." I can't help but say it out loud.

Keelan winks at me approvingly.

Maria says our experience in the tomb chambers was a special one as the other guides are too superstitious and do not enter. She says it's fine to climb a little way up the temples, which we do, lying in the sun drying off. She says spending a little time here will prepare us for the city.

"Vamos. Estamos cerca." Now back on the trail, she tells us we're very close.

She shares more information as we pick up pace, and that it was once home to an estimated 200,000 inhabitants and the capital of a complex society of interconnected cities and settlements.

We turn off the main path and onto a thin trail, overgrown with bent and buckled trees blocking it. Passing a few small pillar-shaped rocks that line the trail, we find ourselves in a small dirt clearing. In the middle of it stands a rock pillar of around eight feet tall.

"Estaella para sacrificios." She points at the sacrificial rock and dots a cross on her chest.

I involuntarily shudder, thinking of the animal and human sacrifices carried out here. We take a moment to reflect. It feels weird, and I imagine the floor covered in thick red blood and body parts. We're glad we don't linger too long and join back with the main path, which lifts the mood.

A dug-out bowl of the forest is to our left. Maria stops.

"Es cantera." A quarry. "Don Ricardo hace mucho trabajo en este."

She tells us Richard Hansen has done a lot of excavations in this as well as eight others where the stones were cut to build 'La Danta', the largest pyramid at Mirador.

Standing in the entrance path leading down to the quarry, I imagine the slaves that would have once extracted and pulled rocks up the causeway to build the pyramids. It sends shivers down my spine. To our right, a small structure stands, made of blocks the same colour as the quarry wall. I imagine it as the quarry foreman's office.

I find myself thinking *Yabadabadoo* in my head, remembering the opening sequence of the *Flintstones* cartoon. Rock and nothing but rock.

James slips off the blue boat shoes and goes barefoot to alleviate the pain from his blister. The sensation he endures is clearly a far cry from Keelan's shoeless freedom yesterday as he winces and ouches his way along the trail. We have covered a lot of ground since we climbed the perimeter wall. I feel miniaturised as I shrink before the idea of the sheer area this city covers.

Maria whistles into the trees and, just like before at Tintal, the sound is returned. We walk down a track, which opens out into a clearing where our basecamp is situated, about two kilometres from the city's main plaza. Monkeys play in the trees around a clearing where more ocellated turkeys peck away in the dirt. She tells us this is where another Maya sports field once was. Black tarps in need of repair form the roofs of three crude log-framed shelters with fire pits. Inside tents of thick canvas nearby, we are given the choice of hammocks or camp mats. Four old men with machetes and string belts wander around the grass swatting bugs. A toilet shed sits up in the trees on the hill. Eric ties up the mules among the trees before going to find branches for them to eat.

"Hay ducha por alla. Jorge te puede ayudar chicos."

Maria informs us a shower is available and that Jorge, one of the old men, will help us.

"OK, amigos, cinco quetzales para cinco litros y se funciona como esto."

Holding a five-litre jerry can, he takes our five quetzals, and we follow him.

The shower hut is built of vertical wooden slats nailed to a square frame. Jorge creaks open the door. A plastic crate has been dug level into the ground for a standing platform and the downhill slope below it allows the water to run away. The shower is a plastic oil drum hung with twine at chest height with a water can hose sticking out of its base. Jorge tells us to pour the five-litre container into the top of the oil drum, get underneath and bet on about three minutes of washing time. Keelan and I laugh, excited to try it. James decides otherwise and returns to camp to smoke a cigarette while Maria prepares dinner. I pre-foam myself and enjoy the cold water spraying my body clean after the last two days of walking.

The evening sky darkens and we're served up a steaming hot, hearty stew of marrow and potatoes accompanied by more clove tea. The three of us relish every mouthful. Maria seems to be a little exhausted and sits with the guards at a picnic table, where she laughs with them over a beer or two. I fall fast asleep after another exhilarating day. Monkeys swing across the canopy in the dark, their blood-curdling howls now just another jewel of this wild place.

LA DANTA

The deafening racket of birdsong wakes us. It rained hard in the night, but the rainfall has been diverted around our tent thanks to the channels dug into the hill.

Maria has instant coffee and breakfast on. Steam plumes rise from a stack of maize pancakes she places in the middle of the table. The remainder of yesterday's pineapple is also part of breakfast. I marvel at her knack for making delicious meals out of virtually nothing.

Keelan takes photos of a furry creature with a long, white-striped tail on the field. It looks intently at us from afar, not in the least bit bothered by our presence.

"Coati." Maria names the creature and hands us a mug of coffee each. She explains how the Maya collected rainwater off roofs and stored it in reservoirs due to the lack of rivers in the area. I think about the same system at Machu Picchu that I saw in the Andes.

Maria waves her spatula at the large field where the Coati animal still roams. "Once a Maya ballpark, now a helicopter pad for archaeologists and rich tourists."

I translate her words, unsure of how I feel about the ancient sports field's new use.

"Hoy, sin prisa." She tells us today will be more relaxed and that we'll have plenty of time to explore.

Leaving the mules tied behind the camp, Eric takes Maria's place. She's probably done it a hundred times before and deserves a well-earned rest.

Eric walks at a steadier pace than his mother, machete swinging at his side. He's on constant alert and tells us to try to not talk too much. We pass quietly under shady, leafy blankets of green that dapple light on us. He tells us the structures are mostly untouched by archaeological research.

He says they belong to the animals now.

Every few steps his ears prick up as if he hears or smells something. He picks out more striped Coatis clinging to trees and then a boar, rustling in the trees that he follows with his finger.

"Muy rico a comer." Good eating. He says he'll let the guards know about that one.

We stop at a set of deer tracks and several areas where the ground has been disturbed. It's fascinating watching Eric move in this environment, the benefits of him growing up here obvious and so invaluable for moving gently around the jungle. We pass many stone structures, abandoned for hundreds of years and partially buried in mulch and jungle, suburbs if you will, once thriving centres where tribes went about their daily business, now reclaimed by thick vines and forest.

"Aqui esta." He holds out an open palm at the end of his outstretched arm.

A dark stone wall in front of us disappears up into the trees.

"La Danta," he says.

We are standing at the base of one of the largest ancient pyramids in the world.

With a total volume of over 2,800,000 cubic metres and 76 metres (236 feet) high, it looms so large that we are dumbstruck at even this mere blip of the first level.

Eric leads us around the base of giant mossy stones to a staircase that climbs and disappears into the trees. At the top of a flight of steps, the edge of a cut stone and rock platform is covered in spindly trees that sprout from it.

This platform covers around forty-five acres.

Each of these stages would easily match the area of a small township. Its immensity is hard to absorb and harder to describe. We climb another flight of stairs and mount another platform.

"This one is four acres." I translate what Eric is saying.

This area has smaller individual stone structures built on it, soaked in a thin, dark green moss and complete with semi-intact mural carvings of animals and jaguar heads. The trail leads to another set of steps that climb to a third platform, hovering on the canopy line at 86 feet. More impressive than the last, this level is home to a central pyramid flanked by two smaller, similar buildings with larger, partially intact carved stone murals. The west face of the larger centre pyramid is bisected by its near vertical staircase. We continue around the base of this upper platform and then come to a steep cantilevered wooden staircase that zigzags its way up the vertical rear eastern wall of the pyramid. Gripping what handrail there is, we cautiously climb.

Eric tells us the jungle floor is two hundred feet below and is home to five kinds of tropical forest.

The wooden stairs deliver us to the top of the world, literally. We are above the surface of the planet, perched on an uneven platform of white stone around 40 square metres and riddled with the roots of a lone tree that grows from it. On the east edge, a waist-high wooden barrier fence has been erected to prevent anyone accidentally tripping on these roots and falling 280 feet to their death.

Standing up here on the peak of La Danta, the crown of El Mirador, it's hard to grasp that the hands of a long-gone civilisation made this colossal pyramid 2000 years ago and that below us a metropolis would have been thriving. My mind drifts to the rituals that may have been performed on this very platform in the sky, perhaps coronation ceremonies I've read of in which priests would draw blood from their genitals to spill onto paper and burn as a sacrifice to the gods.

I feel an uncomfortable tingle in my balls just thinking about it.

Countless giant green hills poke dominantly from the carpet of jungle that stretches as far as the eye can see in all directions.

"Same size as the Egyptian pyramid." I translate to the boys who are now bare-chested and silent as they look out over the vast jungle.

I believe James is now coming to terms with where we are.

I point over to some hills in the distance.

"Nakbe." Eric says. "Muy bonito tambien."

He tells me the green hills are the temples of Nakbe, one of the oldest known settlements of the Maya.

"Un dia me voy." I say I'll go there one day.

He nods, unconvincingly.

"Por alla." He points west at another.

"Pyramid Tigre." The forested silhouettes of the Tiger complex.

He tells us Richard found skeletons at the top with arrowheads in their ribs.

"Maybe from the last wars." I translate.

He points again. "Templo de los Monos."

"Temple of the Monkeys!" Keelan understands.

Eric points out a 'Sacbe' — a slightly raised, darker line of trees down below in the jungle telling us it's another plastered road, two to six metres high and twenty to forty metres wide that runs for around twelve kilometres from Mirador to Nakbe. He adds it's part of the first freeway system in the world.

"¿Quiere fumar?" He pulls a joint from his pocket.

"¡Claro!" Of course!

I draw a few puffs. The weed takes a hold quickly and we spend a long time up on top of the world, staring out across the green carpet in silence. I drift off again, happy I've achieved my goal coming here and making it the milestone marker for turning 40. Keelan and James pass a small bottle of whiskey around before taking photos of each other in muscleman poses and waving an American flag that James has brought along.

I have flashbacks to Jan and Mikal howling at the lost waterfall in Ecuador on the 2009 trip.

Eric and I share a look.

"Los gringos, amigo," he whispers, taking a long drag on the joint and blowing two plumes of smoke from his nostrils.

"Como siempre los Monos."

Gringos, my friend, always acting like monkeys.

WRECKAGE

We tread carefully as we descend La Danta's rickety wooden staircase, gripping what handrail there is. It's a treacherous few minutes. Built by archaeologists years ago, this set of stairs has seen better days.

Back down at ground level, more temples spring from the undergrowth, some looted, some untouched. The sounds of wildlife are more acute and projected shadows dance on the forest floor.

I try to picture past civilisations walking among us and what they'd be doing. Perhaps a group over there to the right, preparing a fire while some women tend to their children in the cluster of dwellings to the left. We wander among the stone structures and pathways in a trance. I never want to leave this place.

Back at the campsite, guards burn branches while others replace leaves on a camp roof.

"Ellos son muy necesarios." Maria tells us how important these men are, patrolling for looters and maintaining the trails and camps.

"Como jardineros." Like gardeners. She hands us each a banana leaf of beans and tortillas.

"What do they eat?" Keelan asks.

She tells us they hunt daily for their food. I fear for the boar that Eric's finger followed in the trees earlier.

At the door of my tent, a rustling sound startles me and I freeze on one leg when I see a metre-long brown snake below my raised foot. Camouflaged in a pile of leaves, it uncomfortably slithers underneath me. I can see by the awkward way it moves that something's not right with it and spring backwards, calling out to anyone who can hear. A guard is at the scene within seconds and grabs a stick, deftly picking it up before flicking it into the forest.

"Barba amarilla," he says. "Se inferma." It's sick.

The snake may be sick, as the guard has said, but learning the thing he's just casually flicked a mere ten metres away from us is a venomous pit viper isn't a comforting thought.

Maria tells us the crashed plane of Richard Hansen lies somewhere in the forest about an hour away from camp. She hasn't been there in ten years or so but as we are so interested in the history, it may be more of an adventure than the Temple of Monos that Eric usually takes groups to.

If she can find Felipe the guard, he'll know how to get there.

"Vamos arriba El Tigre cuando volvemos." She says we'll go up the Tiger pyramid this evening.

Maria finds Felipe and introduces us. The very short, machete-wielding man of around 70 has a wrinkled face and a pair of trousers that are way too big for him. They hang suspended by a piece of string around his waist. He tells us the wreck is a forty-minute walk and if we give him $5 each he'll gladly take us there.

We run to the tent and grab the cash.

With us in tow, he barges himself through a wall of undergrowth and starts to hack away at an overgrown path. How he knows where he's going is anyone's guess and each time I think I know which way he will go up ahead, he does the opposite. We follow closely behind while the melodic 'ting!' of his machete carves us a path.

Forty minutes later, some colours appear that are not in tune with the natural greens and browns of the jungle. I see a panel of blue and then one of white, followed by what look like black letters and numbers.

"¡Aqui esta!" Felipe holds his machete in the air while Maria does the same with her hands.

Sure enough, right in front of us, in a clearing no larger than a few parking spaces, and exactly where it crashed thirty years ago, is the wreckage of Richard Hansen's Cessna aircraft.

Keelan, James and I freeze on the spot.

This is like something out of a film.

But it's not. It's fucking real.

The still intact nose and tail bookend the wire framing of its burnt-out cockpit and the wheels of the landing gear are sunken in forest mulch. One of the wings has been partially sheared off and twisted backwards neatly against the rear of the plane, while the other sticks out of the body still intact. The propellor is embedded upright in the ground around 10 metres in front of the aircraft. Felipe tells us the prop sheared off on impact and has been stuck in the ground right there since 1983.

Keelan is racing around peeling off photos, Maria sips tea from her flask. She tells us they were all lucky to have survived. I translate the story she relays.

"About two miles from the airstrip, the tail hit a tall tree, pitching the nose down and shearing one wing as it plummeted through the canopy. The propeller chewed a path through the branches causing it to cartwheel across the forest floor before coming to rest five feet up in a tree. Now trapped in the air, they could see the fuel starting to leak everywhere, but escaped the wreck before it sent a fireball cresting above the trees."

Sitting on the log with Felipe and Maria, I'm fascinated by the story, surprised that this much of the wreck exists. I ask them about the missing strips of rubber on the tyres and the holes cut in the panels of the plane.

Felipe explains the rubber is good for making things such as handle grips for their machetes.

We marvel at the crash site some more before retracing the route Felipe has cut.

Back at camp, Eric is waiting for us.

"¿Tiene lamparas?" He asks if we have torches. We nod and grab our headtorches.

"Vamos al jaguar." We are going to 'structure 54' – the jaguar paw temple.

I remember some of what I read about this place in an old *National Geographic* magazine. The jaguar paw temple is one of the most intensively studied of the ruins at El Mirador, and part of the Tigre complex on the western side of the city.

Eric tells us when the Maya walked away, they left everything in place.

Reaching a giant sheet of black plastic that stretches up a steep incline, Eric ducks underneath, then holds it up for us to follow him in.

Flicking on our torches, we find ourselves in a white limestone trench surrounded by walls covered in meticulously carved murals, some standing six feet tall, some half-restored and some in original state.

I translate what Erics says.

"They preserved the records of their civilisations on stelae in these images and glyphs."

He shines his torch on different sections, where snakes, birds and other animals are entwined into scenes of war depicting chieftains in head dress. He tells us they've found flakes of stone tools here and that the murals bear the colours and waxy feel of the 'Chicanel' style that is said to have dated to two centuries before Christ.

We stare in disbelief.

The history that's been unloaded on us since leaving Carmelita two days ago is more than a lifetime's worth. We dip in and out of more tarp-covered areas.

"Muy buenas los tarpas," Eric says gratefully, shaking the water droplets off one of the black plastic covers. Sliding under it reveals more Mayan handiwork of giant jaguar faces with noses crumbled off from the beating mother nature has served up over centuries. It's clear why the protective black plastic is so important.

Peeling off a few photos, I pray my film camera will survive the trip. Rained and sweated on, I'm not sure if the romantic idea of my pictures looking like the photos in the old *National Geographic* article was such a brilliant idea now.

Back at ground level Eric stretches his arm towards a giant tree. "Ciebo," he says.

Its above ground system of roots is too tall to climb over.

"Shhh." He commands us to be quiet and listen.

"Voices," Keelan whispers.

The German group meet us in the opposite direction on the trail. They look tired. Eric has a chat with their guide, giving the Germans a chance to speak to us.

"Your food smelt good this morning," the girl says.

"Lunch was nice, too. Tortilla, marrow and beans." James unwittingly rubs salt in the wound.

"We had marmalade sandwiches." She looks like she's about to cry.

Her friend is still covered in red bite marks, and they look more inflamed than the other day. Their guide bids farewell to Eric and again hurries them along before we can talk more.

The climb up Tigre temple burns but is well worth the struggle after another long day of walking.

When we reach the top, a similar flat rock platform to the one on the Henequen pyramid at Tintal is waiting for us.

"Nakbe." Eric once again indicates where Mirador's linked city lays, pointing out a green lump on the distant horizon.

We sit in silence. Birdlife chatters at a deafening volume across the reserve. Eric points out a group of toucans with giant fluorescent green beaks below us in the canopy. I count six of them, easily spotted if you know where to look. We savour our final sunset up in the sky, turning the forest to dark green with the fading light.

We arrive back at camp to the turkeys awkwardly flapping themselves up into the trees to roost. Maria is cooking up marrow and tomatoes. Her motherly nature is as warming as the food and knowledge that she has shared with us. It must be a lonely trip, guiding groups who cannot converse and understand her. It's times like these that I'm glad I spent so many frustrating hours, days, and months learning Spanish.

Before turning in, we shake our sleeping bags, checking for pit vipers.

CAUGHT SHORT

I wake dying for a shit. I think I've overdosed on Maria's marrow. My watch reads 3am.

I've avoided the shed so far, but that luck stops right here.

I gingerly step outside and can't believe my eyes.

An orange glitter fills the air, lighting up the dark night. Millions of fireflies move among the plants in slow motion. I follow their lead, moving slowly towards the back of the camp without disturbing the mules. As the hut draws nearer, it reminds me of the tool shed from the *Evil Dead* movie.

Treading up the muddy incline, I flinch each time shadows deep in the forest catch my headlight beam and play tricks on me.

I'm terrified.

I become snared in a giant web spun across the path. Picking clods of it from my hair, I'm confronted by a pair of large fluorescent blue eyes inches from my face. The eyes are attached to eight thick hairy legs.

The giant spider still hanging in what's left of the web stares at me.

Frozen on the spot, I'm unsure of what to do, but unintentionally blind it with my head torch. I slowly lower myself and weave past it. I duck under more webs as a group of monkeys let out their blood-curdling howls from above.

Who else would've trodden this path at witching hour?

It crosses my mind that I might try to poo against a tree right here, but I push on.

The door creaks slowly open on its rusty hinges revealing a wooden box with a toilet seat. A mixed aroma of strong bleach and waste comes from the deep dark hole.

My head torch startles two Jurassic-sized cockroaches that scuttle out from the hole and over the toilet seat. The prehistoric roaches disappear across the floor and into the dark.

Petrified, I pull down my pants and push out the quickest shit of my life, trying not to think about what else lives in the pit below my naked and vulnerable bum hole.

Plop, plop, plop. *That'll fucking do for now,* I think.

I waddle with toes facing inward like my knees are tied tightly together and gain a clear distance from the hole before wiping my arse.

The glowing embers of the kitchen fire pit guide me as I rapidly breaststroke back to camp through the orange blanket of fireflies.

I never thought it could get worse than the overnight bus toilet in Peru, but there it was.

THE MUSEUM

Farewells are exchanged with the guards and Eric leaves first, leading the mules swaying from side to side as a hum of flies hovers around them. They disappear in a rustling of the trees.

I feel sad as we pack up for the return trip. I could easily do another a day or two here.

Back on the trail, Maria stops and tells us to be quiet, asking if we can hear a squeaking sound. She points to the end of a long branch where a small, bright green frog is making the distressed call. Further along the branch is a tree snake, slowly closing in on the frog.

She moves us on, much to the disappointment of James, who is a little too eager to stay for the fatal moment.

Woodpeckers bash their jackhammer beaks into trunks as rain patters the canopy above. My legs tire at the thought of another full day of walking. The last few days have been brutal. Miscalculating the distance to go, I'm thinking it's a mere forty-five minutes. I am sure my blister and now empty water bottle won't be a problem. An hour-and-a-half later we still don't seem close. My main focus now is solely putting one foot in front of the other. Maria is walking at pace which isn't helping my blister but relief finally comes when she whistles, signalling our arrival at Tintal. Giant, blue flying ants and bright green crickets flutter around the camp as we step among the stone temples and structures for the second time.

A guard saws branches from a felled tree while another sharpens his machete on an oil stone. These men are a unique breed, living so far from civilisation for weeks on end and surviving on what the land provides. As the light drops, birds fuss in the canopy and Eric brings the mules through camp, gifting me with a horsefly bite. I now understand James' pain. A guard returns from a leaf collecting mission. He shows us a near-perfect, black ceramic dish in his hand.

"Where did you find that?" I'm so shocked by what he's holding, I ask him in English.

"¿Donde encontrar?" Maria translates, slurping her tea.

He shows me the dish. Around the bottom it has a series of intricately carved feet.

Maria tells us they find stuff like this all the time here.

"Es ceramica Maya," he says. Mayan ceramics.

We stare at it in disbelief.

He then leads us to an area behind the shelter.

Perched humbly on a ramshackle set of rope hung shelves behind the makeshift camp, ceramic crockery and exotic jewellery are displayed. Obsidian, basalt and granite that may have once wrapped the craniums of infants to modify the shape of their skulls sit next to ancient whistles and weapons decorated with shells from the Caribbean Sea.

I wonder what other priceless treasures lie inside the countless stone buildings that surround us.

*

Two aurora birds perch in a tree above us as we begin the walk back to Carmelita the following day. Of course, Maria has spotted them and shares their position with us. The two birds are somewhere between a parrot and a wood pigeon; they proudly push out red feathered bellies while fanning their wide grey tails, showing themselves off to us.

"Que bonita las avecitas," Maria whispers. "Mira las colores."

Rain begins to fall and two, three, four spider monkeys appear above, swinging from tree to tree, playing with each other.

I ask Maria what she thinks happened to the Maya and why they vanished.

"They terraced fields by carrying mud up from the swampy marshes to grow their crops."

She continues while I translate.

"It's the swamps that brought them here and in turn, the destruction of them and their nutrient-rich soil. This wiped the civilisation out between 100 and 200 A.D. The theory is that gradually, the runoff of the clay into the marshes, created from the massive deforestation for firewood they needed, killed the swamps."

"Why so much firewood? It's so hot here," Keelan asks.

"They needed it to make the lime plaster. They plastered everything, from La Danta to their plazas and house floors, layer on layer over the years." My brain is firing on all cylinders as it translates.

The walking is a slower pace today. Maria is definitely moving in a more relaxed manner. I think we all are. The sight of the water tower at the edge of the village stirs up mixed feelings. The sense of achievement is mired by sadness, knowing this once in a lifetime adventure is over.

We set our bags down at the village comedor and sit alongside a row of rusty-roofed sheds. The cold beer we chug back is followed by a second, washing down a Guanaco chicken stew and a stack of fragrant homemade tortillas. The food wakes up my gut, prompting me to use the toilet.

I fear what I'm going to be walking into after last night's toilet mission, as Eric directs me through a gate to the backyard.

Half-plucked chickens peck a row of rubbish bags that spill out onto the ground and a wooden box of similar construction to the Mirador camp toilet stands in the rear corner of the yard. The door hangs awkwardly by one hinge and a drooping arrow that once guided patrons points towards the ground. Entering the cubicle, I see a hole surrounded by scattered pieces of poo-smeared paper. The scene, combined with the heavy and cloying stench of the rotting household rubbish bags outside, causes me to gag. I try hard to not think of the prehistoric cockroaches and squat, quickly doing my business. Using the few sheets of torn paper left on the roll, I'm out of there in a flash, only glad it's daylight and that I don't have to find my way back through giant spider webs.

After lunch we trudge our weary bodies through the tiny village back to Maria's house, dumping our bags at the gate just like we had a week ago.

In the kitchen area, Eric's daughter sits content in a hammock surrounded with cheap fluffy toys. His wife wears an unhappy look, complaining that she's been doing all the work and looking after the child during his week away. He explains to her that he's putting the money on the table.

Cradling his daughter, he disappears into the backyard and returns with a pod of bananas. We thank him for the past week's adventures, and he hands us a few for the ride back to civilisation.

THE MULE

Keelan, James and I wait patiently at the edge of the village green for our bus. Our six-day trek into Mayan history has come to an end. Stacked high and secured with twine, the pile on the roof of the little bus is a precarious sight as it approaches us. Before it stops, I peel off my last photo on the roll of film in my one-use camera.

Maria our guide hugs me, saying we'll meet again. I will miss this lady. I simply can't imagine the last week with anybody else to guide us. She has made this trip everything I wanted it to be and more.

I feel myself welling up as we break our hug.

The small bus revs its engine and our bags are added to the others on the roof. We are leaving the village of Carmelita and the lost city hiding deep in its vast jungle. We set out on the rocky return to the town of Flores.

Bouncing along through the jungle, the ride is every bit as uncomfortable as it was a week ago. I daydream about that first hot shower and comfy bed drawing ever closer while the bus weaves down side-tracks behind the villages en route, stopping to pick up passengers who flag it down.

Old women with bags of live chickens and farmers and their machetes jump on, dependent on the daily service it provides.

Two dogs are pushed up onto the roof. Their front legs are splayed out and scratching at the windows as their owner shoves them upwards from behind. They let out a bark from above as the bus pulls away.

A girl at a gate shouts to the driver through his open window. "¡Parate! ¡Parate!"

We all lurch forward as the driver slams on the brakes. An old man appears through the gate trying to drag something on a rope. The girl begins to help tug as well. From behind a hedge, the now taut rope reveals a huge, mud-splattered pig squealing for its life. There are now four people tugging at the rope, desperate to move the pig. The dogs bark from the roof.

"What the fuck?" James laughs, as the beast digs its heels into the dirt track.

"No way, dude! Surely that's not coming with us?" Keelan laughs.

The young ticket collector jumps up on the roof with the end of the rope while the three others at ground level struggle to push the now kicking and screaming pig inch by inch up the back panel of the bus. The dogs continue to bark at the scene unfolding, clearly not amused at riding the roof with the pig's company. Snout snot and mud smudges against the window as the men vertically manhandle the squealing porker. Watching from inside the bus, the other passengers don't bat an eyelid. Clearly, they've seen this many times before. The pig, exhausted from the excitement, rolls to rest on the roof where the men rope it down securely.

The rough ride continues. A few minutes later I look over at James who is fast asleep with his mouth open and pressed against the glass.

"Look at the window!" I say to Keelan, who's sitting next to him.

He turns towards his buddy as a yellow liquid runs down the outside of the glass.

"But it's not raining," Keelan says, looking out of the window confused.

"It's pig piss!" I laugh.

The stream of yellow urine runs past his mouth, separated only by five millimetres of glass.

"Dude! What the fuuuck!!!" Keelan buckles over crying with laughter.

The bus rolls to a stop when a loud bang comes from the engine. We are surrounded by fields and not a lot else. The driver sits in his seat punching in a number on his shitty cell phone.

"I'm pretty sure there's no coverage out here," Keelan remarks.

We sit for a few minutes while the driver persistently tries the phone. An old woman up the back shouts at him. "¿¡Gasolina?!"

"Si," he replies.

"We ran out of gas?" Keelan says in disbelief. "Dude!" He puts his head in his hands.

The women all start to gabble between themselves about the driver.

"¡Hay finca un poco atras! ¡Vaya a pedir!" One of the ladies orders him to go and ask for gas at a farm that she saw a mile or so back.

Without looking around, he stays put in his seat, still staring at his lifeless phone.

"¡Esperame! ¡Calma!" He tells her to calm down and lifts himself from his seat before disappearing up the road on foot.

We are left in the middle of nowhere in the blazing midday heat. The man who owns the pig also disembarks the bus. We follow. Sitting down in a small patch of shade, we watch him un-sheath his machete and chop off two giant banana leaves from a tree. He walks to the rear of the bus with them on his shoulder and climbs up the little ladder on the back door. The pig starts to wiggle as the man tucks the leaves under the ropes that are holding it down. The dogs sniff at the pig.

"¡No quiero chancho frito!" he shouts at us, laughing.

"He doesn't want a fried pig," I translate to the boys.

Suddenly, the sky opens from a single cloud that passes overhead and we take shelter back inside the broken vehicle while the roof is pelted with heavy rain.

I ease a little, knowing the pig above will be getting a cool shower. It passes quickly, replaced once more by the blazing sun. We disembark again and share a few tokes of the three consecutive joints the bus boy smokes. We wait in hope for the driver to return with fuel.

We see him at last – he's carrying four plastic milk bottles with a yellow liquid sloshing around inside that I presume is diesel. I watch through my window as he places them at his feet and pulls a length of dirty hosepipe from the cab. He tosses one end of it up to the boy, who's now on the roof. As the driver stretches with his throw, his hairy potbelly flops over the belt that holds up his filthy jeans. Crusty orange particles of crisps in and around his mouth show he's obviously found a store on his search for fuel.

Unscrewing the cap, he passes one of the milk bottles up to the boy, splashing the highly flammable liquid onto his grubby sweat-stained t-shirt.

"What the fuck is going on here?" James is confused at the scene unravelling just outside our window.

"Gravity assisted refuel, bro," Keelan tells him.

Dribble trickles down the sides of the driver's mouth as he seals it around his end of the hose and begins to suck.

"He doesn't need to do that!" Keelan laughs.

"The boy is pouring fuel in from above!"

Sure enough, the diesel flows down the pipe and he cops a mouthful that throws his head back. He spits the liquid out and plunges his end of the hose into the tank. He's wasted half a bottle of the fuel.

"Man, are those four bottles gonna get us home?" I ask.

"It's like three-and-a-half now," Keelan says shrugging his shoulders.

Suddenly a dirt bike roars past, the man and boy who are riding it covered from head to toe in thick mud. Without slowing down, they swerve up the embankment, skidding past us without curiosity.

Shaking the hose and getting every last drop out, the driver screws the cap back on and throws the empty milk bottles in the side verge.

People board and disembark as we skirt a few more villages where again, kids play football in gardens, kicking balls through goal posts made of branches and twine.

The bus comes to a stop at a few menacing looking teenagers on BMX bikes and a fat cowboy on a horse who block our path. A pair of ornate, tall steel gates stand at the head of a track to the left that leads off down to a ranch in the valley. The cowboy circles the bus on his horse, inspecting everyone inside while readjusting the silver revolver tucked in his belt. The horse trots slowly, pained by the weight of this hefty man on its back. The cowboy pulls his horse up to the driver's window and chats with him in muffled tones. I start to fear the worst when the bus boy opens the folding doors and disembarks to chat below the windscreen at the front of the bus. It's as if they don't want us to see what's going on. The cowboy shakes hands with the driver, the bus boy gets back on – and the BMX bandits follow the fat man and his horse through the gates, disappearing into the valley.

"That was weird," Keelan says as we pull away.

"Better not to know sometimes," I reply.

He nods and pushes his earphones back in.

At the outskirts of Santa Elena, the bus is full. An old guy with a bike wheel sits down next to me across the aisle. I think back to the bus to Tikal with Marco in 2009 and wonder if this is the same guy with the same wheel.

It's easily the same scenario: a wheel perched on his lap and travelling almost the same stretch of road I did four years ago.

"Buena tatuaje," he smiles a toothless grin. He likes my tattoo.

"Gracias," I reply.

I tell him it's the national bird of Nicaragua. He chuckles, asking why I have no Guatemalan Quetzal bird.

The bus pulls up at a garage for fuel. How it's managed to get us here on the three-and-a-half milk bottles of diesel is anyone's guess. The driver refuels and the ticket boy runs into the garage workshop. An oil-smudged man appears and takes a brick-sized parcel sealed in brown tape from the boy.

I glance over to Keelan.

The cowboy, and his BMX bandits, now make sense.

3
CROSS COUNTRY

THE CHAVS

CHAV
\ˈchav\
plural
British slang, disparaging:
a young person in Britain of a type stereotypically known for engaging in aggressively loutish behaviour especially when in groups and for wearing flashy jewellery and athletic casual clothing (such as tracksuits and baseball caps)
from www.merriam-webster.com

The three of us are exhausted from the week of hiking in the jungle and are all looking forward to a good night's rest back at the Tres Amigos hostel.

Our allocated dorms split my two American hiking friends. Keelan, my short, intrepid and spectacled buddy, is next door with a random crew, and frat boy James, our other companion, and I are to share a bunk in another with a pasty young British couple.

They fossick through their bags at the end of a double bed they've secured for the night.

"We always getsa room to ourselves." A rough British accent. Shaven-headed Chav is unhappy about our arrival.

Hi, nice to meet you too, mate, I think to myself.

He plugs his electronic tablet into a socket in the wall. Stained into his arms are a few badly etched tattoos. A football team emblem and another that I presume is Woody Woodpecker. As we unpack, he eyeballs us as if to say they were here first.

"We've bin workin' in the Yukkatan inna 'otel resort fer free monfs," he says, like we really wanted to know. "It's lush up there, wevvers great. We love it, don't we, babe." He brings his scrawny missus into the one-sided conversation.

"Yeah, babe," she answers in a similar accent, still rummaging through their mountain of wheelie suitcases at the end of the bed.

How they've failed to gain any kind of suntan while working in the Yucatán for three months is beyond me. I can't help but remember Dean and Mandy, two similar characters Dan and I had the pleasure of meeting in Mendoza a few years ago. These two could easily be related to them, or worse still, their offspring.

"Iss the first time we've shared a room wiv uvver peepul." Chav speaks again, making it clear that he hoped the room would just be for him and his girlfriend.

"Where you lot from?" he asks.

"Reading, originally," I reply.

"Wicked bruv. Safe." He approves of my British hometown. "Yeah, can't wait to get 'ome. See the lads down the pub." His conversation is predictable.

I sigh under my breath, feeling sorry for the future of Britain.

"You American, yeah?" Chav now turns to James, but James doesn't hear him, as he's deep within his exploded backpack, its contents spread all over the bottom bunk.

"Eww! Issa right state this barfroom!" The girl scurries out on tip toes with hands raised like her fingers are controlling string puppets.

James and I share a glance, are hungry and make a plan to leave.

"I finks we gunna jus av dinner 'ere, int we, darlin?" Chav says to his girl.

We didn't ask you, mate.

"Yea, babe," she agrees, not looking up, rummaging in her bags.

"Oi, I fink me fones bin nicked innit!" She kicks off again. Her shrieks fire up the Chav.

"Wot, babes?!" he snorts, puffing up like a pigeon.

We leave them to it and meet Keelan outside in his least creased shirt and smartest shorts.

James's outfit and hot shower have transformed him into Ted Danson from *Cheers* again. At least they've made an effort. I just look like I've returned from five days of hiking.

"Let's go out drinking and meet some girls!" Keenan is bursting with excitement after conquering the hike to El Mirador.

We find ourselves at a little bar completely devoid of all souls. Disco lights flash above our heads as we sit with a watered-down drink.

I swear I see a tumbleweed roll through the place.

We find another bar perched on a rocky outcrop at the shoreline. Sipping a cold beer, dangling our legs into Lake Petén while the sun sets over the surface of the water, I dream of being back on top of a temple again, staring out across the jungle.

Back in the dorm, the English couple are getting into bed and look surprised I'm already home.

"Where's yer American mate?" Chav asks.

"Still out," I gurgle through a foamy mouth, brushing my teeth.

*

"Heeeey, dude, let me in, man."

I'm aroused from my deep sleep.

James is trying to get into the dorm but the Chav couple have locked the door from the inside.

James continues to knock.

"Fa fuck's sake!" Chav boy says, switching the torch on his phone to find the door latch.

Your fault mate. I keep quiet, up on the top bunk.

Opening the door, he's straight back to bed. James follows suit, but not for long. He fumbles his way over to the bathroom, turning on the light, leaving the door open and loudly fire-hosing a piss into the toilet.

"Oi, mate, turn the light off. We're tryna sleep!"

I can feel Chav on the verge of exploding.

James continues, oblivious.

The girl groans. "Fuckin' 'ell, babe, this is a nightmare."

Still hidden up top, I can't help but smirk as the anger continues to escalate below me. James leaves the toilet and makes his way back round to his bunk.

"Hey mate, for fuck's sake, can you please turn the fuckin' light off?!" Chav is fuming now.

"Uh yeah. Sorry, dude." James slurs as he makes his way back to the light switch.

The dorm becomes dark and silent again.

Clump! Clump! The baby blue boat shoes drop to the floor like bricks and James starts a noisy snore.

"I don't fuckin' believe this," Chav says.

"This is 'orrible," the girl adds.

"Iss alright, babe, we'll be onna plane tomorra an' away from all this shit."

We all doze off.

"AARRGGHH! Wot the fuck is goin' on!" Chav screams at the top of his lungs, flicking on the light.

Standing with dick in hand, James is pissing all over their pile of clothes and suitcases at the end of the bed.

Evidently, James has lost directions to the toilet. We are all awake with his splashing sounds.

"Mate! Mate! Wot the fuck are you doin'?!" Chav screams again with his hands on his head, looking like he's about to either burst into tears or have a heart attack.

"Eee's pissin' on arr cloves!" the hag shrieks, now sitting upright. "Do summit, babe!! Fuckin' 'ell, I can't believe this is 'appenin'!" she squeals.

James, still stood in the same position but now with his dick back in his boxers, is clearly out of his mind.

"Mate! Are you fuckin' mental?" Chav is now up in his face.

"It's cooool, maaan, don't stress, duuude," James slurs.

"I'm gonna break yer fuckin' nose yer fuckin' idiot!" Chav is red as a beetroot. His veins look like they are about to burst out of his head while the hag drops to her knees with a towel, trying desperately to mop up what piss she can.

"Eet fuckin steeenks!" she squeals, now crying.

I can't pretend to still be asleep with the volume of the argument spiralling out of control below me.

"JAMES!" I command. "JAMES! GET THE FUCK OUT OF THE ROOM!"

The sheer volume of my voice snaps him out of his daze and sends him fleeing.

Chav is looking a little rattled, obviously forgetting in his rage that I am up here. He grabs a towel and joins the hag to soak up what piss they can. They leave their clothes to soak under a running shower.

"Fuck this, we'll 'av to deal wivvit in the mornin," he snarls, re-locks the door.

His tone softens slightly. "I'm sorry for all this, mate, but your yank mate is a cunt."

I'm surprised at his apology; not so much by what he thinks of James.

THE MORNING AFTER

James nurses a terrible hangover with a Styrofoam cup of coffee. He sits on the courtyard bench where he slept last night.

"I fucked up, right?"

His recollection of the night is vague.

"What should I do?" he asks, looking *very* remorseful.

I suggest waiting until they wake to apologise and offering to wash all their gear.

He nods agreeably.

"It's the least you can do," I add.

The couple emerge from the dorm looking unrested.

"Man, I'm so sorry," he says as they approach him.

"Mate, you're just lucky this guy was there, cos I was gonna break your fuckin' nose," Chav says, puffing up like a pigeon again.

"Give me all your clothes, I'll go and get them washed for you," James offers.

"Nah. Daan't trust ya, mate. Just give us the money cuz we're leaving at midday." Chav holds out his hand.

James slaps a twenty-dollar bill in it. They leave without a word.

"I already booked my bus back to Xela when I woke up. I leave tonight. Fuck this." James crashes out in the dorm.

Keelan and I have breakfast with a couple of older Croatian guys who look like ex-war heroes.

"Vee bought car," they say proudly, dressed for combat in beige desert boots and camouflage army gear.

"Is better to stop vere you vant and see different stuff."

Brave guys, I think. I'm a little envious of their confidence.

They kindly offer us the option of joining them. "Vee are making for zee souse but you can leave us venever you need."

Keelan tells them he's in. I decline, explaining that I have my own itinerary.

A giant blister on my foot from the trek has me limping to the local pharmacy. I buy cream and dressings for it and spend the day researching the next leg of the trip.

The hostel sells bus tickets to San Salvador for 330 quetzals. Although only $40, it's undoubtedly cheaper at the Santa Elena station, but walking that far today on my blister is impossible.

I pay the overpriced fee for a Thursday morning departure.

I hobble with Keelan and a couple of English girls to the local barbeque chicken place. The chatter we have on the way is pleasant but quickly shifts when they ask me to barter in Spanish with the waiter over 3 quetzals.

"Three fucking quetzals! Are you guys for real?" I'm shocked.

"But we asked for legs and wings and he's given us breast."

I stare at them, say nothing and continue with my food.

"Harrumph." They look at me like I've done them a disservice.

Keelan breaks the mood, pointing at a minivan approaching. "There he is! Haha!"

We look and see James is on board.

"Later, bitches!" he shouts at us with his head out the window of the taxi van like a dog with its tongue out.

The English girls harrumph again, wondering who the madman in the van is.

I reflect on my time with James and the random people who cross my path when travelling, all making lifelong memories for good or bad. The boat shoes, the sweatpants, the dorm room piss and his final hurrah hanging out of the van window in true frat-boy style.

I'll miss him – I think. This character of the gringo trail, one more along the path, surely to be replaced down the way by an equally entertaining character – but hopefully not too soon.

A guy called Cooper joins our table, nearly falling from his chair as he sits down. It's clear that he's wasted.

"Yeah, I'm a pro snowboarder and skater but I can't be pro anymore cos of too much heel bruising."

I've never heard of a heel bruise debilitating someone's career before. We continue listening to his boasting for ten minutes, then I tell him I've been skateboarding for twenty-odd years. He promptly changes the subject to hunting black bears in Montana.

The waiter approaches our table.

"Uner pollo por fayyver." Cooper's Spanish is barely Spanish.

Within 48 hours of leaving the Guatemalan jungle, where I was engrossed in intelligent conversations with our guide Maria, I've already encountered the Chavs and Cooper.

Back in the dorm, I fall asleep with the faint whiff of James' piss still lingering.

Keelan hugs me the following morning. "See you, bro. I'm so glad we crossed paths."

"Me too," I reply sincerely.

"I'm going to Nicaragua next trip. You've sold me."

He follows the Croatian war heroes outside and slides into the back seat of their little car.

LAKE PETEN

An American girl sways herself back and forth on a swing in the Flores hostel communal area. "I'm in Guatemala right now! It's sooooooooo cool!" She speaks very loudly into her phone, desperate for attention.

I slip on my boots and go for a walk.

My jungle companions, Keelan and James, have since departed and the time has come to mentally prepare for the next leg to San Salvador. I limp down to the lakeside on the giant blister the jungle has gifted me. Two men quarrel about something across the gap between their little boats. One, a wiry rake of a man with slicked back hair and an ill-fitting button-down shirt, stops his ranting when he sees me and offers up a ride on the lake. I agree to a price, and make his acquaintance.

Denis, my guide and captain, steers us around the lake in his little outboard. He jumps between subject matters, recounting his son breaking his foot playing football and the lake rising by three metres in the last few years. As we float by, he points out the flooded shells of abandoned hotel projects that were built too close to the shore, now occupied by vagrants. The boat slows into the muddy shoreline of San Miguel, a small village of stilted adobe structures. A small cement lane climbs up through the village, but Denis ties up the boat and leads me off track to an overgrown single access stairway. He tells me we are climbing the side of a triadic pyramid known as 'Mirador del Rey Can'Ek' – 'King Kan Ek's Lookout.'

"Nombre Tayasal," he says, as we climb up through the tangled scrub on this higher portion of the peninsula.

Although the summit of the ancient pyramid rewards a great view of Flores Island sitting in the lake, this city, once flourishing with open plazas and pyramid temples, is now buried under centuries of earth and stinging nettles.

SHANE

"Name's Shane."

The guy next to me at the bar speaks in an Aussie accent. The 45-year-old had set off from Australia as soon as his daughter turned 18. "I signed the house over to her so I could live my dream. Holed up in Santa Marta near Cartagena for a while as a diving instructor."

"So what brings you here?" I wonder how he has ended up sat in this bar next to me in the north of Guatemala.

"Ah, I got myself a Colombian girl. Just did a diving stint in Europe so I'm on my way back to see her, thought I'd check this place out on the way."

Shane is a friendly guy, and a bushman of wisdom. He's a welcome change from the younger set of travellers. His park ranger stories of wrestling crocodiles in northern Australia are too cliché to be anything but true. I sit fascinated by his tales before booking a taxi that will take me to the Santa Elena bus terminal in the morning.

THE BROWN BUS

The driver doesn't flinch at the wing mirrors his taxi clips as we descend through the narrow streets of Flores at the crack of dawn. Swerving out onto the perimeter road, we cross the causeway before skidding to a stop outside Santa Elena's terminal a few miles away. Today has started in northern Guatemala and will hopefully end in El Salvador.

A street light flickers and only a few faint shadows move in the morning mist. In the grimy station, a brown bus reading 'Frente del Norte' along its side has seen better days. I look at my ticket. It bears the same company name. *Surely not mine,* I think, picturing the long-distance Tica buses I've ridden in the past.

The 'San Salvador / San Cristobal' destination card lodged in the windscreen confirms my fears.

Seven passengers board the bus before heading south, which passes through many small towns that nest at the foothills of a large mountain range. The driver honks his horn at pedestrians as he squeezes the beast through village market stalls that encroach the highway. We pass a large truck enveloped in beer advertisements. Sat in a small entrance stoop in its side, a short man hunches with a pump-action shotgun propped on his potbelly, presumably to deter any hijackers with a thirst. Sparsely populated greenery flashes by for an hour before the edges of the highway become busier with an African / Caribbean feel. A continuous stream of people can be seen walking the roadside, all wearing bright splashes of colour and balancing baskets of green and orange mangos, yellow bananas and other tropical fruits on their heads. The traditional woven dress of Guatemala seems to have all but gone now we are nearing the edges of the Caribbean. Crossing a bridge, I can see to my left Lake Izabal and to the right, the Río Dulce that slides underneath us, connecting the lake to the Caribbean. Little boats sail along downstream while others propel themselves across the current with large barge poles in dugout canoes.

Across the bridge, we pull into a township bustling with life where a small group climb aboard who look like the cast of Scooby Doo, minus the dog. They bleat in American accents at the top of their voices. I think of the many times I've seen this group before, albeit in different forms. They half-finish their waters and drop the bottles on the floor; these then roll around under the seats every time the bus stops, slows or makes a turn. One keeps repeatedly rolling into one of the girls' feet standing in the aisle – and she still doesn't think to pick it up.

I hate them already and they've only been on the bus ten minutes.

I stay distanced so as not to be associated with them. I sink in my seat, buying some plantain chips from a bus vendor who climbs aboard at a dusty stop. She's beaded in sweat and pushing her way up the aisle. A passenger crushes past the Americans in a bid to get to the front of the bus. As he does, a revolver tucked in the back of his pants is made visible. This whole time, he's been on the bus, a few seats away, with a loaded gun. I wonder who else is packing.

I begin to feel scared as we close in on the border with El Salvador.

The group continue to bleat on at volume, taking selfies with their expensive phones and dancing embarrassingly to the music playing through the buds that dangle from their ears. The passengers surrounding them would probably have to work for a year to afford the electronics on show. I don't fancy their chances in San Salvador. Another stop, another vendor, this one selling candy pushes her way up the crowded aisle. I buy a handful of sweets from her, passing some through the gap in the headrests to a small child in front sat between his parents.

"Hey chico. ¿Quieres?" I hand him the sweets.

His parents nod. The little boy shyly takes them.

Two men who boarded at Río Dulce are working their way through the bus, preaching to individuals. One of them has a bright green parrot on his shoulder. They zone in on the Americans and begin to lecture them.

"You must be careful and not to be so flamboyant with your things." They try to clue them up on the dangers of El Salvador and how to conduct themselves.

"You must always stay in a group." They stress these facts to them.

The Americans bombard them with questions, now sounding very worried about their destination. Their idea of San Salvador being a 'chilled-out surf town near the beach' has been crushed.

"Guys, there are no backpacker hostels in San Salvador," the parrot preacher informs them.

A white and green sign outside reads 'Bienvenidos a San Cristobal' as we enter the outskirts of the border town. Shifty characters sift inside hedgerows that squeak and scratch the bus sides as it squeezes down the wafer-thin road.

Armed soldiers in black ski masks and bulletproof vests outnumber the shifty-looking money changers who surround the checkpoint building where we are asked to get off.

Alighting, I'm now on my own. Not too sure of which lane to take, but not wanting to make a false move in such a sensitive place, I weave through the confusing zig zag of roped-off lanes while the empty bus drives through to the other side. Stamped out at the Guatemalan border booth, I follow the blue and white lines that guide us effortlessly through to the El Salvador point, leading off in various directions. My palms are sweaty and money changers hover at the edges of my peripheral.

The El Salvador customs booths number three. A hand beckons me over from the dark barred window of one of them.

"Documentos," he says calmly.

I hand over my passport and it's passed back almost instantly. I re-board the bus, confused about the lack of an entry stamp.

"No es necesario," the conductor says when I ask.

"CA-4." He reminds me of the visa link held between Guatemala, El Salvador, Nicaragua and Honduras.

I let out a sigh of relief as our bus moves off but it's only in gear for seconds. Literally seconds; now more masked and armed soldiers board, demanding to search our bags and documents.

BIENVENIDOS, CHERO

Masked soldiers in black uniforms search the bus. We've just re-boarded after crossing through the San Cristobal checkpoint. We are now in El Salvador.

As quick as they get on, they disembark, eager to search the vehicle behind.

Floppy-eared cows share the road with broken-down trucks that the bus narrowly avoids as it swerves its way south. Giant cloud-shrouded volcanoes of green, strike juxtapositions with waterfalls of household rubbish that pour from elevated sections onto the roadside.

I've read that 75 percent of the population live on less than a dollar a day here.

My anxiety level runs high as the bus is sucked into the smog-stained bowels of San Salvador. The driver finds an empty bay in a busy row of idling buses at the terminal. The door swishes open to the familiar gang of taxi drivers grabbing at us as we disembark. Picking the least menacing looking driver, I ask if he knows Santa Tecla.

"Si, si, no es lejos." The short guy says it's not far.

He pushes a pair of round spectacles up the bridge of his nose. The address I have seems familiar to him and he says it will be a $12 fare. Led through a dark, low roofed alleyway in the station, we pass two women who stare at me with puzzled faces.

I can't help but think about Buenos Aires in 2009 and the gun point robbery Dan and I had walked into as I tread this new unknown.

The air in the alley reeks of warm human shit but opens out onto a side street where his tricked-out yellow taxi awaits. I throw my bag in the boot and jump in. The dash is plastered in stickers and a tangled clump of rosary beads hangs off the rear-view mirror. He fiddles with his radio, and I ask him if he can play a local station. He appears pleasantly surprised by my question and turns the dial to tune into some Reggaeton. I sense that he's as nervous as me, and I go about lightening the mood, asking his name, where he lives and the usual ice-breaking questions. This seems to put him in a more relaxed state.

"¡Uauu!" Osmin says, when I tell him I'm from England.

"You know dee Beatles? ¡Muy cool!" The drive is filled with chatter as he shows me photos of his baby daughter, Angelica and informs me I'm the first 'extranjero' he's ever driven.

We reach the outskirts of Santa Tecla, where he drives in circles for fifteen minutes around the little town. His directional skills are worrying me. I've come so far today and can't let this guy fuck it up this close to the finish line. I give him Jacob, the school program director's phone number and minutes later, a smartly dressed man standing on the corner of a quiet intersection flags us down. He bends down at the window and surprises me when he greets me in good English.

"Darreen! You made it!" he says.

I grab my pack and thank Osmin for getting me here safely, give him fifteen bucks and tell him to keep the change. He seems as happy as me that we've found our destination. Maybe it's the three-dollar tip.

"¡Bienvenidos, Chero!" he says, pulling away and sounding his horn.

I'm not quite sure what 'Chero' means, but I take it as a compliment.

4
EL SALVADOR BEGINNINGS

HOMESTAY

Jacob's a smartly dressed man in his late twenties. He ushers me into a jeep in his driveway near the intersection where Osmin just dropped me off.

We pass through semi-deserted streets of Santa Tecla in Jacob's jeep before pulling up at a big steel gate. He knocks a smaller door on its left-hand side that sets a dog off barking. I hear a muffled female voice.

"¡Titi! ¡No! ¡Titi! ¡Callate!" The voice commands the dog to be quiet while a series of clanging locks unbolt the metal door. Standing with a white Scots terrier at her feet is a tall slender girl with long dark hair.

"Darren, this is Amelia," Jacob says.

"Hola, Darreen." She stretches the 'e' of my name just as Jacob has while shyly stepping back to let us in.

The dog takes no interest in either Jacob or me but sees its chance and makes a dash into a patch of long grass up the street.

"¡Titi! ¡Titi! ¡Venga!" She stamps her foot, ordering the mutt to come in.

The small dog trots back inside the gate.

Among the few sparsely positioned pot plants in the empty concrete courtyard, an older round lady greets me.

"Hola, guapo. Soy Gina," she says.

"Ella mi hijita Amy." She points at her daughter.

"Y estes son Titi y Zim." She points again to the scruffy terrier and a tiny tabby cat that darts erratically around the plants.

"We see us here tomorrow!" Jacob looks at his watch and takes flight.

"¡Cuidate de Gina!" 'Be careful,' he laughs. "She loves the extranjeros!"

Gina laughs as he shuts the gate behind him.

"¡Mama!" Amy squeals with embarrassment.

I remember how anxious I was before moving into Malena's house in León a few years ago but this is far from awkward. I feel instantly welcomed among these strangers in what will be my home for the next two months.

"¿Donde estas su esposa y sus hijos?" Gina asks of my wife and children. She stares up into my nostrils from below, looking shocked when I tell her I have neither.

Rowdy birds chatter in the tall trees growing from the other side of a tall red brick wall. Topped with razor wire that runs along one side of the courtyard, the wall sprouts green leaves from the cracks in its cement. On the opposite side of the yard, two doorways in a bright blue wall lead into separate rooms. Through one, a very simple kitchen is equipped with a chest of drawers slopped in a shade of purple, a large gas stovetop connected to a bottle that stands on the chequered tile floor and a small vinyl-topped dining table with two plastic chairs. The evening sunlight streams through a barred window.

Two more doors at each end of the room lead to other parts of this maze-like dwelling. The door near the stove reveals a bathroom, its best features a water pipe poking out from the wall and a seatless toilet bowl. The other room can only have been built around the bed. The double mattress pushes against three of its four walls.

"Es tu cuarto." Gina informs me this is my room.

"¡Excelente!"

I'm standing in what will become my own little slice of peace and quiet for the next couple of months. The tiger print blanket spread over the mattress swallows my bag.

"OK nos vemos en escuela mañana." Gina will see me tomorrow at school.

She asks Amy to look after me, giving her a stern look. Amy nods and continues to feed the animals, commenting that I must be hungry, too. I tell her I haven't eaten a pupusa in four years. She gasps as if that's unheard of. (The pupusa is El Salvador's national dish and best described as a thick maize flour pancake with a savoury filling.)

"¡Entonces, vamos!" She throws on a hoody to leave the house.

Various grocery stores and ATMs – the ones I should use – are pointed out as we walk my route to school. The deserted street blocks remind me of Managua in Nicaragua. The first bank she shows me is still under construction. The car park has water pipes sticking out of it and the windows still have crossed adhesive tape stuck to them.

"Que raro," she remarks. How weird.

She pauses for a moment, confused before walking in another direction turning into a little coloured street lined with closed roller doors hiding shopfronts. I'm beginning to think she may not be the most reliable information source regarding my new town.

"Aqui esta." She looks up to a second-storey balcony overlooking the bustling plaza.

A flight of white tiled steps delivers us there. Round, orange plastic stools supported by white metal poles are bolted to the floor and surround rectangular tabletops in the same plasticky orange colour.

"¡Bienvenidos! Sentar por favor." A man greets us and directs us to a table with his open palm.

He hands us two sticky menus with the other. The pupusas advertised vary in fillings. Cheese, beans and pulled pork, and a list of 'Licuardos' on the opposing page. Amy explains they are thick juices blended from ice, fruit and sugar. We share light conversation over dinner before returning home via the town's main street, 'Paseo del Carmen'. She tells me that it comes alive with bars and restaurants on the weekend nights and that townsfolk set up market stalls along the sidewalks.

"La iglesia esta abierta." Amy leads us through scaffold towers that wrap the exterior repairs of the Iglesia del Carmen, an old wooden church that is in dire need of renovation.

Its vast interior shows the true damage that the 2001 earthquake caused. It's like standing below deck of a shipwrecked Spanish galleon. Cracked and dirty stained-glass windows let in little light and crumbling concrete walls hide behind flaking pastel green wooden plank cladding. Fluted wooden pillar façades cover original poles that support an arched roof where wires hang precariously above us. We throw some coins in the donation bucket and continue home.

The thin wall shudders as I close my bedroom door and a silent elation overwhelms me. I made it!

What a day. The bus, the border, Osmin's taxi and my new home.

I punch the air once, twice, many times like a boxer warming up. Jab! Jab! Jab!

Thank god no one can see me.

INAUGURATION

Six chimes of the Santa Tecla church bell wake me to my first morning in El Salvador. I'm in the comfort of my homestay house. I gingerly turn the squeaky stopcock tap embedded in the bathroom wall. It releases a freezing cold sting of water that blasts me as I edge myself into the cubicle; this ensures I'm soaped up and out of there in under a minute. Wrapped in a threadbare towel, I hover with open hands over the blue flame of the stove while a coffee pot brews.

A tall dark man casually strolls into the kitchen, also with only a towel around him.

"Buenos dias," he says, grinning a white, friendly smile before slipping into the bathroom.

I stand frozen on the spot as the bathroom door locks.

Who was that?

Has he just wandered in off the street for a quick wash?

I'm unsure of what to do while this mystery man soaps himself up in the shower singing at the top of his voice. I drink my coffee and wait.

Re-emerging, he introduces himself as my roommate and Amy's uncle, Manilo. He shuffles off to another bedroom in the corner of the courtyard in his towel. I wonder how many other family members they've forgotten to mention live here or perhaps just pop in to use the bathroom before work?

Titi and Zim sit patiently, expecting to be fed.

"No tengo nada," I tell them, sipping my bitter coffee.

Amy startles me as she enters the kitchen and commences pouring food into their bowls.

"¡No Titi! ¡Es tuya y es de Zim!" She pushes the dog away from the cat's bowl with her foot.

There is a knock at the door. It's Jacob, the volunteer programme director.

"¡Buen dia! ¿Como estamos?" he greets us energetically.

A well-rehearsed speech follows in an effort to convince me about the 'Travel to teach' programme and how my fees will be used to benefit the school. Titi sniffs him suspiciously as he hands me a cheap cell phone and a photocopy of a faint town map outline with two X's marking the volunteer house and the school.

"Meet me at dee school in quarenta minutos," he says. I do exactly that.

En route, I am greeted by stall owners calling out their products from the bowels of the municipal market. Cheap clothes, plastic tat and bootleg CDs are waved in my face as I walk through the intimidating disorientation of junk.

The school is painted in sky blue and dirty white shades with a small flagpole that rises upward from a concrete slab where tufts of grass sprout from its cracks. Navy blue letters run vertically above the main doors and read 'Escuela Municipal' and a faded blue sign attached to the wall bares the almost unreadable peeling words:

Centro Escolar Margarita Duran
Ministerio de Educación
Gobierno de El Salvador

This is the place where I'll spend the next few months trying to fool my students into believing I know what I'm doing. I'm overcome with a mixture of intrigue, nerves and anxiety. I wonder what lies behind that school entrance door and what tomorrow will bring.

Jacob knocks the two giant blue steel doors of the school's entrance.

"¡Hola hola!" he calls out.

A shutter slides open in the door and a pair of eyes peer out at us. It feels if we are about to enter a prison. The hatch slides shut, a bolt unlocks and the door creaks open. I step inside and am transported into a different world.

A series of numbered dark blue classroom doors in the perimeter walls surround an outer raised red tiled floor, sheltered under a roof that's supported by blue and white concrete pillars. The sun blazes down on an eerily empty concrete netball court in the centre, where along one wall, a row of sinks hang.

A small wire cage in one corner houses a tuck shop that looks like an old chicken coop and diagonally across the court from this is another caged area where a cook is busily stirring a giant wooden spoon in a huge steaming pot.

Behind a blue door bearing the number '5A', I walk into a scene scarier than yesterday's border crossing. Entering the dimly lit space, it's mayhem. Paper litters the floor and girls shriek at each other arguing over pens and pencils.

"Introduce yourself to them, you'll be fine," Jacob tries to reassure me over the din.

He grips my shoulder.

"Son niñas." He smiles. Just girls.

Two American women standing near the whiteboard are taking the class and point to me causing thirty little heads to turn 180 degrees and stare.

Jacob prompts me, squeezing my shoulder.

I nervously address the class. "Buenas niñas, soy Darren, el voluntario nuevo."

"¡Gooood moooorniiiinggg teeeeechuuuurrr!" they bellow together, startling me a little.

"¿Y cuantos años tienen ustedes?" I ask their age.

"¡OCHO!" they shout back, laughing. '8'

"Que bueno. Mucho gusto a conocerle y nos vemos mañana." I keep it short, saying I'll see them tomorrow.

The reality of what I've signed up for hits hard.

Standing in front of thirty 8-year-olds whose sole focus is to see how many of your buttons they can push is not what I'd initially envisioned.

INTO THE FIRE

Thousands of butterflies flutter in my stomach while I sit waiting in the school foyer for classes to start the next morning. The walk to school in unfamiliar surroundings only added to them. This is a huge step for me. I'm very anxious about what lies ahead.

Vicky, a girl from Utah, is introduced to me by Jacob. Something about her vacant stare stirs religious connotations. A short, rotund woman with a stern face approaches me, with Gina at her side.

"Hola," she says. "Soy Lola."

"Darren, es Directora." Gina introduces her as the school principal.

I have a similar feeling to when I was 10 and being called into the headmaster's office for throwing stones at windows.

I guess she's just sussing me out. After all, I'm here to teach the girls in her care.

"Es muy alto." She remarks in a concerned tone to Gina about my height. I'm glad to be wearing long sleeves as I dread to know her stance on tattoos.

Lola's oversized tablet phone rings and she disappears into her office to take the call.

"Sentate." Gina guides me with her open hand into a staff room seat.

She explains that the American women volunteer teachers, who were teaching yesterday's class where first I introduced myself, are receiving their diplomas in front of the whole school today.

The din from the sea of excited girls at break time is deafening. Groups of them run around playing ball, skipping and chasing, while others sit in circles talking.

Lola returns to the foyer area. Her presence silences the noise of recess. Sitting on chairs in front of the whole school, the two women cry tears of joy as they listen to the schoolgirls and teachers thank them. The microphone transmits a metallic sound through the tannoy system.

Tears flow as one by one the classes make their way up and hug the departing teachers. I'm beginning to realise the impact it's possible to make as a volunteer. But will I be able to make the same impression? These two women are actually real teachers back in Nebraska and it causes me to question my ability. They stick around after the ceremony to watch and help me in my first lesson.

"We've been helping the girls to cut out pictures from a pile of fashion magazines we brought with us from the States."

"OK, great, we can get into that." I go along with their suggestion. "But do you think I can introduce myself with a slightly off-theme topic?"

"Dude, you go with whatever you feel is right." The woman puffs through a pair of rosy cheeks.

"Hola, niñas. ¿Como estan ustedes?" I ask them how they are, gaining their full attention.

"¡Bien gracias!" they reply in unison.

So far so good.

"¡OK! ¿Este es que?" I draw a crude world map with a piece of chalk on the giant green chalk board.

"¡Una mapa!" comes the reply.

"¡Si!" I reply. "¡Excelente!"

My next question has them all silent and bewildered. "¿Donde esta Nueva Zelanda?"

A few point at different areas on the map but most of them stare at me like stunned fish.

I tell them it's a small island near Australia.

Still silence.

I mark the spot and ask them to copy the map down in their books.

The Nebraskans leave quietly without raising the attention of the class.

This can only be a good sign.

"¡Teeecher teecher ya termine!" A small girl with plaited hair lets me know she's finished.

This opens a floodgate of twenty students all wanting their pages marked as well. Hands fly up as they rush me at my desk. Overwhelmed, I desperately try to mark each book thrust in my face but thankfully am saved by the end of class bell going off.

"¡Gracias teechuur!" They leave in a stampede.

Going through the same map and country routine with the next class, I'm starting to realise the magnitude of the responsibility I've been handed. They bicker and squabble over pens and paper, but I ignore them the best I can, unsure if being stern is the right or wrong thing to do.

The ring of the bell is music to my ears once again. They quickly pack up and filter out of the classroom.

I feel exhausted as I walk home.

Gina is tending to her plants in the yard. I ask her what level of discipline is acceptable with the disruptive students.

"Eres el jefe Darren. No van a morder."

Her words are wise. I must remember them tomorrow: You're the boss, they won't bite back.

My homestay roommate, Amy, drags me along to the supermarket on the other side of Santa Tecla. The barred windows and lack of other pedestrians as we walk is unnerving. I'm once again reminded of the eerie and empty backstreets Dan and I nervously walked through in Nicaragua's capital Managua a few years ago.

A man with a crooked stick and a strange eye asks for money but Amy whisks me inside the supermarket.

I weave cautiously among the exposed rusty corners of racking and buy tuna, tortillas and a chewy bone for Titi. People stare at us curiously while we shop.

The folding door of the bus has no glass and stays half-open as we return home.

Blue packaging string holds our seats to the frame.

Jacob calls to say I should join the volunteers for dinner this evening.

I insist that Amy comes with me, much to her distaste.

Jacob picks us up as the skies darken.

'La Gran via' is a large beige, neon lit shopping mall and cinema complex. Various international fashion brands and fast-food joints occupy identically shaped, glass fronted stores. It feels very westernised. Inside 'Cebolline's' restaurant, the table is comprised of volunteers all about to return to varying mid-west states of America and a couple of new arrivals. The long bar is shadowed by several TV screens hung from the ceiling playing Mexican music videos at a dinner-spoiling volume, while families and couples eat very un-Salvadoran dinners of pizza, curly fries and steaks. Jacob sits at the head of our table where two carafes of margaritas are placed. He's clearly enjoying the attention of the female volunteers.

WHITE MEN CAN'T DANCE

Still unsettled in my new surroundings, I'm far from prepared for the evening my homestay family have in store for me.

"¡Esta noche vamos a bailar!" Gina changes the subject of teaching to dancing.

She does a little twist, wiggling her arms.

"Hay fiesta grande para la maestras. Te invitamos."

A teachers' party for the staff of the Santa Tecla school sounds like a great way to immerse myself with the locals. After all, it is only my second day in El Salvador.

"Pero necesito ropa elegante." She says I'll need smart clothes.

I mention that I don't own any.

"Aiii, chero!" she advises Saint Martín Plaza is the place to go for a new suit.

I find a giant recycle shop overflowing with used clothing. I sift through piles of garments sent down from the USA to be re-sold; the enormous measurements of the altered clothes say a lot about the state of American health. Racks and racks of giant waist-banded jeans don't give me much hope I'll find anything that fits.

After a long arduous process, I manage to find a pair of beige chinos that just about reach my ankles. I figure if I walk a certain way, I can minimise the gap between the top of my shoes and their hem. Slinging them over my shoulder, I finger my way through the racks of nightgown-sized shirts and find one with vertical stripes in a faded tinge of blue. Tucking the shirt into the trousers, I exit the changing booth to search for a mirror.

And there I am, looking back at myself in my new ensemble.

The tucked in nightgown shirt looks like an air cannon is inflating it, and my beige high-wading slacks stretch desperately downwards in an effort to reach my socks. Just like 'Superman' exiting a phone booth after his transforming spin, I have also emerged anew, a completely different character.

But rather than appearing as a superhero, I have stepped out as a Mexican gardener.

"¿Todo bien?" A young man approaches me as I stand speechless, still staring at myself in the mirror.

"Si, todo bien, gracias." I lie and purchase the outfit for three dollars.

Back at home, I make a burrito while Titi and Zim sit at my feet, waiting for any scraps that fall on the floor. As I'm washing up my dishes. Gina arrives with two other teachers dressed very elegantly.

"¡Hombre! ¡No hombre!" She sounds angry but I'm unsure why.

"¡Amy le va a hacer!! ¡No lavar!" She scolds Amy for letting me wash up, embarrassed in front of her friends. I refuse and carry on.

"Tenemos que ir." She grabs the dish brush from me, throws it in the sink and hurries us out the door.

Amy has also spruced herself up, wearing a tight-fitting black dress and choker. Leaving the house, they float along elegantly in their finery while I awkwardly try to keep up in my high wading chinos, waddling along behind like a penguin.

We arrive at two tall wrought-iron gates and walk up a driveway flanked by equally tall bushes. A flight of white marble steps end at fluted columns draped in wide red satin ribbons. Either Gina has led me to believe it's a small affair or more likely, I've misheard her. This grand entrance crushes any thoughts of my 'intimate teacher party'. At the top step, we are greeted by a butler in coat tails who passes us each a silver gift wrapped box with a red bow. Amy tells me it's a small gift.

I look up to see a huge crack running down through the middle of the roof gable.

"De la ultima terremoto." Gina sees me staring at it: from the last earthquake.

Inside the palace and staring out across the sea of people, I'm clearly the only foreigner. Females dressed in beautiful gowns dominate the head count. I can't believe my eyes, it's like we've time travelled to the roaring '20s. Lola, the school principal, introduces me to a short man in glasses who everyone waits to shake hands with.

"Darreen, es Oscar." She seems ecstatic that I'm meeting him.

"Hola, Darreen." His voice is sincere as he shakes my hand, putting his left one on top to strengthen the bond.

"Bienvenidos a nuestro país." His welcome to 'our country' feels very heartfelt but also official. He continues on to the next person.

Round tables are carefully set with white tablecloths and place names. Each one with a sign allocating it for a specific college, school or group. A band sets up their equipment on a huge stage while smartly dressed waiters bring ceviche in fluted glass bowls to the tables. One by one, the head of each table is asked to go up to the stage and read their speech about what their school or institution has achieved in the past year.

The room erupts in applause as Oscar takes the stage.

Amy leans over to me. "El es el Alcalde de Santa Tecla, será Vice Presidente del país," she whispers.

This man standing in front of us and commanding the attention of the crowd is the town's mayor, Oscar Ortiz, and, according to what Amy has just told me, the future vice president of the country.

To have already met the man who could be running the country after only two days is certainly not what I expected. I sit and listen attentively while he delivers his speech, commending the room on their brilliant work in educating the youth of the country.

A line of cantina girls in blue feathery costumes take the limelight and begin to dance. Long slender legs kick and twist in tights and suspenders to the rhythms of the music. A gorgeous girl in a flamboyant red head dress joins them and begins to sing. The tables slowly empty and filter onto the dance floor until there are only a few random people left sitting. I'm one of them. Even if I wanted to, I could not possibly dance in the second-hand clown suit I've worn to this grand affair. I watch all this from my seat.

A beautiful young woman in a shimmering emerald green dress approaches me. I look behind expecting to see someone else, but no one is there.

The woman stands over me and smiles shyly. "Bailar conmigo." She orders me to dance with her.

Before I can answer, her smile broadens, and she grabs my hand and drags me up and through the empty tables to the dance floor.

As Oscar the mayor sways and twists like a natural, I know that my 'puppet on a string' dance moves are about to embarrass me. Thinking swiftly, I take the woman's hands and let her lead.

Smiling faces fill the dance floor as she spins and shuffles me through the crowd. Everyone wants to shake my hand and know my name. I'm overwhelmed by the attention. The girl in green passes me on to another equally pretty girl in a blue dress who continues to spin me around. I oblige as she shakes and sways, gyrating her hips, while I try to copy.

And then another girl, as beautiful as the last. I lose myself in her deep dark eyes. I'm shared around for a few more songs but manage to squirm my way back to the table for a rest.

But the girls don't give up.

Every one of them wants to dance with the novelty gringo. It's a relief when the whole room sits back at their tables. The waiters appear with plates of roast chicken, potatoes and green beans stacked on their arms while the music takes a mellower tempo.

But no sooner have I finished my last spoonful of ice cream than girls begin to line up to dance with me. I'm dragged back in the writhing tangle of the dance floor, passed around again like a rugby ball.

"¡Vamos afuera!" A beautiful girl shouts into my ear over the loud music, dragging me outside by the arm.

Standing among the fluted pillars out front, she whispers in my ear. "Soy Lucy," she says.

If I was ever going to fall in love immediately, it would be this moment, here, with Lucy. She asks if I'm a teacher, too.

"Mas o menos." I tell her more or less, explaining my volunteer status. "¿Y donde esta su esposo?" I ask of her husband.

She's a single mother.

"Me llama mañana." She writes her number on a scrap of paper and leaves in a taxi. I clutch it, her soft voice still in my ear: Call me tomorrow.

Finally getting a breather, I chat to an old bald guy. He's the husband of one of the teachers and speaks good English. Originally from El Salvador, they'd moved to the US when the country was at war but have now moved back and are renting their house in California.

"With the rent from the house we can live pretty happily down here," he says. We talk until the party wraps up.

Before we leave, another girl hands me her number on a scrunched-up piece of napkin.

"Es mi amiga, allá." She points at her blonde friend looking sheepish across the dance floor, and tells me she's shy: "Es tímida."

I put the napkin in my pocket. We leave as a torrential downpour hits.

"Vamos con Lola." Gina hurries us to a tiny white Suzuki jeep with black smoke puffing from its exhaust. Squeezing into the vehicle's back seat, the three of us fidget and manoeuvre our limbs to get comfortable. Lola clicks the passenger seat back and jumps in shielding herself from the rain.

"Hola, querido Patricio." Gina greets the driver, an old man wearing spectacles and an Arabic scarf over his head.

"Hola, mamacita," he replies in a rough sexy voice. The women giggle.

"El quiere mi leche." Gina makes everyone laugh except for Amy.

"¡Aii mama!" she shrieks, embarrassed at her mother's claim that the old man wants her milk.

As the Suzuki lurches forward, I can't quite believe the evening that has just transpired. If this is El Salvador's way of welcoming me, then the next two months are going to be quite the ride.

Patricio's face presses against the fogged-up windscreen as he crawls us home at snail's pace.

ACCULTURATION

Amy's dog Titi rolls in front of me hoping for a belly rub as I shuffle through the courtyard to the bathroom. Surviving the ice shower, I wait patiently shivering while the coffee pot rattles away on the stove. I swig back my mug before heading off to school.

From the top of the small sedan, a loudspeaker wails the metallic tones of a sock salesman. The megaphone continues, fading off down the street as the old car creeps along the curbside.

I push open the door of an internet café. A little bell tinkles at its top and a scraping sound grates the floor. It's a pokey little shop of individual booths where a few teens sit playing online games.

"Tengo una página." I ask to print a document.

The girl behind the desk looks at me like I've asked her something in Albanian. Her eyes slowly follow my pointing finger to the printer that she probably didn't even know existed under her desk.

"No funciona," she mutters.

Of course it's broken.

I bid her farewell and venture out to find somewhere else to fulfil the task. The overflowing lean-tos and back alleys of cluttered streets are confusing, but I find San Martín Park where I'd bought my Mexican gardener outfit for the school ball. Old buses line the kerbs of the square while vendors drape jeans and socks for sale over the park fence.

I spot a 'Ferreteria' hardware store and try my luck. Rolls of gaffer tape hang next to ladders and coils of rope, every item jostling for space on the overcrowded walls of the small store. Two girls and an older man serve customers but seem to be ignoring me as I look around, perhaps in fear of the game of charades they'll play with a gringo who can't speak Spanish.

"Hola. ¿Como estan ustedes?' I greet them with a smile and startle the old man.

"Hola, todo bien, gracias. ¿Que busca?" He asks what I'm looking for.

"Tengo una página a imprimir." I tell him about the printing.

"Ah, no puedo." He can't help me, but he directs me to a stationary store on the other side of the park.

Through the crowded sidewalk, I duck into a covered walkway flanked on one side by thick brown fluted columns. A sandwich board reading 'Papelería' directs me into a dark arcade. Paint peels from the wall and the tile floor cracks with each footstep. Sat on the window ledge of an empty shop space and picking through a Styrofoam bowl of food with a plastic spoon is a bony-framed man in a loose brown uniform. Leaning against the ledge next to him is a pump action shotgun with a worn rubber reload grip that looks like it's seen some use.

"Hola, amigo." He greets me with a smile and shovels an overloaded spoon of the orange soup into his mouth. "Sentate." He beckons me to sit with him.

I perch myself on the ledge next to the shotgun. I tell him I'm English. He asks if I know the Beatles. He slurps another spoonful of food and wipes bits of orange rice and soup from his face.

Scrawling his number and name on an unused napkin, he puts it in my hand closing my fingers around it.

"Jorge," he says, shaking my hand.

I ask him why he has a gun. He stops eating and fixes my eye.

"Estamos en El Salvador chero." He raises his eyebrows: We are in El Salvador friend.

"Soy una guardia de seguridad. Es peligroso chero. Cuidate." He tells me: "I'm a security guard. It's dangerous. Be careful."

I tell him I'm going to the office store. He nods and digs his spoon back into the bowl.

The girl behind the counter looks like she's suffering from the effects of a sedative. Her droopy eyelids and blank expression are not filling me with confidence that I'm going to be able to complete my mission. I sit down, open my emails and click the print icon once more but the computer shuts down and restarts. I try again. Same. I try once more and hear the printer whirr to life under her desk. Bingo! We wait while the machine whirrs below her. The fact that a page isn't appearing from the slot doesn't seem to faze her.

"¿Hay una problema?" I ask.

She says she doesn't know and that she's never used it before. I ask her if I can look. She pushes herself backwards on her wheeled office chair. Squeezing past her hairy legs, I shuffle along on my hands and knees under the desk for closer inspection. Judging by the cobwebs and dust inside the machine, I surmise it probably hasn't been opened since the 1980s and is void of an ink cartridge. Without wanting to confuse the poor girl anymore, I thank her (for what, I don't know) and leave empty-handed. Jorge is still slurping away on his bright orange soup outside.

"¿Quieres?" he offers me a spoonful.

"No, gracias." I wave goodbye.

Back in the blinding sun, an air of desperation hangs over the streets that surround the park. Mounds of vegetables are peeled by old women in white headscarves while makeshift wire racks hanging from cable ties, display plastic clothes pegs, egg whisks and other household utensils. Brightly painted flames and religious slogans adorn the sides of the noisy buses that belch dark clouds of smoke from chrome exhaust pipes. It feels like I'm in a market of yesteryear but the goods on offer are of a tacky western influence. Cell phones and SIM cards, walls of pop CDs and the latest films only just released in cinemas across the world, already dangling in DVD cases for $2. The pungent smell of mothballs and mould engulf me as I enter a used clothing shop. It feels like an abandoned department store with the fittings ripped out.

"Los Rolling Stones. Meek Jagger." A young assistant replies appropriately when I tell him where I'm from.

I can see a pattern developing here.

He asks me to help him with his English. Obliging, we spend fifteen minutes going through some simple phrases and words which he writes down on a piece of paper.

Back outside in the park, people outnumber space and eyes follow me as I look for somewhere to rest. I wonder if the other volunteers venture out from the house at all. I perch on the end of a bench where a man and a young boy are sitting, and I feel lonely for the first time since waiting for hiking buddies in Flores.

"Chero," one of the men says, tapping me on the shoulder.

I turn around to look at him. He bears signs of a hard life. With a wrinkled face and a worn collared shirt, he asks where I'm from.

"Inglaterra," I say.

"¡Meester Bean!" At least his reply isn't related to the 'Fab Four'.

I do wonder if he thinks I'm Mr. Bean, though.

"¿Y usted?" I ask him where he's from.

"Aqui, no mas," – 'Here no further,' he says. "Mucho gusto chero." And with that, he slowly pushes himself to his feet and walks off followed by the young boy.

Making myself more comfortable on the bench, I feel relatively safe here. Not one person has begged or asked me for money but it's clear to see that these people are below the breadline. I sit at the bench alone and soak up the life of this little town quietly going about its business.

VOLUNTEERS

Jacob and I make our way to the 'volunteer house' to check up on a girl who has fever and vomiting.

I'm not overly excited to visit a sick German, but with nothing better to do, I join him. No more than five blocks from the school and situated in a colourful street of barred windows, the place is a far cry from my homestay accommodation. Shiny mopped floors, air conditioning, Wi-Fi and a couple of hammocks in the backyard far surpass the grass growing from our cracked courtyard and the seat-less toilet. This is how the volunteers live, in an all-American house with all-American amenities. The kitchen has a blender on the bench and a tall bookshelf in the lounge holds a selection of reading material left behind by previous tenants. Stephanie, a mousy-haired German girl, only pulls one ear pod out as Jacob introduces me. She half-heartedly smiles before continuing to tap away on her laptop from the comfort of the leather couch.

The place is well kept, thanks to their cleaner, but I feel integrating with Salvadoran life would almost certainly be hindered if I were to stay here. I wait while Jacob kisses up to the girls and their every whim, cracking a few cheesy jokes with one of the new arrivals, an American girl called Vicky as she blends a smoothie in the kitchen.

"You can use the Wi-Fi, amigo," he says.

Stephanie looks at him with disdain. She's clearly not happy about his offer.

Erika, the sick girl Jacob is there to check up on, appears from a room and, in a demanding tone without so much as a hello, insists that he bring her more bottled water for the cooler.

MONICA

I grab an ice-cold Coke from a chilly bin that its vendor uses as a seat. The faded parasol shading her is tied with twine to a power pole and hangs precariously at eye level over the crumbling sidewalk. Folding myself in two, I stoop down, pay her and continue. Further on, a wrinkled old lady sits inside a shop in a tattered wicker chair. The floor is wall-to-wall black and white chequered tiles. A dusty glass cabinet contains an ancient tool of some description, two tea towels and one used leather shoe. I give her a confused nod as I pass.

The animals greet me on my arrival at home. Amy prepares to leave for her night shift at the veterinary hospital. She inquires after my plans for the evening.

I imagine how boring I must sound, staying in on a Saturday night to read a book.

She does a bad job of hiding a look of pity as she leaves.

Swinging in the hammock desperate for company, I open the slip of paper I was given at the teachers' ball.

Monica – 2307–5546.

One ring and she answers, telling me to meet outside the 'Cafetalón Park' at 7pm.

"¡Nos vemos!" She excitedly hangs up.

Fuck. A date on my third night in the country. I danced with so many girls that night, I can't even remember what she looks like.

On the way to meet her, I wander through Paseo del Carmen. It is alive with market stalls. Among the wares I see assorted crockery, glazed donuts and a hot drink called horchata on offer. I discover our meeting point is by far the worst place to do so. A river of cars crawl past, queueing to get into the town's only parking lot. I wait in the rain, until a little red car pulls up. I don't recognise the blonde woman waving at me from inside the steamy vehicle but I'm guessing it has to be her. I climb in.

She wastes no time and tells me all about her day as she navigates us through the awful traffic to 'Cebolline's' in La Gran Via mall. It's the same place that Jacob had taken our volunteer group and I figure it's a safe bet.

For that matter, it's the *only* place I know.

Long straight blonde hair falls elegantly around Monicas face, and she wears a cream halter dress.

Dressed in ripped jeans, a white t-shirt and my only boots, I'm punching well above my weight here.

Candlelight illuminates the restaurant. Pizzas and curly fries are carried to tables as we continue our conversation over drinks. She tells me in detail how she married very young, is now divorced and living with her two teenage children. Before our food arrives, I'm startled when she reaches across and holds my hand, telling me she has a problem with the way I dress and that I should be at least wearing a collared shirt.

I'm not sure if her direct approach is admirable or offensive and my mind races, unsure of what I'm getting myself into. She giggles a lot on the way home, telling me she's so glad that she's 'found me'. Staring out of the windscreen as she erratically swerves along the road, I try to process her comments throughout the evening.

Is she comparing me to a rescue pet? Or perhaps a cherished long-lost earring she's recovered in a crease of her sofa.

Outside the house, she continues with her forward approach and asks to come in, but in fear of taking things too fast, or possibly her barricading herself inside and holding me hostage, I decline politely and motion to leave the car.

"¡NO!"

She startles me again, commanding me like a dog and grabbing me by the forearm with a talon-like grip. Prising her claws free, I exit the car and wait at the gate until she drives away. I am desperate for company and yes, *I* phoned *her*, but perhaps I'm not that desperate after all.

CHANCHITA

"Tiene la Marie Cruz esta tarde." Gina tells me Marie Cruz, the teacher of my next class, will stay with me during lesson as the girls are a disobedient bunch.

My anxiety raises in anticipation of what the afternoon holds.

Back in the school, I briefly see the German girls Stephanie and Erika who were shifting around the volunteer house. Still prickly and clearly looking down their noses at me, they disappear into another classroom.

Marie Cruz is a lovely lady with small round spectacles. She embarrasses me, telling her girls I work in the film industry with lots of famous actors. And then, contradictory to what Gina has told me, says she has a sore throat and leaves me to teach alone.

Thankfully the girls are fascinated by my movie work, asking me about Brad Pitt and other famous people. It seems Hollywood has the world at its mercy as they obsess about what stars of the big screen are like.

Although mostly attentive, interested and keen to learn, their attention slips away quickly and the majority are quick to cause trouble. One in particular thinks it's funny to snort like a pig when my back is turned. I let it go a few times but eventually lose my cool.

"¿Tenemos una chanchita en clase?" I sound stern when I ask them: *Do we have a little pig in the class?*

The large square table in the back corner where most of the disruption is coming from bursts into laughter.

I pick out who it is in a heartbeat.

"OK, a la oficina por fa." I pull my draw card, calmly telling the girl to go to the office.

Her face changes from a grin to a look of fright.

"¡No! ¿Porque?" she squeals.

"La chanchita, no mas. ¿OK?"

She nods remorsefully.

And just like that: no more oink.

VEGAN

The German girls Stephanie and Erika bombard Jacob with questions about a weekend away for the volunteer group to some islands in El Salvador's Gulf of Fonseca.

It's clear they're going to be very much out of their comfort zones. They insist we all chip in to buy food at the supermarket, stressing that all the vegetables have to be washed and sealed in zip lock bags. Their behaviour is rude and insulting. I imagine sitting before a carefully prepared traditional meal, while the girls unzip their plastic bags and nibble on their sweaty prewashed carrots.

I'm a little anxious being with this group for a whole weekend, but don't want to miss the opportunity to see the country. Jacob's description of our host reminds me of the rough salty old man known as 'Captain Quint' in the *Jaws* movie. A man I can imagine will make the German girls squirm with disdain.

I convince my homestay family's daughter, Amy, to come along, assuring her I'll help with the costs.

My little phone rings. Dreading Monica's number on the screen, I'm relieved when it's Gina's.

"¿Que haces Darito?" She's wondering where I am.

"En camino a casa." I tell her I'm on the way home.

She says we'll be going to a teachers dinner at the art museum tonight. Amy has been at school this afternoon acting as a substitute teacher but is distraught after having her purse stolen. Gina calms her daughter, inviting her to the dinner and reassuring her that we'll get it back.

The museum is opposite the entrance to the Cafetalón Park where Monica had met me. Its small slit windows are barred and the white exterior brick work is reminiscent of a jail house.

"Este," Gina begins, "Fue la jaula," she confirms my observation. Inside, an exhibit of young Salvadoran artists is on show. Unique works of art hang in each tiny jail cell that are designated to each artist. Gina leads us inside to a half open room where a long table and chairs have been set up, where a group of ladies ranging from 40 to very old sit. Lola, Maria Cruz, Janine and a few other teachers I recognise from Margarita Duran are here. Lola hugs me and introduces me to a lady who was the principal many years ago. A stack of pupusas are then served with curtido, the pickled cabbage that always accompanies the dish. I spot a tiny cockroach flat and torched in amongst the cheese as I tear my pupusa open. Gina sees it too but I don't want to make a fuss and eat the chunk where the little critter is embedded. She gives me a look of admiration that I've not brought it to anyone's attention. I appreciate the invite even if my food does contain an insect. The women then all wait to see my expression as we are served 'pastelitos' – pastry pockets containing caramelised plantain. They look satisfied when my face lights up after taking a bite. Amy and I excuse ourselves, heading out to the rear courtyard, where inmates would once have had their hour of exercise. An old lady's face bearing a sad expression is spray painted on a high white block wall that runs the width of the yard.

Jacob calls. The German girls are having a birthday dinner tonight. I accept his invite, again begging Amy to come with me. I'm relieved when she reluctantly agrees.

Stephanie is having her drinks at a swanky vegan restaurant. The fact such a place exists here is a shock. Amy says it's popular with the wealthier folk from the city. I doubt many from this little town have eaten here.

Two maître d's who think very highly of themselves look us up and down as if to say we're in the wrong place, but Jacob calls out across the empty restaurant from their table. We join them and the current conversation – still about the groceries for the Gulf of Fonseca trip.

I order drinks for Amy and me, saying we've already eaten at the teachers' dinner.

"Vat teachers' dinner?" Stephanie seems annoyed.

Jacob glances at me like I've just stirred a wasps' nest.

"Vere vas it?" Erika is also curious.

"Oh, just a small gathering at the museum for a previous principal."

They continue to pick at their over-priced rabbit food.

A new volunteer by the name of Angel joins our table. Hailing from Portland, Oregon, she resembles a transparent sea cucumber. Short, frail and very limp looking, she could benefit from a good, nutritious meal. She's in the wrong restaurant for that.

"I won't be coming," she says. "I'm meeting up with my boyfriend who lives here." Then she adds, "We met online."

Amy and I down our drinks and make to leave but Stephanie hastily gets the bill and starts to divide it. I do not want to be in the middle of this complicated scenario and slap a $10 note on the table for our $6 drink bill. "Keep the change," I say.

SAN SALVADOR

The church bells of Santa Tecla wake me.

"¿Dormiste bien?" Gina asks how I slept. She's already tending to her plants in the courtyard.

"¿Oiste?" I comment on the hooting sound, asking if she hears it too. She loves the sound of the bird.

"Muy tropical." She points up in the branches pinpointing a blue and green long feathered bird. I think of Maria and her knack for spotting animals on the Mirador hike.

Gina joins me for a stovetop coffee. It's sweet she's come to check on me before she goes to school. She still teaches there from time to time. I ask her about the hundreds of mosquitos that hang around the yard. She tells me they lay their eggs in the sink water.

Flash cards go down well with 8th grade and I manage to get through the forty-five minutes relatively unscathed. I catch Jacob at recess and ask about powder for the mosquito eggs in the sink at home.

"Ah, just go to the cook, she will give you some." I can tell he's becoming tired of my questions regarding simple amenities for the house.

"N'ombre." The cook has none and directs me back to Jacob.

Later that day he gives me a guilty look when I tell him what the cook said and he says we can go get some in the city.

"It's good trip for you and Vicky, but you must stay close to me."

As the taxi drives towards San Salvador the heavens unleash a torrential down pour. Gina calls me, frantic, wondering why I've been so stupid and gone to the city on my own. I explain I'm with Jacob in a cab but her concern for my safety still worries me. We pass a fork in the freeway, where an overhead sign directs Santa Tecla traffic to the left and San Salvador to the right. Quietly, I'm hoping we take the left and just go back to familiar surroundings.

The taxi veers right passing through a confusing labyrinth of industry, where corrugated iron fences hold in tall steel racks that overflow with car parts. Tatty neon signs on tall poles sprout high into the grey sky, advertising fried chicken. Underwear and cell phone covers are displayed in the eroding shopfronts below them.

We pull in suddenly to a guarded parking lot behind the giant Catedral Metropolitana and make a dash in the rain, ducking into its covered entrance.

The hollow, lofty insides are dimly lit by a huge chandelier hanging from the centre of a domed roof where painted angels frolic in a blue sky. Its bulbs blink over two rows of hard wood pews facing a wooden pulpit where a pastor reads passages from the Bible. Behind him, eight colossal murals depicting religious scenes reach high up the walls joining the angels on the roof. I can only imagine what it's like on a bright sunny day, very much different to today's dark brooding space where people kneel praying.

Downstairs in the crypt, the roof is low and the air is cold. The tomb of Archbishop Oscar Romero fills the entire space. At each of the four corners of the tomb, beautifully sculpted bronze figures in hooded capes guard the central horizontal statue of the dead Romero with his archbishop's mitre. According to some, a design inspired by Romero's statement shortly before he was assassinated.

"If they kill me, I will rise again in the Salvadoran people."

An advocate of anti-government corruption, he spoke out against the social injustices, poverty and the assassinations and torture tactics being carried out at the time. Worshipped by the poor and reviled by the right-wing government, he was shot in broad daylight by a death squad while offering mass in the chapel to support the country's poor.

This erupted El Salvador in a thirteen-year civil war that claimed an estimated 75,000 lives.

The mood down here in his crypt is palpable. Its cream-coloured arched low roof and thick pillars feel very much like a bomb shelter. We pay our respects before venturing back outside.

The 'Centro historico' area should be, in theory, one of Central America's most architecturally interesting places but after years of empty government promises to clear up the chaos, the situation has only grown worse. The smog-stained paintwork of the ancient and ornate building façades surrounding the main plaza and its park are masked under tin and tarp roofs, propped up with makeshift struts and rope. The rain, still falling in buckets, is running off in torrents from a gutter-less mass of awnings, giving these tired buildings a tangible air of despair. People shelter under them and stare at us miserably. It seems the pavements are meant for every purpose except walking. To find an unoccupied stretch would surely be impossible.

Braving the rain, we head across the square to the Palacio National, the building that housed the government before the 2001 earthquake. Six fluted columns stand proud along its frontage, and I seize my chance to buy a coffee outside from a little lady sheltering under a yellow and green segmented parasol. The brolly has seen better days but the oversized yellow raincoat she's wrapped in keeps her dry. Her trolley is loaded with hot water urns full of coffee that swing from the sides. She grabs a Styrofoam cup, fills it with piping hot coffee and passes it to me.

"Quince." She hands me a little paper tube of sugar.

I give her a dollar for the 15c drink. Her eyes light up and she dots a cross across her chest. I dash with my drink up the stairs of the Palacio's entrance. An ornate foyer of brown and black chequered floor tiles welcomes me in. The coffee is warming and sweet but as I take a second sip, Jacob calls over to me.

"Hey, no drinks inside."

I leave it at reception.

The old government house is a national treasure of Salvadoran history. Climbing a marble staircase with wide fluted bannisters, we are directed through a series of regally decorated rooms of differing colours. The ornamental plaster architraves, cornices and ceiling domes hark back to the early 1900s when the building was originally constructed and, unlike many of the buildings I saw on our way into the city, has been tenderly looked after and cherished. Each room has a line of free-standing informative photo boards showcasing earthquakes, political points of interest and geography. I find myself being drawn to the windows that look out over the plaza. The colossal Catedral Metropolitana stands off to my left, surrounded by a shamble of streets, shaken by the earthquakes that periodically level everything. I peer down, watching the old American school buses that jostle with each other, barely missing the canopies of corrugated iron that entrap the wet, crowded streets.

Older façades hidden by crude lean-tos overlap each other while the long burnt-out neon signs of theatres are the only reminder of the past's grandeur. I see the steeples of the dark grey Calvario Church in the distance across the rough layer of wet corrugated tin and Jacob laughs when I ask if we can go there.

"They'll kill you for your pupusa." He smiles and wags his finger.

Grabbing my coffee on the way out, we follow Jacob through more tiny, improvised lean-tos of wood, tin and cardboard hiding modern bike and guitar shops. Vendors compete with each other, desperate to make a sale.

Across from the Palacio through a small side street stands another large church in an equally large plaza. 'El Rosario' looks like a giant, dirty wind turbine. Its smog-stained, dark grey concrete is possibly the most brutally industrial architecture I've ever seen but stepping inside and out of the rain, the interior is anything but that.

The resting place of the Father of the independence of Central America, 'Padre Delgado', has a stained-glass roof running floor to floor in a giant arched rainbow. White ribbons fixed to the ends of each wooden pew eerily flap in the wind, while a pyramid of candles flicker at the altar. Surrounded by these candles stands a life-sized wooden carving of a Catholic nun, her hardwood grain difficult to make out in the dimly lit space.

As if perfectly timed for our visit, beams of sunlight suddenly cast coloured rays through the rainbow of stained glass. Blue, green, yellow and red bolts of iridescent splendour illuminate the nun's face. I'm impressed that such beauty can come from a building so ugly.

Back out in the rain, I break away from Jacob and Vicky to take a photo of an old theatre. Vagrants sleep on cardboard in its doorway and above, a once neon sign reads 'Libertad' in a vintage font.

Snapping off a few shots on my disposable camera, I turn round to see Jacob backdropped by the domed roof of the cathedral and shaking his head at me, clearly unhappy that I left his side.

"Cuidarte, no es seguro aqui." He sternly warns me it's not safe here.

We duck into a cake shop by the name of 'Napoles'. The interior is a time warp to yesteryear. Wooden panels line the walls where famous poets have been coming to drink coffee and eat pastries since time began. A mouth-watering display of baked goods perch in a glass cabinet that runs the length of the shop.

I choose a few to take home and watch as they are carefully boxed and ribboned.

LA LIBERTAD

My breakfast looks like a train wreck. Beans, broken egg yolks and triangular tortilla chunks jostle for space in the frying pan while the coffee pot gurgles away. The cat and dog patiently wait for scraps.

"Vamos a la playa." Still in her pyjamas, Amy appears from her bedroom and suggests we go to La Libertad, a nearby beach only a half-hour from Santa Tecla. I've been living in the homestay house in El Salvador for several weeks with Amy by now, and I have grown to trust her guidance. Amy and her mother Gina take good care of me. If Amy says we should go to a beach, then that's where we'll go.

She yawns, rubbing her eyes and shoos the pets out of the kitchen. She must have only had a few hours' sleep. I heard her come home from her shift in the early hours.

"Bueno, dar media hora y vamos." She says we'll leave in half-hour or so.

We wait in clouds of black exhaust smoke as buses roar past on the cracked asphalt road. Their whale tails and fancy spray jobs make them look like stars of a 'pimp my car' show.

"¡Vamos! ¡Setenta y ocho!" Amy calls out as she runs for the Number 78 bus.

We wriggle and squeeze our way up the aisle. Familiar with these squashed scenarios, Amy slides into a gap while I'm left standing and crushed with the other upright passengers. I am clearly still a novice at such matters. Next to the rear door is a turnstile, preventing people sneaking on and riding for free. I wrestle my way to it and utilising the empty space above it, perch my self on top like a pigeon. A mother and her child stare at me with blank expressions as I squat above them. I feel a tap on my shoulder and sense I'm in trouble, but it's an old man who points at the bird tattoo on my arm and smiles, with a thumb up.

"Gracias," I say, smiling back in appreciation.

The bus rumbles on, passing through San Salvador and honking its horn, desperate to fill every inch of its interior. Wearing a red and white striped headscarf, an old wrinkled woman kneels on a seat up front and twists herself around. Gaining the full attention and necessary height above her audience, she begins an ear splitting, high-pitched preach about the dark path joining the street gangs will lead you down. She delivers her well-rehearsed speech forcibly.

People in the aisle unlock themselves from each other at each stop and eventually I see my chance, hopping down from the turnstile and taking a seat next to an old lady with a large wok of live chickens on her lap. Through the string net that's stretched over the top of it, the birds' heads poke out, bobbing and swaying with the bumpy road like those dashboard bulldog figurines. The old lady pulls the string signalling she wants to disembark. This is going to be interesting. She plonks the wok in my lap and pointing to the top of her head, asks me to put it there when she's down the stairs. I do as she says. Another man whistles to the driver, prompting the bus to move off.

The old woman disappears in the dust cloud with the chickens still poking from the top of the perfectly balanced wok. I'm impressed by the ease of what just happened and the manner in which it was executed. I'm not even sure chickens are allowed to ride the buses back at home.

The road narrows between rows of stores and market stalls as the bus reaches the bay of La Libertad. Small fishing boats bob in the waves tethered to a wooden pier. A large flaking sign at its entrance reads 'El Malecon'.

Under the wharf's tin shed lean-tos, fish are gutted, filleted and washed with deft skill by fishermen in blood-splattered aprons. Pelicans perch atop its piles driven into the seabed, watching the fisherman at work, anticipating the guts and carcasses they'll scavenge. An abundance of shellfish, red crabs and octopus are arrayed on flat wooden tables while rotund men vend silver sardines overflowing from plastic buckets that swing from their arms.

Children play in the waves that smash onto the pebbly beach either side of the wharf and a clutter of open-walled restaurants provide shade for local surfers who lounge around in deck chairs waiting for the swell to improve. Further towards the north end of the promenade, the buildings become more deserted and show heavy signs of neglect and erosion, flaking away in the breeze like dried out pastry crust. I reminisce back to the empty shells of the hotels in Las Peñitas, Nicaragua.

"¿Hey you want habitación? Venga, venga." A surfer offers us a room.

We decline and continue to the end of the promenade, passing through a small, thickly-painted teal blue gate. Makeshift crosses in their whites and blues jostle for space with statues draped in flowers among the cluttered disorganisation of tombs in the overcrowded cemetery. We wander the site for a while in silence. I think what a calming and pretty place to be to laid to rest it is.

Back in the town's centre, we stay vigilant while shifty characters hassle us for loose change. A taxi pulls in, saving us from the chaos. Windows down, the car swerves and twists at breakneck speed back to Santa Tecla. I feel the wind in my hair and bob my head to the music while the driver raps his rings on the steering wheel to the beat.

Later that day, Amy's mother comes to the homestay house.

"Mire," Gina says, showing me the newspaper. "Babosos," she continues. Fools.

I take the paper and read the article she points to.

Refusing to pay a gang territory tax, three drivers of our Number 78 bus to La Libertad have been shot dead in their seat during the last three weeks.

I lean back in my chair, remembering the old lady and her chickens in the netted wok.

5
EL GOLFO DE FONSECA

ISLAND HOPPING

Amy is up before me and excited about leaving Santa Tecla for the first time in a long time. We are to visit the Gulf of Fonseca for a few days with the volunteer group.

Jacob and the girls pull up in a minivan. The girls have scored the best seats. I remember holidays when I was younger, how the German families would wake up early to lay out their towels and secure the best beach lounges.

Amy puts her earphones in and snuggles up to her bag.

Thick jungle is divided by the vast green slopes of a string of twenty-two volcanoes that run through the middle of the country. Villages pass by, some plastered in MS13 gang graffiti, some in 18th Street. I think back to the Number 78 bus in the newspaper headlines and wonder if I should be worried.

Giant melons and coconuts piled high on wooden tables at the roadside flash past as we swerve to avoid the potholes that pepper the road. Brown cows munch at the grass verges, sometimes wandering in our path, causing the van to brake and send us flying. Three hours later it descends into La Unión. The port town has seen better days and could do with a good lick of paint.

We pull up to a concrete structure perched right at the sea wall's edge. Its peeling sign reads 'Recuerdos perdidos' – 'Forgotten Memories' – perhaps of what it used to look like.

Walking along a narrow, curving harbour sea wall, we are helped by a barefooted man down onto a flatbed cart fixed to a single car axle. The German girls hold their woven handbags above their heads trying to steady themselves. The grubby man, now ankle-deep in brown mud, takes the two front poles in his hands and, with a heave, pulls the now laden cart into the water, dragging it until he is waist deep. A clutter of small motorboats bob in the waves, one manned by a shirtless old man and a young boy.

"¡Hola, Chentillo!" Jacob calls over to the old man.

"¡Buen dia, amigooo!" he shouts back, scooping us towards him with his cupped hand.

The man continues to drag the flat bed cart to the boat until the water is at his shoulders. We climb aboard. The young boy flits around the boat like a butterfly, directing us to sit on the planks that run across the hull. Our bags are thrown into our laps and the idling boat engine fires into action and digs the back of the boat into the water as we lurch away from the man and his cart.

Jacob introduces us.

"¡El CAPITÁN! ¡Chentillo!" he says with pride.

"¡Es mi nieto!" the old man shouts over the roar of the boat, steering with one hand pointing at his grandson, Maycol, a child of no more than 10 years old who is hanging from the roof bars like a monkey.

Just as I expected: this salty old sea dog before us is a dead ringer for Captain Quint from *Jaws*. A prickly mat of grey bristle sprouts from under his nose and a shiny sun-bronzed potbelly the size of a basketball sticks out proudly over the top of his yellow board shorts. A pair of blue boat shoes on his feet remind me of James' jungle-trek footwear and are comfortably tapping to whatever music is playing in his head.

The German girls have settled and are looking out across the deep blue ocean that meets a cloudless sky. Amy is off in her own world, stripped down to her orange bikini top, and lying back with the wind in her hair like she's in a 1980s pop music video. A cooling mist sprays up either side of the little boat from the cutting water as we pass through the gulf.

A long concrete pad sits on pillars to our right. Jacob informs us it's the new dock and pier that was meant to be finished last year to alleviate 'Acujutla' – the already overflowing port further up the coast to the north. Two giant grey naval ships are moored to it and backdropped by fluorescent green hills that gift us a glimpse of Volcán Cochague's peak in the distance. Crudely painted along the frigates' sides are the words 'Se vende' – *For sale*. Off to our left, we look at Honduras' small Pacific coastline while front left, the giant blown crater of Volcán Cosigüina in Nicaragua's north stands proud.

"Do you have your passports?" Jacob calls out over the roar of the engine with a smirk.

The German girls start to panic. "You didn't say vee ver leafing zee country!" they shriek.

"It's joke!" he says, pointing at a line of orange buoys that bob on the surface.

"These are the El Salvador / Honduras border line. Armed gunboats patrol these waters, so we have to stay on our side!"

The girls are not impressed by his humour.

Our first stop is a small island called Zacatillo. Palm trees bend lazily over a white, sandy coastline and out in front, an idyllic cove appears.

"¡Maycol!" Chentillo grunts at his grandson to drop anchor.

The tiny boy jumps out into the waist-deep water with the giant claw on his shoulder and lobs it up into the shallows. With the help of the tide, he drags the boat a little further in. Amy, Jessica (another volunteer) and I jump off and wade to shore while Jacob and the others struggle to do the same.

"My shoes!" Erika whines about getting wet. She and Stephanie are none too impressed at having to walk in the ocean.

Two colourful wooden shacks with galvanised tin roofs sit raised up on platforms in the sand. One has a bar inside where Cumbia music plays and the other houses a shaded porch area with deck chairs. It's paradise. Stephanie and Erika are straight in there with the towels, commandeering deck chairs as a portly man welcomes us with a big smile.

"¡Hola! Soy Edgar," he says. "¡Venga venga!"

He asks if we like the music playing.

"Do you hef any European stuff?" Erika asks.

I cringe.

He happily obliges and throws on an old chart mix while they lay slathering themselves with sun cream. Finally, some lively Honduran music takes over from the Euro sounds.

"¡Que bicha!" Edgar claps Amy along as she sways to the music in her bikini.

He sways a little himself, happy to have our company.

I stroll up the beach, staring out at Matate Island and Volcán Amapala that poke from the horizon behind young Maycol now splashing around in the waves. A couple of stray dogs join me, sniffing in and around where the beach joins the jungle. We reach a large, white fibreglass yacht resting forlornly in the sand. Void of any windows, it seems to be a completely sealed unit apart from a large hole that's been roughly sawn out of one side. It seems way too far up the beach to ever be taken out to sea again. Even the dogs are a little hesitant as we circumnavigate it before heading back towards the group.

"Ok! Time to leave!" Jacob claps his hands and shouts to us all, now spread out over the beach.

"Gracias, Edgar!" We thank the barman and wade back towards the little boat.

We haul ourselves up into the boat again, and Maycol un-snares the anchor and throws it back on board before climbing in himself. Stephanie and Erika wade towards us with their arms held high like they're walking waist deep in fish guts. I help to drag them up into the boat. Amy smirks as they land with a thud on the hard wooden bench seats.

I ask Chentillo about the boat on the beach. He takes a swig of beer.

"Abandonado, amigo. Narcotraficantes — cocaina." He looks at me, knowing I've understood and smirks.

He takes another swig of his beer and pushes the throttle to warp speed, lunging us back out into the waves.

ISLA MEANGUERA

Salty sea dog Captain Chentillo skirts an indeterminate coastline in his fishing boat. Jacob, our volunteer programme director, has certainly chosen a very isolated and beautiful place for our group to spend the weekend.

Rock-walled jetties stretch into the choppy water as we continue to follow the island's edge. Dark green, dense foliage twists its way up the island's steep cliffs.

The boat slows to a gurgle, whirring into the calmer waters of a tiny cove where a fishing village climbs up the hill. Fishermen lean on their vessels set in the sand of the little beach. They sip from beer cans as Chentillo steers us over toward a concrete plinth on the left side of the cove.

"¡Hola, mama!" Maycol shouts to a grey-haired woman before jumping off and tying the boat to a piece of rebar that juts out of the platform.

Chentillo's place is a prime spot, an unfinished, grey concrete structure with an older original house set back from it.

More rebar wire pokes from the tops of cinder block pillars that sprout from the upper level. Unfinished plaster abruptly stops halfway up. As we unload our bags, Stephanie's and Erika's silent disapproval is palpable. Amy and Jess are already chatting away to the grey-haired lady. She tells us Chentillo and her family live on the ground floor.

A flight of stairs void of any handrail leads to a huge balcony that hovers ten feet above the water. Three hammocks are strung between a centre pillar and scaffold bar guard rails cling to the edges.

A large room at the rear of the deck contains beds in various conditions but no sooner have we dumped our bags we are back out on the water.

Steering along the coastline as dusk falls, Chentillo informs us we are about to see some magic.

The boat slows, Maycol jumps up and starts to shout and clap.

And then, as if from nowhere, giant prehistoric silhouettes blanket the sky above us. The sound is deafening as the creatures drop from the trees that hang over the water. They swoop and dive bomb the boat.

"¡Pelicanos!" Maycol is swinging around the boat like a deranged monkey, howling at the now angry pelicans, pointlessly disturbed from their roost.

EL GOLFO

Back at Chentillo's house, Jacob begins his tour.

"Aqui es baño." He leads us through a badly hung, paper-mâché door into the bathroom.

Wrapped in emerald-green tiles, the small cubicle resembles the bathroom at Amy's back in Santa Tecla. The seat-less toilet is familiar as well as the shower pipe sticking out of the wall above it.

"No funciona bien." He tells us it doesn't work great.

"Pero bastante." *Good enough.* Whatever that means.

"Tira papel hygenico en la basura por fa."

Amy and Jess nod, but I sense how the German travellers squirm at the thought of discarding their used toilet paper in the open waste bin. That volunteer house probably has the best toilet in Santa Tecla. I conceal the smile at the corner of my lips.

Stephanie and Erika quickly grab the double bed, leaving the rest of us to share out the singles. When I sit down on my mattress, my weight brings my body down, down down. I nearly touch the floor. Attempting to rise out of it again is like trying to escape one of those 'ball pools' in McDonalds play areas. I look over to see Amy, already swinging in a hammock on the deck and dozing. She's none too bothered with the sleeping choices.

"OK, vee need to eat. Jacob, ver is zee feesh?" The girls ask like he already has some prepared.

He looks over to them with his mouth open. "You have food, no?" he replies, smiling nervously.

"Vee hef vegetables and snack bars but vee can't just eat zis! Can you go to zee supermarket and get some feesh? And vere is zee barbeque?"

Now I laugh out loud. I can't help it. Tragi-comic travel, especially the supermarket bit.

The girls stare at me.

Jacob's organisation is in general pretty shit, to say the least. Simple items like the mosquito powder for the homestay house took a couple of weeks of pestering before it arrived. I'm not surprised in the least that he's expecting us to fend for ourselves here. I quietly suggest he asks Chentillo about a barbeque and some fish. Twenty minutes later, he returns with a smug face and a net holding two silver fish.

"Ewww! Are zey are alive?" The girls squirm.

"They were about a minute ago by the looks," I say.

Amy and I gut the fish on the dusty concrete floor while the girls turn the other way.

"Vat about zee barbeque?" they ask.

"Ah yes, we have wood downstairs. Amy, traer los palitos." Jacob asks Amy to fetch the firewood. He scoops up a handful of fish guts and throws them off the side of the balcony into the sea.

Stephanie and Erika look like they're about to puke. We prepare a crude stack for a fire but the matches Jacob strikes fail to light the damp newspaper. He hurries off downstairs and returns with a china cup full of red liquid that he pours onto the pile of wood. He's clearly unimpressed at the amount of 'hard work' he's having to do. When he strikes another match, the red fuel almost catches his hair alight with the fireball it ignites.

"¡Aiiii!" he screams, rolling over backwards.

"Are you trying to kill us?!" Stephanie squeals.

The little stack of wood is now burning away in the corner of the balcony, and we wrap the fish in foil and throw them on. The girls take out some plastic plates and unzip their sterilised vegetables.

We flick the two tin-foiled fish off the fire; they are a charred, sad sight. Riddled with bones, they do not exactly offer sustenance. We pick through them. The girls try to snatch the meaty parts but are politely fended off by Jess and Amy who do their best to share out what meat there is.

Jacob has clearly had enough. He pours water on the fire and disappears downstairs for the night.

I wake in the balcony hammocks to the girls moaning about the lack of breakfast. They reluctantly nibble on their zip lock vegetables. I follow Amy and Jess into the empty village to try to find somewhere to eat. The mud brick houses of the village sleep silently. We take a breather, leaning on a faded Coke mural painted on a store's exterior wall before continuing up a narrow brick road to a crumbling shop at the top of the hill.

A lady standing in the doorway, wearing baggy boardshorts, welcomes us in. "Bueeenaaas." She drags out her "Good morning" in a friendly slow drawl.

"¿Tienes huevos o plátano?" Amy asks her for eggs and plantain.

The woman swats a fly from her head. "Si, casi nada, pero si." She purses her lips in the direction of a near empty shelf at the rear of the store.

We scrape together four plátano, six eggs and a squeezy packet of refried beans.

A rising sun glints diamonds on the calm surface of the tiny cove as we tread our way back down through the village to the house. Captain Chentillo is downstairs looking a little hung over, cooking up some eggs on a makeshift hotplate while a big pot of refried beans simmers away.

Amy approaches him raising the plastic bag of food. She asks if we can cook. He yawns, nods and rubs his eyes. A large green parrot sits on a perch outside and nibbles at its claws.

"Que lindo parajo." Amy admires the bird before entering the little cook house.

The dirt floor of the hut is complemented by black soot-stained cinder block walls and tin ceiling that hovers inches above our heads. A clowder of fuzzy kittens appears from behind a pile of flattened cardboard boxes in the corner.

"Awwww," Amy croons, bending over and putting her hand out.

The kittens retreat behind the cardboard and start to meow. She fries up the food, offering Chentillo some, who gracefully declines but tells us to throw any scraps to the kittens.

"Gatitoooos, gatitooos," Amy coos, like she's talking to a baby.

The kittens appear one by one from behind the box, stepping gingerly, and take the blobs of plátano from her hand.

Back upstairs, Jacob is lying with the girls on a mattress they've dragged outside. Stephanie cuts us a look.

"Vere hef you guys been?"

"A la tienda," Amy replies. The shop.

The girls don't answer and continue slurping soggy cereal from their little plastic bowls.

Jacob pipes up. "Today we go to Al torre del energia al cima." A walk to the pylon tower at the top of the hill.

After Stephanie and Erika finally choose their outfits, we set off. Their backpacks are stuffed, as if ready for a week away.

OVER THE HILL

A man called Horacio leads our troop up and out of Meanguera village, passing the faded Coke mural where children and wild chickens are congregating. The track steepens and changes from cobbles to a scoria dirt path. Chentillo's grandson Maycol sniffs out the route up ahead like a bloodhound.

"¿Sabes la ruta al cima?" I ask him if he knows the way. He nods without looking back.

I put my trust at the mercy of the child. He stops in the shade of a large tree.

"Mira," he says to me, pointing up into its leafy branches. "Mango."

He hurls a stick hard up in the air. He jumps up and down as four giant mangos hit the ground. "¡Aiii!"

As we close in on the summit, a dog barks, loud and frenzied. Maycol stops to listen.

"¿Es salvaje?" I inquire if it's wild, worried it could attack us at any minute.

"No, esta bien," he says confidently, continuing through the grass, now taller than him.

The barking grows in volume, but Maycol trudges on until reaching a clearing dominated by a power pylon riddled with satellite dishes. A perimeter fence surrounds it, and there is a small white house where the dog is chained to a pole. While we sit and wait for the others, it chokes itself as it lunges and gnashes at us.

Exhausted and out of breath, the group finally catch up, falling into piles at the side of the path. With their arrival, the dog starts barking again.

"Vere is zis dog? I hope is not dangerous." Stephanie aims her concern at Jacob.

"It's OK," he says, sweating profusely. Horacio tells us to follow the fence line and stay in single file. The bush opens at an area with views looking out over the gulf to Volcán Cosigüina in the north of Nicaragua. This volcano had a violent eruption in 1835 that blew a huge part of the crater away and the largest pieces of rock form the small group of islands in the gulf known as 'Islotes Cosigüna'.

"Hay serpientes aqui, cuidado," Horacio warns us.

"Snakes!" Erika yells.

"¡Aiiii!" Amy lifts a foot off the ground.

"No te preocupes." He tells us not to worry.

From the tower, we follow a smooth track of round rocks and meet with a pair of feisty bulls being held back on ropes by two men in cowboy hats. They struggle, using all their strength to control and steer them into the bushy embankment to let us pass. Stephanie and Erika squirm and wriggle while the men wrestle with the bovines.

The track narrows and the jungle thickens either side of it. Two young girls no more than 15 approach on mules loaded with straw baskets. The track width makes it hard for us to pass but, pressing ourselves into the jungle foliage, we manage to successfully get past. They carry a cargo of freshly cut corn cobs. We say an 'Hola' from our squashed position in the bush. They smile back with white teeth. A steep rocky channel carves its way through the vine strangled jungle and ends at a barbed wire fence. Maycol leads the way, pushing on, climbing over. Suddenly he lets out a scream.

"¿Que pasa bicho?" Horacio asks him.

"Mi cuella, mi cuella," he whimpers, crying in agony and holding his neck.

He pulls his hand away, and we can see he's been bitten or stung by something that carries a strong venom.

"It's like big wasp." Jacob translates, looking at the swelled lump on Maycol's neck.

It's clear that Horacio is now lost by the way he's hesitating and looking in all directions. We are surrounded by undergrowth and there is no path in any direction. The treacherous terrain has taken us off route and he begins to hack his way through the bush with his machete. The ting of his blade stops as he hesitates and listens. Another dog barks angrily close by.

"Ah, la casa," he says.

The dog is clearly not happy we are on its territory.

Suddenly, a blue wooden panelled house appears within the shaded canopy of bush. Perched on a flat shelf, halfway down a heavily wooded slope, a woman stands outside next to a washing line of wrinkled clothes. Horacio shouts across to her in incomprehensible Spanish.

"¡Oyeee chucho callate!" She hushes the dog tied to the house, hitting it with a stick.

We skirt the house cautiously. It's in bad shape. Creeping rot climbs the wooden weatherboard walls and the revolting smell of the rubbish piled in the backyard makes me gag.

A little further, the sound of waves bring relief to the group.

"Aqui no mas," Horacio says. "Playa Mahjual."

The jungle opens out to an untouched paradise. Huge turquoise waves crash onto the shore and a line of giant trees hang heavy with green shelled coconuts, mango and papaya. After the hike, the cool ocean is invigorating, and I wallow in the shallows until a rogue wave pitches me into an underwater double backflip that deposits me with a crash on the beach. Jacob and Horacio laugh as I stagger up to the shade of the trees, rubbing my head. The Germans are there, hiding from the sun. They don't ask if I'm ok.

Horacio climbs up a coconut tree, cuts some bunches down and drags them over; then he chops their tops and hands them around for us to drink. It's not long before Chentillo comes humming round the point and anchors the boat in the chest-deep water.

"¿Do vee hef to get out to zere?" Stephanie is not keen on wading to the boat.

Dragging two more giant bunches of coconuts down to the water's edge, Amy and I wade out to the boat and are first up and in, struggling to get over the side with the coconuts. The girls wade through the water in single file with their bags up above their heads before being dragged up the side of the boat and tossed in.

COCOS LOCOS

Our few days on Meanguera Island with the volunteers has been made unforgettable by Captain Chentillo and the various people we have encountered. Back at the little store in the village I buy a bottle of rum as a thank you and join Chentillo and the green coconuts we've brought back from the beach, piled high next to the cook house on the ground floor.

His friend joins us, a Navy sailor based at the island's small naval barracks next door.

"OK. Coco locos," Chentillo says, twisting his machete round his hand like a twirling baton.

He places a coco on a table and, with two swift chops and a little twisting of his blade point, creates a hole in its top before adding a healthy dose of rum. Turning on a little television set, he pushes a DVD into the player and a Salvadoran music video mix appears on the screen that puts a huge smile on his face. Now loosened up by the drink and music, the sailor has his arm around me and is sharing dirty jokes from his little cell phone while Chentillo sways with the groove of the song playing on the TV. He is now swigging the rum straight from the bottle. He rubs his shiny belly as he howls along to the music. The coco pile is drastically reduced as the evening progresses and the two guys' eyes pop out of their heads every time a woman in a yellow miniskirt and high boots appears on the screen.

The woman twirls around in her frilly yellow dress, shaking her boobs and ass while the two men either side of her fall off the stage. This has Chentillo and the sailor in stitches, slapping their thighs and bending over in agony. I wonder how many times they've watched this DVD as they laugh hysterically like it's the first time.

In the midst of all this, Erika comes down with a grimace on her face.

"¡Uuyyyweee!" The men cheer at the sight of a female but she's not impressed.

"It's very loud," she says. "Can you at least change zis terrible song?"

6
BACK TO SCHOOL

Being a teacher. Santa Tecla.

MARGARITA DURAN

The excitement of the Gulf trip is soon forgotten on Monday morning back in Santa Tecla. Entering the school foyer, Lola, the school principal, spots me and quickly changes her smile to a frown when she sees my bare arms.

"Disculpame pero no tengo camisa limpia." I apologise for my short-sleeved shirt. I'm aware of the school policy to keep tattoos covered because of the affiliations they have to the gang violence associated with this country.

"Esta bien." She says it's fine but turns to her sister and fellow teacher Janine. "Es como mara."

Janine laughs at her comment that I'm like a gang member because of my arm tattoos.

"¡Lola! No es mara," she says. "¡Es gringo!"

Amy is in the foyer and introduces me to Angel, the girl I'd met briefly at Stephanie's vegetarian restaurant birthday. Looking at her now in the light of day, her skin is still almost transparent and it's a wonder her frail little body can stand upright.

"Hi." Her limp hand slides from my grip like a piece of seaweed when I try to shake it.

She'd be an expert at getting out of handcuffs.

"I'm not starting today." She says in her croaky voice. "Jacob is taking me to see my boyfriend."

She is void of all eye contact when she speaks.

"Your online boyfriend?" I ask, remembering her telling us before.

"Yeah. We met online, and he invited me down here." Jacob shares a glance with me before they leave.

I can see why his attention is directed more at the volunteers in the house than me. How they'd survive without him is beyond comprehension. He really does have his hands full. I'm glad he can see I'm a little more independent.

"Goood morning teeechuur, how are you?" Class 1b comes alive as I enter the room.

As I walk among the desks during class, they try to stroke the bird tattoo on my arm, scared it's going to come alive if they touch it. They are not used to seeing such things.

I mark their work with ticks and smiley faces. They rush to each other's desks to compare them.

Oops, bad idea, I think.

"OK!" I raise my voice, quietening them down and ushering them back to their seats.

"Tengo pegatinas." I show them some sticker sheets that I've bought at a dollar store.

"¡Ooooo por favor teechuurr!" Like stampeding bulls, they rush and jump up at me trying to grab them.

Another big mistake. D'oh!

I hold the stickers above my head, telling them that the first one to copy my three sentences from the board gets a sticker. They sprint back to their desks and write as fast as they can. Bribing them is probably not the best teaching method but it certainly calms them. I hand the stickers out as they complete their task.

Chaos fills the yard during lunch break. Students sit on the floor in circles, talking and eating berries from plastic bags while a long line queues for the ever-spinning jump rope. The old lady sits on a crate behind the wire cage in her tuck shop preparing little 15c bags of mixed sweets. She eyeballs me suspiciously as I enter the cage. Pouring some Coca-Cola into a plastic bag, she seals the open end around a straw and passes it to me.

I spy the German girls talking to Amy and approach them, but before I can fight my way through the rabble of lunch crowd, they quickly disappear.

"¿Que pasa?" I ask Amy what they wanted. I could tell they were up to no good.

She says they'd asked for $25 towards the weekend trip to the gulf. Practically a week's wages or more for her. I can just imagine them fuming about having to pay for a 'local'.

Monica's number flashes on my phone's tiny screen as I pull it from my pocket. She wastes no time with her interrogation to why I've not called her. I make the conversation short. I need a break from her persistence.

"Loca. No te acerques." Gina advises me to stay away when I ask her advice.

During school I tell Jacob about the Germans asking Amy for money. He's embarrassed by their behaviour and agrees that Amy should not be contributing. He reluctantly gives the cash to Vicky to pass on to Stephanie.

Gina shows up at home with a large black bag steaming from its top. She pours an orange soup into bowls and rips open another bag of warm tortillas.

A car horn sounds outside.

Monica? Surely not.

"La loca." Gina jumps to the same conclusion.

Anxiously I watch Amy open the door.

"¡Hola, Darreen! ¡Oye Gina! ¡Vamos a bailar!" The last thing I expect to see is the principal, Lola, hanging out of the driver's window of her little jeep begging us to go dancing. Gina and I politely decline.

AIMLESS WANDERINGS

"¡Hay chuchos muchochos!" Amy arrives back from her night shift at the veterinary clinic.

She tells me she had fourteen of the president's dogs staying for the night while his house was fumigated.

Today's teaching schedule in school gifts me an extended hour break at lunch and I decide to watch a junior football game in Santa Tecla's Cafetalón Park. On the way I stop at a stall and buy a plastic bag of coconut water. Charging ten cents more than the going rate the old lady gives me another harsh reminder that I'll never be a local.

Sipping from my plastic bag I watch the quick-footed kids kick and pass the ball around. The game inspires me to seek out a couple of football shirts I've seen on offer in town.

Wire racking laden with shirts leads me down an alley into a fake football shirt heaven. Tops in every colour imaginable line the sky-high racks on the walls.

"¡Chero chero!" The vendors hound me, pointing at shirts with large hooks fashioned from coat hangers gaffer taped to the end of long wooden poles.

"¡Cambio cambio!" they call out, shaking the change in their fanny packs for the large dollar bills they presume I'm carrying.

A guy in a Hawaiian shirt decants me through a back door.

"Adentro, adentro," he says. "Ellos tienen las mejores." They have the best.

It's an ominous feeling and for a moment I'm unsure. Did anyone see me going into the alley from the main street? I'm slightly worried. But then we pass through a wall of vertical plastic strips, and I'm in the back of another sea of t-shirts.

"¿Que booko?" A voice startles me from behind.

The doubt I had on entering resurfaces when I turn around and find myself face to face with a Quasimodo-like creature staring at me with his mouth open. He tries to speak but nothing comes out. I turn to make a bolt for the door, but a plump woman in a cotton pinny blocks my exit. The money in her apron pocket jingles as she walks.

"¿Que busca?" she asks, slurping the remaining dregs of a bottle of Fanta through a straw.

I'm relieved she just wants a sale and say, "Alianza San Salvador." The national shirt.

Fingering her way through a rack, she pulls out the white and sky-blue strip emblazoned in bread and plumbing logos.

"Diez," she says, taking advantage of my want for the polyester advertisement. I oblige and leave through the front of the shop with a new overpriced shirt, slightly rattled.

LA LOCA

Torrential rain pours from the gutters of the Santa Tecla house. Amy's uncle, Manilo, arrives, making a dash across the courtyard clutching a large sack while shielding his head with a newspaper.

"¡No! ¡La Titi no le gusta!" Amy informs him that the dogs hate the food he's bought.

"¡Es un perro, no es humano!" He angrily tells her it's a dog, not a human.

Amy tells him to change it.

"Ya esta cerrado." Manilo goes to his room muttering that the store's already closed.

My phone rings. Amy looks at me with a smirk, knowing it can only be Monica.

"¡Hola, carino!" comes her voice down the line. "¿El dia, como fue?" she asks of my day.

"Todo bien, gracias." I reply in a short tone, not wanting to be stuck on the phone for hours.

"¿Y vos?" I silently curse as I make the mistake of asking how hers was.

The next ten minutes are filled with every moment of her existence since we last saw each other.

I try to get a word in edgeways, failing miserably at avoiding another date with her.

"¡Oooooo, Darreeen!" Amy laughs as I hang up the phone.

I go outside. I swipe the mosquitos that hum around the concrete wash tub in the yard. The powder that kills the eggs they lay in the water is not working. Monica calls again, insisting we go for dinner.

"I meet you at house," she says. "I can remember where is."

'Course she can. I tell her again that I can't. She asks what else I could possibly be doing.

Her manner is a turn-off. If she was a just a little less pushy, I might be into her. We stick to meeting the following evening.

"¡LOCAAAA!" Amy laughs again, aware of the pickle I've got myself into.

The following evening, Monica calls me from her car. She's outside the house. I'm not sure how long she's been lurking out there. Dressed to kill in a short leather skirt and black heels, she holds on tightly to my hand as we walk into town. She asks why I've never been married or had children. I tell her the right woman has never come along. She squeezes my hand tighter and struts along on her little stilts.

The delicious smells of a small comedor entice us. The easy-wipe, bright plastic tablecloths are stapled down, and pastel pink walls are adorned with paintings of volcanic landscapes, Virgin Marys and rosary beads. The other patrons seem curious about us. Warm tortillas, pulled pork and little side plates of salad are delivered to the table while Monica continues with the marriage talk.

I refuse her when she asks to come into the house on our return, merely out of respect for Manilo and Amy.

"Mi auto," she says, dragging me by the hand over to her little red car.

The passenger door has a bunch of branches shoved through the open window and the seat is saturated from rainwater.

"Lo hago los jovenes." She bursts into tears and tells me this is the work of kids on her street.

I listen as she sobs through her stories of woe while the wet seat soaks my jeans. I tell her we can meet on the weekend.

I watch through a slit from behind the gate, making sure she drives away.

DISOBEDIENCE

My volunteer partner, Vicky, decides to not show up for class. She's clearly forgetting that the class's work is in her bag. I know how much they are looking forward to the lesson and I do not want to be the bearer of the bad news. The slim teacher who always tells me off for buying cakes for the staff room wears a face that looks like it's sucking a lemon. She leaves me to figure out how to keep the girls occupied without the appropriate material.

Vicky finally shows up with the pages but it's way too late. I've drawn all the clothes on the board and have managed to find some flashcards in the desk. She apologises, explaining that Jacob had said there was no need to go to class.

Hearing this infuriates me. His lacklustre approach of late has taken its toll on me.

I leave a message on his phone, explaining my disappointment and the disorganisation and unprofessional manner he's conducting himself in, especially as the kids are the ones who suffer.

The next time I see him, he looks sheepish and hands me a volunteer programme polo shirt as if it's going to smooth things out.

Completely ignoring me for the first ten minutes, a few of the girls in the afternoon class don't even open their books and spend the whole time talking, taking photos of each other and applying lipstick.

"¡A LA OFICINA!" I pick out the four most disruptive girls, sending them to Lola's office.

They whine, trying to change my mind, but I stand my ground and calmly march them out the door.

The remaining girls sit in stunned silence while I continue to write on the board.

A few moments later, Pamela, their teacher, returns. A broad lady of senior years, she commands their attention with a booming voice, unloading her rage on them. She explains how I'm working for free and that I've spent a lot of money to travel here solely to try and help with their English.

The girls sit frozen.

I sit frozen.

"OK, niñas. No mas." She readjusts her now dishevelled poof of grey hair and leaves the classroom.

THE BOG SEAT

I detour over to Plaza San Martín before the day of teaching and buy a newspaper from the small stand. Shaded from the Santa Tecla sun by his parasol, the old man smiles as I hand him a coin, perhaps wondering if I can even read what I'm buying. I continue on to the bakery and pick up some treats for the staffroom.

The thin-as-a-rake teacher, Liana, says I am trying to make them fat.

"Too late!" Gina, my homestay mother, laughs as she and the others tuck in.

The ladies enjoy their coffee and cake over a few gruesome gang stories in the newspaper.

Lunch extends well beyond the hour, cancelling my afternoon class. Girls line up in the foyer to skip while others play card games sat in circles on the tiled floor. Another group is playing a game of 'Twister' on a piece of old tarp with numbers penned on it. They bend and twist around each other on all fours, tumbling over and laughing. I imagine how ecstatic they would be at the sight of the real 'Twister' game and its coloured plastic sheet.

Spotting Jacob, I mention the lack of a toilet seat at the house, but he gives me a 'why are you asking me' kind of look. Before I can recite his speech about the volunteers' money going directly to help the homestay families, he's out the door.

Fifteen minutes later, he's back with a toilet seat. The swing tag reads $6 – he's clearly sourced it from a second-hand shop. It'll do the job. He also has a bag of grey powder for the mosquito eggs in the sink. I rush home, excited about fitting the seat before anyone else arrives. The animals curiously sniff me as I lie under the toilet bowl fiddling with the screws.

"¡Hola hola!" Gina is first to show up.

I tell her to look in the bathroom. She looks confused as she heads in.

"¡Aii Darreen, que fantastico!" she calls out, approving of its comfort. She laughs when I tell her about hassling Jacob for it.

"Amy le va a gustar, creo." She says Amy will be pleased.

We brew a cup of green tea and wait for her arrival.

Gina tells her to look in the bathroom as she arrives. She looks confused but heads to the toilet.

"¡Aiiii que chivo!" an excited shriek comes from the bathroom.

"¿Y como fue?" I ask her how it was when she reappears.

"¡Uuuau!" she says, "¡Muy lujo!" Wow! Luxury!

Manilo arrives and goes through the same motions, spending a good half-hour in there. Gina laughs when I say we're not living in the stone age and a girl shouldn't have to sit on the rim of a toilet bowl. Manilo finally emerges and stretches his arms above his head.

"Oooff. Gracias, Darreen." He smiles.

CONFISCATION

The 12-year-olds are taught by the very loud and joyful Janine, the school principal's sister.

She leaves as Vicky and I arrive and, squashing our confidence, wishes us luck.

We teach the same routine with the clothing, adding in a few cut-outs from fashion magazines and asking the girls to label them in their textbooks. It's a quicker pace than the 4th graders and the moment I turn my back to write on the board they start up, moving around and forming groups and not concentrating on the job at hand. They ignore Vicky as she tries to herd them back to their seats.

"¡YA! Enough already!" I shout, exhausted by their disobedience and letting my temper get the better of me.

They snigger at this, knowing they've pushed the right button.

I confiscate a girl's phone. She starts to cry.

"Es teléfono de mi Papi," she whines.

"Mío, mío, mío," I say – mine, mine, mine! – taking another two more away from her classmates.

Now all three girls are crying.

I put the phones in my pocket and return to writing on the board, but another girl across the room starts to groom herself pouting and applying lipstick. I confiscate that too, causing her to burst into tears. That's four.

The lesson is a shambles, the girls have seen to that, as has my short-tempered way of dealing with them. Addressing the whole class, I attempt to calm the atmosphere.

"No soy diablo." I tell them I'm not the devil.

They chuckle. Good start.

"Pero quiero que ustedes aprender por lo menos, algo en la clase." I take a more sympathetic tone as I emphasise that I want them to learn at least *something* in my class.

"Awww teeechuuur," they croon. They can see how upset I am.

Their empathy quickly fades as the volume increases again but we are all saved by the bell, as the girls spring from their chairs and line up for their confiscated things.

"Gracias, teeechuur." They thank me as I re-disperse their belongings.

Four rows of empty desks and chairs are now quiet.

I breathe a sigh of relief.

Whose fucking stupid idea was it to go to El Salvador and teach kids?

SAN ANDRES

A pile of black rubbish sacks cooks in the heat of another Salvadoran day. The smell is revolting.

From the dusty lay-by, Gina, Amy and I watch the bus we've just departed noisily pull itself back onto the highway and disappear. A floppy eared cow munches the grass verge.

It seems we're in the middle of nowhere.

"Allá." Gina points across the road at a six-foot chain-link fence with crisp packets stuck to it.

We follow the fence to a pair of open gates leading into a dry area of scrub.

Inside, a security guard with an automatic rifle sits next to a diagonal-striped yellow and black sentry hut.

"Tres por fa." Gina asks for three tickets.

"¿Y el?" The guy looks at me. He points at the price board screwed to his hut: '$1 Salvadorans, $3 Extranjeros'.

"Es chalateco, mi primo de Chalatenago." Gina lies, saying I'm her cousin from the mountains.

He stares at me, unconvinced.

"Verdad, es mi tia." I go along with the lie: She's my auntie. Then I have the urge to explain more. "Mi mama Salvadoreña, papa Ingles. Raza Mixta."

Whether he believes me or simply can't be bothered arguing, he accepts a dollar.

Two glass doors slide open automatically and we step into a cool interior of sandstone. It's a modern structure with a low-pitched roof housing shiny glass cases that display crockery, jewellery and other artefacts found at the site.

The informative placards written in both Spanish and English educate us on the history of San Andres that dates back to around 900BC when the area was an agricultural community. In the third century, it was evacuated due to a volcanic eruption but then re-settled before a city was built by the

Maya in the fifth century. Then for more than 300 years, the site known as the valley of Zapotitán was ruled by the Maya until being taken over by the Pipil descendants of the Toltec tribes of Mexico.

Our exit is hastened when the room floods with school day trippers. Noisy over-excited kids tug and chase each other around the cabinets while their teachers try to regain control.

Through the exit, three imposing temples constructed of giant volcanic tuff blocks stand in the centre of an open field, their browning, stained concrete surrounded by green jungle, hills and farmland. The structures are around three stories high and 'protected' by a few crude fences of sticks and loose barbed wire. A plaza where royalty would have once reigned is now a relic of a civilisation lost, crumbling and tired with tufts of grass sprouting from its cracks.

The pointed peak of San Salvador's volcano sits majestically behind them while abundant birdlife sings across the clearing. We lie in the grass a while, looked down upon by the temples and a blue sky.

The three of us are practically asleep when, without warning, the rumble of the school group appear at the top of the hill like an attacking army, rolling, falling, running and screaming down its slope like deranged monkeys.

The kids are more interested in jumping around in the grass and play fighting than admiring the ancient majestic temples standing before them. I wonder what their Pipil ancestors would think of their behaviour.

The teachers seat themselves near us and scratch through the channels on a portable radio. Our serenity is lost. Thus ends our visit.

Outside the main gates, it's not long before a bus pulls in. We pass through the town of Lourdes. A dust of commotion blankets the small bus terminal. Gina sticks her head out of the window shouting into the crowd.

"¡Hermana hermana!" She spots another sister, loaded up with sacks of potatoes.

"¡Te llamo!" the woman replies. She waves, says she'll call Gina. She's still holding her potatoes. Behind her is a mural of a red devil. Its fist makes a horned gang sign and the letters 'MS13' are sprayed in 6-foot-high letters.

"Este mural," I say to Gina. She can sense my worry.

"Ah solo las maras." She replies calmly – 'Just the gangs.' She says it will be painted over soon.

"No nos molestan." She adds they don't bother her or her sister.

"Pero, para ti, es peligro."

I am disquieted by what she has added: *But for you, it's dangerous.*

ISLAM LUNCH

Jacob tells me I'll be teaching alone for the foreseeable future. No volunteers are scheduled to be arriving in El Salvador any time soon. Not that I care, but I feel his attention is solely directed at the volunteer house guests and little of it is allocated for me. Vicky has been put with Stephanie and Erika as they need extra help and Jess only works with the younger girls. I vent my frustrations to Amy while we walk home.

"Necesitas un choco," she says.

I look at her puzzled.

"Aqui esta." She points to a little hole in the wall up ahead.

Peering inside, I see a lady who stands behind a freezer.

"Dos con choco y mani por fa," Amy says.

From the freezer, the lady produces two frozen bananas on sticks and dips them in a pot on a gas stove behind her. She lifts them out; they are coated in melted chocolate. She then wipes them through a tray of crushed peanuts. Amy hands the lady fifty cents. Her gesture is a reminder I need to stop sweating the small stuff.

Gina calls, insisting we go with her to a lunch party at a friend's house. Amy has other things on, but I agree.

Twenty minutes later, I'm in the lounge of a house surrounded by a group of Persian people.

Today they are celebrating a man called 'Bāb', the founder and leader of the Bahai religion who reigned over Iran from 1844 to 1863. The group uncomfortably fills the room and, one by one, read passages out loud from the Bible. It feels special to be so welcomed into such a private affair.

The dining table is crowded with giant bowls of food, and we form an orderly queue. I dig into a huge bowl of rice with sultanas, and then spoon a clod of a bubbling potato, cheese and rice bake onto my plate. Another large tray of a mince casserole and three large silver pots of tea wait for us at the end of the buffet. I get acquainted around an oval table with others, all very interested to know what I'm doing here. Gina introduces me to an older lady wearing a treasure chest of gold rings and necklaces. She was the first person to set up a Bahai programme in El Salvador many years ago and followers from all over world come to help. The lady enlightens me on how they were the first religion to set up education programmes for women. I listen fascinated as she explains the Islamic revolution of 1979 and how the Bahai followers were persecuted during this time. Time passes quickly among these kind and generous people, and I leave with a little insight into a new group who have shared their food and stories with me.

"Buena gente," Gina says as we walk home. *Good people.*

GINA

The multi-coloured plastic chairs and tables of the Santa Tecla food court are reminiscent of a 1980s Pizza Hut. It seems much of the USA's discarded material makes its way down to El Salvador in various shapes and forms. Gina and I slide into a booth and pick a noodle dish each from the menu. Gina was once principal of the school, and the experience and advice she shares with me is invaluable for my teaching.

She explains the students and their families are all living well below the poverty line and simply unable to afford regular education. The importance of the volunteer programme for Margarita Duran is immeasurable. Around 70 percent of the schoolgirls work in the markets after school and some parents hardly ever let their kids attend, choosing to make them work full days.

In light of this, she conducts regular searches to try to talk sense into them.

Today is one of those days.

A lady with a guilt-ridden face brings our noodles over and Gina starts to lecture her like a naughty teenager. Questioning her for not sending her child to school, she tells the woman to give her daughter the opportunity to make a better life for herself. The scene is awkward, but Gina seems well-versed in such matters. She changes the subject, suggesting we grab soup from the markets for dinner. Entering the dim light of the municipal market, I see various girls from school, one by one. They look embarrassed that I'm seeing them working in these dank alleys, bagging vegetables and bootleg CDs.

I see one sat on a stack of toilet rolls. It brings tears to my eyes.

"Es Emely." Gina snaps me from my sorrow.

She introduces me to another previous student who is attending college and working at her mum's vegetable stall in her spare time. The girl with flawless caramel skin and stained apron is beautiful.

"Bicha, dame diez tortillas, cinco elote y zanahoria por fa." Gina lists her vegetables.

"Ella fue traviesa." She says Emely was bad at school.

The girl laughs sheepishly as she passes us the bags of produce.

Back outside in the light of day, speakers on top of little Honda vans advertise cell phone deals and blast music at full volume while girls in tight red dresses force feed flyers to the public. Across the street, cheap fake jeans lie draped over the iron spiked fence of the crowded park, and with them, another girl from school sits slouched on a stool wearing headphones and looking embarrassed that I've seen her. She strokes a fuzzy yellow baby chick in her hand.

Gina prepares soup in the kitchen while I swing in the hammock holding back tears after what I've seen this afternoon. I am now more determined than ever to be a teacher to remember.

Jacob informs me a new volunteer has arrived and that he'd appreciate it if I went over to the house and made him feel welcome. I'm happy at the thought of this new help with classes and I head over there to make his acquaintance.

En route, I sense something behind me. I don't look back but quicken my pace. Moments later I jump in fright, bombarded with the cries of a woman blasting from a beat-up little Honda van with two giant megaphones taped to the roof. In an attempt to wake the whole of Central America, the woman shrieks into a handset from inside the vehicle.

"¡OFERTA! ¡OFERTA! ¡¡¡Pollo!!! ¡¡¡Polliiiitooo!!!" She's obviously mistaken that I want to buy some chicken.

The dented vehicle drags itself past me and up the street, while the old hag inside continues to wail.

Shaken by the megaphone outburst, I ring the bell of the volunteer house, but it seems no one is home. As I turn to leave, a tall, dark-haired guy wearing glasses comes to the gate.

"Can I help you?" he says in an American accent.

Jacob obviously hasn't told him I was coming to say hi.

"Hey bro, I'm Darren, I'm a volunteer at the school."

"Ah OK, I'm Chris, come in." He seems subdued, indifferent.

He sits down at an open computer and starts to type.

Great start to this meeting, I think.

Chris is clearly not wanting to chat, so checking my emails via the Wi-Fi, I upload a couple of pictures from the San Andres trip and leave.

"OK, Chris, great to meet you."

No reply.

I let myself out.

THE RETURN OF MONICA

It's Friday night in Santa Tecla.

Gina, Manilo and Amy are busy and I'm spending the evening with Titi the dog and Zim the cat.

It's a little depressing, but the animals will be better company than the likes of 'cardboard Chris', the apathetic American new arrival who has the volunteer house across town to himself. I could wander down to Paseo del Carmen but what I really long for is company. Solitude is beginning to sink in and I desperately try to lose myself in a book.

There's a knock at the door.

I call through the iron gate, fearing another Jehovah lecture.

"¿Quien es?"

I hear a female voice but can't quite make out what she's saying. Opening the door, I'm surprised to see Monica.

"Hi," she says in her cute voice.

"I just need to explain why I was crying the last time." She invites herself in.

She stands over me explaining herself, dressed to impress in a short mini skirt and beige leather jacket. Feeling a little claustrophobic, I stand up, but she jumps on me wrapping her legs around my waist like a boa constrictor. I let caution to the wind and succumb to her advances as she starts nibbling my earlobe. I throw her onto my squidgy mattress, and the woman turns wild, ripping my clothes off. We give each other everything we have in my tiny little room.

"¡PAPI RICO! ¡¡¡PAPI RIIIICO!!!" She howls like a mad banshee as we roll around on the bed.

Titi, now on the other side of the closed door, is barking, scratching and trying to get in.

"¡Titi! ¡Callate!" I shout at the dog to shut up, now pinned to the bed by Monica.

I'm trapped between two wild Salvadorans, one clamped on top of me and one howling at the door.

"Shhhh. Monica, shhh. La perra no le gusta!" I try to calm her. The dog is freaking out.

We abort the mission, and head outside instead. A quiet bar ends our evening of passion. I have broken the golden rule and succumbed to lust. A decision entirely not fair on Monica. Whatever was between us is now unavoidably stronger.

I need to end this before I do more damage.

We have another drink and watch a drunk guy in a gold chain, stumbling around with a microphone in his hand singing karaoke. He staggers and bumps into tables miming along to the 50 Cent song, 'We're gonna party like it's your birthday'. The only words he knows are "Izzz yurr burrdey" that he repeats over and over again.

"La loca." Gina predicts the caller when my phone rings the following morning.

"¡Hola, carino!" Monica is clearly ready to get into a long chat, insisting we go for dinner.

I cowardly tell her I'll have very little cell coverage because I'm going to the mountains in Chalatenango for a couple of weeks. She hangs up. I'm expecting the phone to ring again but it stays silent.

"Buen hecho." Gina pats me on the back with a 'good job'.

And just like that, I never hear from her again. Well, not until a year later when she tracks me down on Facebook.

The message simply says she is ready to fall in love again and will wait until I return so she can bear my children.

CHAOS

I'm earlier than the Santa Tecla market stalls, still wrapped in tarps. The people on the streets look old, scarred and desperate. Taxis begin to line up kerbside. A bus honks and I jump in fright.

The Citibank ATM is surrounded with rough-looking, bare footed people who lean against the bulletproof glass cubicle. Stepping over them I try to make my transaction as quick as possible.

$400 in $100 bills spits out of the slit and I scrunch it up and stuff it into my pocket quickly, zipping it tight. Withdrawing the machines limit is a safer idea than taking a little out every few days. I figure having people become familiar with my routine is not wise. I hastily make my way back to the house, hoping I'm not followed.

Back in my room, I stash the money in a plastic envelope before sticking it to the back of the framed picture that hangs in my room. I walk to school, relieved the money run was a success.

During class, little by little, the girls get up unannounced and leave.

"Un momento," I call out, a little offended that they are taking off without my permission.

"Va para bebida de arroz." The girls still at their desks tell me the others have gone for a rice drink.

"¿De donde?" I ask where, still confused.

"La cocina," they reply. The kitchen.

With a military precision, girls from every classroom filter towards the canteen cage in the corner of the yard and line up. The fact that half these children probably don't eat sufficient food out of school hours is reason enough to not question it disrupting their lesson with me.

I ask one of the girls if she can get me one, too. She looks at me stunned but skips off towards the kitchen cage. When she returns, the class all watch with a tense anticipation as I sip it. The drink is warm, sweetened and flavoured with cinnamon.

"Que rico," I say, after drinking a mouthful.

The girls seem happy that I like it almost as if they've not seen this happen before.

Jacob is in the school foyer at recess.

"Entonces," he says, raising his eyebrows.

"¿Que pasa con la chica loca?" He inquires about Monica.

"Todo bien." I don't want to share information with him.

His vibe seems almost jealous of my meetings with her.

"You have fucked her?"

I stare back at him speechless. What a bizarre question.

"¡Hombre, todas las bichas locas!" He tells me all girls are crazy.

I think we both know who the crazy one is here, I think to myself.

I manage to escape from Jacob, but the 6B classroom is hot as hell. It has only a few missing bricks that act as air vents around the top of the walls. To add to the inferno, the class turns to pandemonium.

I become so focused on the work I'm marking that I fail to notice what has transpired in front of me. I look up to see a girl holding a table above her head while another is standing on a chair.

"¡OYE!" I shout at the top of my voice, silencing the whole class.

"¡A la ofincina! ¡Ahora!" I send another one to Lola's office.

"¿Por que, por que?" The others whine and plead with me to not send her.

This scenario is getting boring, but I've had enough of them trying it on. The bell rings and I've one more class to deal with: The oldest: 9th grade.

I walk in and look around. I can see this is going either way. Pulling out the paperwork from my backpack I get going.

"OK, vamos a seguir con el sujeto de ropa."

Obviously bored with the clothing subject, they answer with a collective "Uugghhhh!"

Tired from the day of lessons, I switch my plan and draw four semi-trucks on the whiteboard, labelling each one.

Ropa.
Maquillaje.
Efectos especiales.
Luz.

Wardrobe, makeup, special effects and lighting trucks of a film crew.

For the entire lesson the girls are transfixed on trying to guess in English and Spanish what each truck needs to contain in order to service a film production.

Suddenly they are a joy to teach.

"Teechuur. ¿Los actores, todos son gays?"

A girl's question surprises me as the class erupts in laughter. They spend the next ten minutes throwing actors' names at me in hopes of finding out which ones are gay.

Back at home, I swing in the hammock absolutely exhausted after a huge day and reflect on what my time as a volunteer teacher has taught me about the Salvadoran education system so far.

1. Lessons start fifteen minutes after the official bell due to the time it takes to herd them to class from the play area.
2. Random suited vendors can wander in at any time unannounced and sell CDs, DVDs and chocolates while the class is in session.
3. Pandemonium will ensue the moment the girls see that you are distracted or concentrating on something with your back turned.
4. Warm rice milk is served in the cook's cage sometime between 9:30 and 11am on sporadic days and students can leave their desk without asking. If it's a good day, the mug of goop comes with a splinter of cinnamon stick in it.
5. ALL actors are homosexual until proven otherwise.

MANILO

Tall, dark and immaculately dressed, Manilo combs his slicked hair with the bathroom door open.

"¿Vamos a comer?" Desperate for company, I ask him if he wants to go eat.

"Tengo una Pupusería," he says. "Con las mas ricas del pueblo."

I think it's a big call that he promises the 'Best pupusas in town' after seeing how much competition there is in this little place. We walk to an intersection of graffiti plastered walls where he points at a sign reading 'El Paseo'. A white tiled floor is complemented by equally clean white walls and Formica bench seats and tables. A wall-hung television set plays a football game above us.

"Buena suerte," Manilo greets the couple behind the counter with familiarity.

The girl, skinny and very pale in complexion, wears a full grill of braces and has strawberry-blonde hair tied back in a bun. The man is of similar smart dress to Manilo.

"¡Hola, Mani!" the girl says. "¿Y quien es tu amigo?" She asks who I am.

"Un voluntario Ingles," he says, "Quedando conmigo." An English volunteer staying with me.

"¿A la margarita?" The man directs his question to me, unsure of my Spanish.

"Si. Estoy ensenando las niñas en Margarita Duran." I am comfortable with my explanation: 'I teach kids at the school.'

The man smiles. "¡Habla bien chero!" He congratulates my Spanish and hands us a menu.

The couple's little girl toddles around adorably, chasing a fluorescent ball in the empty part of the dining area. A young indigenous woman pats out the masa dough for the pupusas on a large wooden bench top. Clouds of black smoke waft in on the wind from the buses that idle at the junction outside. Two plastic baskets of the maize pockets, oozing with stringy cheese, are slid onto our table. Manilo dollops a spoonful of warm curtido on them from a large jar. Curtido is a local specialty: a shredded cabbage, beet and carrot salsa marinated in apple cider vinegar.

He tells me a little about himself. He's separated from his wife, but they have two kids. He travels the country working insurance sales. He likes his job and gets to see the kids on the weekends.

I stretch the conversation out for as long as possible, knowing I'll be alone again the moment I arrive home.

BOQUERÓN

The Number 103 bus to 'El Boquerón' idles in the heat of Santa Tecla's Parque San Martín. The driver is in high spirits. His gold teeth glint as he smiles at me and winks at Amy.

She scrunches her face.

"Bicha bicha, no te morde." *Hey chicky, I don't bite.* He giggles.

She ignores his comment and asks how much the fare is. I hand him our 47 cents and find a seat.

Lady vendors push and shove their way down the aisle in the heat while the driver has fun flirting with them. They sit on the dash with baskets on their laps, clearly loving the attention.

Electrical shops barter alongside vegetable stalls as the bus moves slowly through the crowded street, gently pushing pedestrians aside and up onto the narrow sidewalks. A man with a naked mannequin on his shoulder shouts at the driver as he's nudged out of the way. Reaching the edge of town, the bus winds up around the side of the giant volcano and through tiny communities that line the edges of the road. Old women with roast chicken and tortillas take advantage when the bus pulls in to pick up passengers, thrusting the food through the windows in hopes of a sale. A group of men clank up the aisle with giant machetes that hang from belts made of twine. Dressed in loose chinos and thin cotton shirts, they ride with us after a hard morning's work in the coffee plantations that carpet the slopes. The driver navigates the impossible bends in the road and makes light work of a five-point turn outside a tiny shop at the top.

"Vamos," Amy says.

A bent and twisted sign, dented from air rifle pellets, informs us we are at 1800-metre altitude but still a one-kilometre walk short of the summit. Birdsong becomes louder the further we climb up the twisting lane and we reach a young girl at the entrance gate with punnets of fruit set up on a table. Behind her, a small building contains information boards telling the history of the site and the villages the eruptions have wiped out.

Past the building, a well-manicured path is flanked by a rainbow of tropical flowers and leads us onto the ridge of Boquerón's crater.

The view, ringed with purple flowers, is spectacular. Eagles soar through the thermals casting shadows over 'Boqueróncito' – a smaller crater resembling a brown cereal bowl, nestled below in the centre of the larger crater. Signs warn of the dangers of descending into the 5-kilometre-wide and 558-metre-deep crater, including, in no particular order: *loose*, *steep*, *uneven paths* and *daytime robberies*. The following line then in complete contradiction to the previous, mentions the serenity of camping down there.

I listen in to an old guy in a fishing vest peppered with pockets talking to a small group of visitors through his few remaining teeth. He divulges that in 1917, the area suffered a huge earthquake that lasted two hours. This literally left 90 percent of the capital's housing damaged or destroyed and started the eruption that swallowed up the lake that would have once been below us, leaving only the little Boqueróncito cereal bowl we can now see. He notices me listening and switches to a different language.

"Es Caliche," Amy says, her ears pricking up, telling me he's speaking a more native dialect.

"Como los Pipil," she adds, referring to the distant descendants of the Aztecs.

The guide glances at me smugly – I am sure he knows I can't understand. He herds his group away to another section of the ridge for more privacy. Enjoying the clean fresh air and silence of the volcano, Amy finally starts to descend the stairs; she has a class at four and needs to be back in time.

The girl at the gate is still sitting by her fruit. Her slices of watermelon seem to have an awful lot of pips in them – until she waves her tea towel and a swarm of flies rise into the air. I choose the less fly-ridden pot of red 'Mora' berries and munch on them as we make our way down the outside. We pass a dozen houses with barred windows built above road level. Their makeshift chain-link fences lean out awkwardly over us. Carefree dogs and chickens wander outside the tiny, barred hatch of a store where we sit at the roadside waiting for the bus. Gurgling up the hill, it appears, brightly decorated in turquoise flames and adorned with a purple whale tail. It awkwardly U-turns, lets us on and stops at several tiny villages to pick up more passengers as we descend. Local farmers, vendors and school kids greet each other warmly as they board and disembark.

Watching these interactions gives me a warm feeling seldom felt in the world I'm from, where a daily commute occurs over many years with the same people, people who never learn each other's names.

A HAIRCUT

The cracked Santa Tecla pavement outside a barber shop sprouts grass.

Two large glass windows stand either side of a stoop where a fly mesh screen fits a door opening.

A boy sleeps on a sheet of cardboard next to his mother outside. She sits on a crate next to a basket of vegetables for sale.

The tinkle of the doorbell ensures that everybody stops and stares when Gina shoves me up the stairs to enter.

"Sentate." A large man directs us with his scissors across the chequered floor to two empty chairs.

"Gracias." We nod at the men already sitting reading newspapers and join them.

The walls are covered in faded photos from fashion magazines depicting differing styles of cuts.

> 'Francesa oscura'
> 'Buzz'
> 'Estilo hongo'

A barber shaves tramlines in a boy's head, brushes him off and spins him slowly in a red swivel chair. He takes a hand full of coins from his father.

"Ven por fa." He beckons me over with his brush and wraps a cloak around my neck. Gina waits and watches me like I'm her 8-year-old son.

"Un cortar militar, por favor." I ask for a short back and sides.

He obliges and trims my messy mop into the first styled haircut I've had in probably ten years. The rubbing alcohol he applies stings my cheeks and he fluffs a cloud of talcum powder around my neck with a soft brush.

"Doscinquenta." He asks for $2.50.

"Muy caro." Gina grumbles at the price but not quietly enough.

The barber shoots her a glare. The little bell at the top of the door tinkles as we leave.

Our food is slid to us on paper plates at the pupusería overlooking the plaza that Amy had taken me to on my first night. It feels like a lifetime ago but in reality only a month or so. Below us, market stalls are roped and sealed in black tarp for the night, and a little digger buries its scoop into the rubbish cage, emptying its bucket into a small truck.

A red sunset glows over boys on bikes fitted with baker's racks that sell the last loaves of the day. A family wander home carrying crates on their shoulders. The mother pushes a coffee cart with a parasol and chair tied to the side. A small boy drags a full crate along the road with a length of rope while his younger sister stomps angrily along with her arms folded, annoyed that she has nothing to carry. We finish our food and continue home. A woman up ahead looks at something in a tree.

"¡Segue Segue!" She shouts up into the branches at four grubby children clambering around grabbing mangos.

Powerlines run through the branches, metres away from the kids snatching at the fruit.

Gina holds me back with her arm when she senses I'm about to approach the woman and alert her of the danger.

"No, Darreen, no," she says.

"Deben comer los niños."

The kids need to eat.

AND THEN THERE WERE THREE

Two soldiers at the Santa Tecla army barracks in the town centre talk about me as I pass. They glance over in my direction mid-conversation. I smile but they ignore the gesture. I have walked this route every morning for over a month now. They must wonder about my routine.

The welcome I receive from the lady at the bakery has become personable. After coming in most mornings, she now chooses my treats for the staffroom.

"Estos." She picks fifteen multicoloured meringues with her tongs and plops them in a paper bag.

The teachers scold me jovially when they open the bag.

"¡Estamos engordando – La liana no le gusta!" They laugh saying that the thin teacher Liana wouldn't be happy that I'm trying to fatten them up.

Jess, Angel and I are the only volunteers currently at the school. Chris, Vicky and the Germans girls have left. Jacob seems more relaxed.

The whole school assembles in the courtyard and sings the national anthem. Lola gives a stern speech about being ladylike, addressing the miniskirts and makeup that some of the girls have been seen wearing outside of school hours. The crowd is silent but the town is small. The girls in question must realise the speech is directed at them.

Gina has warned me that the more silent and badly behaved girls usually come from violent or troubled home lives. I take this on board and naturally, without being too obvious, pay them a little more attention, helping them with their studies. The other girls can sense this but are far from envious, understanding the reasons why. The care these kids show each other is admirable.

I'm coming to realise that being a 'teacher' is a lesson in itself. I'm learning as much if not more than the girls.

Back in class, I'm reminded of this.

"¡Teeeechuuur!" A small girl with plaits down either side of her head speaks up.

"¿Si?" I reply.

"¿En su país, porque la gente solo tiene tres dedos?"

The class can see I'm confused by her question and all start to laugh.

"Si teechuur, ¿Porque solo tres dedos?" They all now point at my drawings on the board inquiring as to why the people only have three fingers where I'm from.

"¡No!" I look at my anatomically incorrect drawings.

"¡Es mi culpa, disculpe!" I apologise and correct the finger count on each of the hands.

These interactions give us so much connection and they respond well, associating with my foolishness as I act out particular sentences, phrases and words in a humorous way.

It's a small victory, learning I can hold their attention.

Fellow 'real' teachers.
Lola to my right, Gina to my left.

7
HIGH COUNTRY

Gina and I in her brother's garden.
Las Pilas, El Salvador highlands.

SAN SEBASTIÁN

The 05:30 chicken bus transports Gina and I to the Guadalupe church terminal in San Salvador. The place is already alive with chaos, but Gina navigates like a pro. Her sister Noreen waves from the back window of a taxi.

"¡Holaaa!" She hurries us through the gridlocked vehicles.

We squeeze in, joining Noreen. Green countryside and a few dusty villages pass by on the way. I still don't know where we are going, but I'm happy to be on the road again.

Nestled in the highlands of the San Vicente province about two hours west of San Salvador, the small town of San Sebastián creeps up on us. It commands stunning views of Volcán Chichontepec.

The taxi pulls up in a brisk temperature outside the only original building left standing after the 1986 earthquake. The rest of the town has since been rebuilt in a traditional style. A crisp and fresh air hangs silent in the clean streets of this immaculately kept place.

"Tenemos que firmar algunos documentos." Gina says they have to sign some important papers.

The driver, a portly fellow with a pair of well-shined shoes, runs a comb through his slicked grey hair. He suggests we eat while the ladies do their business.

The town plaza is dominated by a blindingly white cathedral. On its left is a small pupusería where a pretty young woman with hairy legs strips corncobs into a large barrel of water. She pushes a bunch of logs further into an oil drum stove that heat a huge pot of water on top.

"Ella haciendo masa." The driver tells me she's preparing the corn to make flour.

The conversation is light. We discuss the weather and our favourite food.

The plaza is typical of a small town such as this but deathly quiet, only broken by a tuk tuk that whisks a round woman with wicker baskets full of fruit and vegetables away down a narrow street.

Gina and Noreen join us and grab a juice. They tell me the town is famous for its hammock weaving.

We enter a narrow doorway into a grotto of colour. Beautifully woven hammocks line the shelves of the low-roofed store. Gina files us through and out the back. She seems to know where she's going.

A wooden beamed roof flanks either side of a yard looking out over a lush green valley and Volcán Chichontepec's double peak dominating the skyline.

Golden bolts of sun beam through the red dust floating in the air where five weavers work at their hand-driven looms. A gentle creaking sound fills the space as they pump the pedals below their machines.

We stand silent, admiring this scene from yesteryear, watching as beautiful colours of wool are spun together through each loom. I could easily stay longer in this peaceful space, but the ladies are keen to keep moving. I buy a few table-throws before we are back out in the blazing heat of the day.

A colourful procession appears out of nowhere, injecting life into the street and passing us in full swing. A pickup truck with megaphones follows the dancing crowd and blasts traditional music while a seven-foot Gigantona doll spins its pigtail hair and floppy arms. I feel for the person inside its framework and how hot they must be controlling it while carefree children skip alongside. The colourful procession circles the plaza before disappearing off down a narrow street.

The route home passes through Soyapango. Here, 18th Street and MS13 graffiti slogans battle for space on the cinderblock walls of the corrugated shanty town. We melt back into the countryside once more until passing a 'Welcome to Ilopango' billboard at the roadside. The sign has been defaced to read 'Welcome to Marasalvatrucha13'.

No one in the taxi seems to notice it. Maybe they care not to notice it.

We are once again engulfed in lush green countryside.

Ciudad Delgado is the next habited area – a thin strip of a shithole that the taxi driver takes a shortcut through. He certainly likes running the gauntlet. We slow down at a rusty, faded red railroad crossing sign and bounce over two buckled train tracks that cut through the middle of the town. The train line is now a narrow slit flanked by shacks where dogs wander freely. It seems impossible that at some stage in the past a freight train would have fitted through here.

I think back to the old rusting locomotives in the train cemetery in Bolivia's Altiplano.

As we reach the fringes of San Salvador, the driver, seemingly still unsatisfied with running the gauntlet, takes another gamble, short-cutting through a barrio affectionately known as 'Tutu'.

Gina whispers something to Noreen. I can sense her concern.

We pass a group of teenagers. I can see their tattoos spell out gang insignias.

They eye us up as the taxi speeds by.

LA PALMA

Alighting from the bus on a quiet street in the city, Gina, Amy and I step into the blazing heat of the afternoon sun. Amy tells me a guy was robbed and shot dead last week right where we're standing. I walk with pace to our destination.

Inside the Museo Anthropologia in San Salvador, we find ourselves surrounded by artefacts of the Nahatual and Pipil people. Masks, jugs and life-sized terracotta figures fill the room. Gina points out items from the Chalatenango region in the highlands and that it's the coldest place in El Salvador.

I laugh at the thought of somewhere being cold here.

"Hay nieve." Gina assures me it snows there.

I laugh again.

"Vamos mañana." She says we're going tomorrow.

I've come to know Gina well. She is a strong-minded woman with friends and family scattered far and wide throughout the country. I have no doubt we'll be in the mountains in a few days.

She proves me right, saying her brother Alberto lives in a town called 'Las Pilas' close to where it snows. She hasn't seen him for ten years.

She returns an hour later with a chilly bin and a tent.

"¿Vamos a campar?" I point at the tent.

"Quizás." Perhaps. She's not sure how much room there is at her brother's house.

I prepare a small backpack with essentials for tomorrow's trip while Gina packs the chilly bin with more food than we'll need.

A swishing sound wakes me. It's still pitch black. Through my tatty piece of fabric curtain, I see Gina in the yard sweeping. I can see she's also done a load of laundry that's hanging out to dry and has made a start on breakfast. This woman never sleeps.

We are out the door at 5am and into the already full bus. Through the window, corroding balconies and razor wire spirals loom over markets lining the narrow crumbling streets. These important arteries that feed the heart of the city hurriedly prepare for a busy Saturday under architecture that once was regal, but now is neglected, and flaking paint.

We arrive at another chaotic terminal. Like a mother hen, Gina leads us through the carnage where a long line of people stand carrying buckets. At the front of the queue, a wooden caged pickup truck is stuffed with goats. White milk splashes into tin buckets as hands squeeze teats from wherever they poke through the cage.

We are pushed into another old bus and squashed up the back. I keep hold of the chilly bin inside the cramped vehicle as more dilapidated buildings flash by outside. Clumps of electric wires hang above the streets on poles that supply the city its weak current of power. Gina narrates the things that pass by.

"Es Iglesia San Francisco." She points at a church.

The faded, pastel-green church is constructed of vertical wooden planks that are split and peeling.

She says the wooden structures survive earthquakes because of their flexibility.

Fortunately, the squashed ride is short, and we are sucked into the whirlpool of Terminal Oriente in the north of the city. Rubbish swirls along the gutters and hungry bus ticket touts pull and shove us aggressively towards buses that lurch in every direction. I yank Gina out of the way as one reverses. At the back of the lot, two rotund women in aprons wash clothes in large concrete sinks under a tree.

"Esta." Gina points at two green and white buses parked next to the washer women.

The header sign above the windscreen of one reads: 'Fra. El poy', the border with Honduras. The other: 'San Salvador-La Palma'.

"La Palma," Gina says, pushing us up on.

The sweaty bus slowly fills up in the prickly heat. We hand over the $1.65 each to travel to the edge of the country. I ask her how far it is.

"Quatro horas en bus niño, mas o menos." Four hours.

I think back to the hostel ticket booking in Flores and the $40 fare to San Salvador. I figure it would have been less than $5 if it wasn't for my blister and I could've walked to the terminal that day.

While we wait, vendors slowly fill the aisle offering up their goods. Pre-cut salted mango in small plastic bags and cheap jewellery hanging on cardboard sheets are waved in our faces.

The bus fires into action and crawls out of the city towards the mountains. Every six blocks or so, new vendors replace old, squeezing up the aisle to sell their wares.

Sitting in front of Gina, Amy and I are completely unaware of her close encounter with one of the vendors, until she leans forward and tells us about it a while later. She recounts how he bent over her seat and grabbed her necklace. Thinking quickly, she tugged down on it, snapping the chain and sending it inside her blouse. Outsmarted, the vendor hastily escaped from the bus in the aisle confusion.

"¡Mamaaaaa!" Amy is annoyed that she hadn't said anything sooner.

"Ai niña. ¿Que pudiste hacer?" she says, knowing there was little Amy could have done. "Es idiota." We all nod and agree: he was an idiot.

Gina has lived through the country's brutal civil war of the 1980s. I imagine this is a mere hiccup in the life that she has seen.

The bus cuts through the green lowlands and passes a few small villages before we start to climb. The engine screams louder the steeper the road. We arrive in a drastically dropped temperature in the tiny village of San Ignacio, a grid of cobbled streets and low-roofed shacks. Curious teenagers in cowboy boots and starched denim jeans stare at us. Gina steps below street level into a low-roofed comedor. Inside, a warming cabinet displays two silver Bain Marie trays containing chicken and a rice, yucca bean and corn dish. A little television set crackles away above us.

"Tres por fa." Gina orders three helpings and I grab us Cokes from an ice box.

Sweat beads from our faces as we tuck into the delicious hot meal. The lady shoos a pig from the front door. The bus outside revs its engine and sounds it horn.

"¡Vamos!" Gina cries, springing up.

Smaller than the previous buses, this one coughs and splutters as it claws its way up the hills in very high revs at a max speed of 5mph. We are accompanied by a soundtrack of Reggaeton, Snoop Dog and Eminem at full volume, blasting from the speaker boxes that sit in the overhead luggage racks. A young girl with braids sits in front and sucks on an ice pop, clinging to her mother. As she finishes, she tosses the stick and wrapper out of the window slit, watching it flutter away. Stretching her hand out behind her, her mother pulls a can of drink from her bag, opens it and pops a straw in the top for the girl, who, on finishing the drink, does the same again. Her mother is fully aware of this and doesn't bat an eyelid. Gina and I both scowl at the young girl.

The engine starts to scream again when the one-lane road turns to dirt and follows a mountain ridge. The temperature drops more as we dip into thick low-lying cloud, at times revealing green volcanoes and lush lowland vistas of Honduras that stretch far across the invisible border line. Gina, now concentrating on the road ahead, assures us we are close and suddenly, springs from her seat.

"¡OK vamos!" she makes a beeline for the front, dragging the tent.

The bus stops abruptly and deposits us in the middle of nowhere.

"Aqui esta," Gina says. She turns around and follows a narrow dirt track.

LAS PILAS

The small community of Las Pilas sits on the Salvadoran mountain border with Honduras. Following Gina up the slippery mud track, dogs bark viciously from the adjoining properties. They don't like the smell of us city folk.

The white mongrel on the right yanks at its rope tying it to a tree, while a brown one to our left throws itself at the chain-link fence between us.

"Awww, chuchitos, calmase." Gina tells them to calm down, seemingly unaware they want to rip us to pieces.

We have arrived at the house of Gina's brother Alberto. A small, teal green place, built of cinder block and capped with a corrugated iron roof. Bars over its windows are painted in a dark green that match the front door. It sits in the middle of these mountains.

We knock at it, and hear footsteps.

It slowly opens on a weathered lady's face that warms slightly at the sight of Gina. Hugging Amy, she comments on her height the last time she saw her. She flattens her hand at knee-level.

"Es mi hermana Mariella." Gina introduces me to her sister-in-law.

"Hola, mucho gusto." I smile and shake her hand.

She tells us her son is at military band practice but will be home soon. Amy asks of the instrument he plays.

"Trompo." She walks towards the back of the house.

Through the terracotta-tiled hallway, we pass two steel doors with hatches. They could've been salvaged from a prison. In the kitchen, two wooden tables sit against the back wall. One is piled with freshly washed clothes and the other has a stack of plates on it. A door in the back wall leads through to a bathroom area with a dirt floor.

I ask if I can go.

"Si. Adelante." Mariella points me in.

Two concrete cubicles with phlegm-spattered walls don't reach the ceiling. In one is an open-topped oil drum with a purple plastic bucket bobbing in it. The waste bin for toilet paper is near to overflowing. There is no handle or chain to flush the toilet. I figure the purple bucket is used to scoop out water from the oil drum and pour down the pan to flush.

"¿Alberto donde esta?" Gina asks of her brother as I return from the toilet.

"La iglesia." Mariella says he'll be home from church soon.

She boils a pan of water and shares it into a few cups of instant coffee powder and sugar.

"Ah caliente, muy bueno." Amy cups the hot mug with both hands.

The front door suddenly clicks shut and Mariella's manner changes as she scurries over to the wet pile of clothes and throws them in a basket. A short potbellied man in a dress shirt and tie appears from the hallway corridor.

"¡Hermano!" Gina says delighted.

"Hermana," he replies, far less enthusiastically, loosening his tie.

I'm curious about his manner, especially as she's just travelled so far to see him. She hugs him and introduces me.

"Bienvenidos." Alberto firmly shakes my hand with a sweaty paw.

"Voy a cambiar mi ropa. ¡Tengo hambre!" He growls at Mariella to make him food, turning around and walking back off down the corridor.

She hastily sets about making him a sandwich. He returns barefoot wearing a stained wife-beater with his belt undone. Without asking, he opens the bottle of rum I've gifted them and pours three glasses. Gina and Mariella reminisce, talking in an incomprehensible speed.

We walk to the village with views of the Honduran highlands. The hills surrounding us sprout maize plants, peach and apple trees. The dirt street climbs a little and then brows over a hill before dropping into a neglected cobbled lane. A piglet is tethered to an orange shipping container. The box has a hole cut in the side for a serving hatch with a flap fixed by hinges and propped open by timber struts at either end.

This is a very small community. It reminds me of Pachijal in Ecuador.

A group of youths on the main corner of the village's street stare at us. Smiling and waving, I greet them.

"¿Como esta ustedes?" I try to be friendly.

"Todo bien." They reply in a tone that tells me it's all I'm getting out of them.

Villagers clear from an outdoor stage on the school field as we pass. Children and parents spill out of the gates and flood the tiny street. A lady tells Amy we've just missed the Saturday afternoon kids play. We U-turn and walk back to the container shop, parking ourselves up on the kerb outside. Amy chats away to the boy inside while Gina and I drink a Coke.

Back at the house, Alberto is now watching a wildlife programme on the television and Mariella brings us bean and cheese boquitas with tortillas. The dynamics between the couple are awkward. She seems a lovely lady but also very subservient.

Alberto spits a few times into the corner of the living room. I'm reminded of the phlegm on the toilet wall. No one bats an eyelid at his revolting behaviour. I can't believe what I'm seeing, this lump of a human, stained with food and slumped in his chair with his belt undone, gobbing on the floor like it's nothing.

He's the village priest, for fuck's sake.

EL PITAL

Sounds of tinkering in the kitchen wake me. I roll over and look at my phone. It's 04:45 am. I can see my breath it's so cold. Thank god for the multiple sheepskins I've slept under.

Mariella has already made coffee and warmed up beans and tortillas in the kitchen.

"Es tuya." Gina hands her the chilly bin, not wanting to carry it on our long return bus ride to San Salvador.

The distant hum of a bus sounds our departure from the Salvadoran highlands. We hurry our last few mouthfuls, say goodbye and jump on at the foot of the muddy driveway.

The barking of the neighbouring dogs fade as practically empty, the bus pulls itself back into momentum and through the icy cold dawn, dropping us an hour later at a lonely intersection where a dirt street leads off into the hills flanked by tin and wooden shacks.

"Es Río Chiquito," Gina says. I'm glad at least one of us knows where we are.

A thick cloud blankets the empty street. Not a soul stirs. Two plumes of smoke rise from a chimney.

I'm not entirely sure why we've got off the bus or if it was a wise decision.

"Es por alla, pero vamos en camioneta." Gina points up the hill, telling us we'll hire a jeep.

I ask her what's up there.

"El Pital." She senses my confusion.

"El lugar mas alto del pais. Entonces, nieve." I had no idea: the highest point in the country.

She's adamant to prove to me snow exists here. Blowing warm breath into my hands, I feel I may get to see it. I pass Amy my coat; she is now also shivering in the little bus stop where we've taken shelter. She pulls the hood up as the rumble of an engine in the distance grows nearer.

A guy pulls up across the road in his pickup truck and sits motionless, staring into space. Approaching him, I ask how much he'll charge to take us to the summit. Tilting his cowboy hat up from his wrinkled face, he says in no uncertain terms that it's a long way and will be $35.

Gina approaches to haggle. "No es lejos y $35 es demasiado caro."

His face grimaces. He's not doing deals with this woman at this hour of the morning.

We return to the shelter and continue to wait in the cold. From out of the fog, I see a dog limping towards us. It looks in bad shape. As it comes closer it reveals the terrible extent of its injuries. Its three intact legs are carrying a mangled fourth front one that's far beyond the point of ever healing. Red raw sores along its side and hip bone leak pus. We can see the poor thing has been hit by a car. He is malnourished beyond words, and its fur is stretched tight over the rib cage. He has a permanent smile from the left cheek having been ripped away, exposing jaw and teeth. Saliva runs freely from the gaping hole in its head. I can't believe this thing is still alive. It's literally walking roadkill.

"Pobrecito." The sight upsets Amy and Gina as the mutt continues on its three-legged way, hobbling off into the mist.

"¡Café!" Our mood is lifted as Gina twitches her nose like a rabbit, trying to detect the origin of the brewing coffee's scent.

"Allí." She points up the dirt road to the house where smoke twirls from the chimney stack.

Ducking through the low-framed door, she greets the three women inside. They giggle while serving us piping hot tin mugs of coffee at our little wooden table. I dig my spoon into the sugar jar. A guy enters the store and approaches us.

"Trienta al arriba." He offers his truck: a ride for $30. Word has travelled fast.

"¡Muy caro! No gracias." Gina refuses again, shooing him away.

"Es buen precio." He ignores her and directs his offer at me.

"No. Mas barato." She refuses, telling him we're going to walk.

He tells her she's mad. "Es muy lejos. Como tres horas, talvez mas." Three hours to walk.

"Ai, mentiroso." She mumbles 'liar' under her breath.

We set out on foot climbing further into the mist. Occasionally a blue hole of sky appears in the blanket of thick cloud either side of the ridge we follow. Gina refuses when I ask to carry the tent she's had balanced on her head the whole way. I think she's regretting not taking the $30 offer.

Nestled in the hillside at the end of a red dirt driveway is a white house with a terracotta-tiled roof surrounded by well kept fields of cabbage.

"Aqui no mas." I call a break. I can sense Gina is tired.

We sit at the edge of the drive flanked by terraced maize fields and agree to finish our climb here.

Amy says she read about tourists camping at the summit and being robbed in their tents in the night.

I think we've made a good decision.

Back at the intersection, half a dozen trucks are now parked up. Gina haggles with the group of drivers, trying to secure us a $25 ride to San Ignacio but the old men are firm with their refusals.

A round-faced guy in hiking boots joins us. In an accent not from these parts, he tells us the bus isn't for another two hours.

A young boy approaches us with a sheet of plywood under one arm and a crate in the other from which he sets up a little fruit stall. He neatly stacks his oranges and pineapples in little pyramids.

Gina pushes herself to her feet and tries her luck again with the truck drivers. She confers with them before waving us over.

"¡Vamos!" she cries! "¡Veinte cinco! ¡No mas!"

CHECKPOINT

At a cross-junction in the mountains of El Salvador, we wait patiently in the rear tray while the group of truck drivers bicker between themselves.

With an ingrained need to always get a bargain, my Salvadoran homestay mother Gina has opened a can of worms, haggling the price with one of them, much to the other's disdain.

Soon we are moving. I stand up and brace myself against the headboard rack, looking forward over the cabin's roof. The truck swerves and twists its way, descending through the sharp hairpin bends of the valley, stopping briefly to scoop up two more backpackers with thumbs out. The two hikers are from Honduras and have been camping up at El Pital for the night. Although they had no altercations with thieves, they do confirm what the truck drivers had said, telling us we would've been walking for at least three hours to get to the summit.

I catch distant glimpses through the trees of pastel-coloured houses and it's not long before we coalesce with narrow cobbled streets, bouncing along in the back of the truck like cattle on their way to market.

Climbing down from the tray of the truck that has reached its destination, we walk the remainder of the way into San Igancio.

"Hay mucha historia en este lado del país. Historia terrible."

I feel a history lesson coming from Gina.

She recounts the government-backed death squads that wiped out whole villages in this area during the conflicts.

One large massacre took place at the Sumpul River on May 14, 1980, in which an estimated 600 civilians were killed, mostly women and children. The escaping villagers were prevented from crossing the river by the Honduran military, and, with nowhere to run but back the way they came, were killed by Salvadoran troops in cold blood.

Less than a year later the Salvadoran army began a 'sweep' operation to eradicate anyone not captured. Survivors of the sweep, again mostly women and children, attempted to cross another river into Honduras but hundreds were killed by aircraft bombs and machine gun.

She leads us through a little artesian market where hand woven hammocks, painted wooden dolls and other hand-crafted items hang from the stalls. Odours of hot food waft through the air. Climbing the steps of the church, she informs us we are standing where the first peace talks were had between the guerrilla group and the government in the 1980s.

Small open doorways on either side of the street share a glimpse of Salvadoran mountain life. Gina pokes her head into one and asks directions to the plaza from an old man in cowboy boots rocking in a chair. Another man sleeps in a net hammock strung across the living room, while a dog lies on the cool terracotta tiles of the floor underneath him. Ornate façades surround the main square, and a white fence edges a grass area with a white and blue bandstand. I make the mistake of asking a man with a strap of belts over his shoulder the price, but Gina herds Amy and me away before he can make a sale.

"Muy caro," she says, pushing us up into another bus. Very expensive.

We transfer at the small town of La Palma to our final bus and pay a mere $1.67 each for the three-hour ride ahead. Twenty minutes later, the bus is stopped in a sandstone canyon by six wiry men in camouflage military fatigues, floppy brimmed hats and AR-15 rifles.

The soldiers do not board; instead, they just watch the bus. The silence is palpable.

Gina's stories of the death squads during the revolutions aren't helping my paranoia as they continue to stare at us inside.

Finally, one stands on the bottom step at the door. "¡Hombres! ¡Baja!" he barks, ordering all of the men off the bus.

I'm instantly transported back to this exact scenario in Colombia. I've a pretty good idea of what's coming next.

Obeying his command, we all shuffle single file to the front. The women stay put.

I can feel Gina's apprehension. I'm scared.

Outside, the soldiers wear dead-eye glances as we're lined up and told to put our arms above our heads, spread our legs and lean with hands against the cliff face. It feels like we're being lined up in front of a firing squad. The soldiers work their way through the line, patting us down, presumably checking for weapons or drugs.

"¿De donde usted?" the soldier that searches me asks where I'm from.

"Londres," I answer, remembering I still travel on my British passport. I don't want to confuse the issue, even though he probably has no idea what I'm saying anyway.

"¿A donde va?" He seems not satisfied with my last answer, now wanting to know my destination.

"San Salvador," I reply.

"¿A donde viene?" He asks where I've come from in the same flat tone.

"El Pital," I say.

He repeats his question in a sterner tone. I can see he has no patience for this interaction.

"¿Que país? ¿Que fecha?" What country did I come from last and what date?

"Guatemala, cinco de Agosto," I quickly reply.

"Papeles, documentos," he snaps.

I'm now sweating. I have no ID on me. The soldier is getting angrier.

"¡PAPELES!" he barks, waking me from my freeze and holding his palm out flat, inches from my face.

To make things worse, the other guys still with their hands on the rock face look in my direction with worried expressions.

Gina appears in the door well. She tries to explain my being here, but he's not interested.

"¡Sentate!" He orders her back to her seat as one of the other soldiers pushes her back into the bus with his rifle butt.

I remember I have a passport copy tucked in my shoe but tell him it's in my bag on the bus to avoid him seeing where I pull it from. I don't need to make him angrier.

He flicks his head towards the door. "¡RAPIDO!"

I'm clearly running out of time with this guy and his short fuse. Rushing onto the bus, I pull the paper from under my insole and fly back down the aisle, but as I unfold the damp page, it rips. Gina, now against orders and back at the front, is explaining that I'm volunteering in a school helping children, but he's not listening, focussed on the piece of sweaty paper. My details are ripped in two and the passport photo looks like a fake Picasso painting.

"¡Necesita fecha en documentos!" he snaps, asking for my stamped copy with entry date.

Everyone is told to re-board, except me. Gina is still pushing the volunteer card but the guard is not listening. Turning to me, he passes me my ID, now limply hanging between his thumb and forefinger.

"Obtener copia sellada," he says. 'Get a sealed copy.'

His tone has changed, as if he's exhausted from the interaction.

"¡Va!" he guides us up onto the bus with the barrel of his gun before whistling to the driver to move on.

No one had said a word to the soldiers beyond answering their questions and they'd not made the slightest effort to be civil, nor had they checked the women or baggage locker belly. The whole scene seemed to be merely a demonstration of authority. Shaken by the situation, I'm glad it's over. I think everyone else is too.

The bus continues and a middle-aged guy gets on with a box of Caramelo sweets for sale. He starts to tell the passengers that since his time in prison, he's found the lord and has seen the error of his ways. He walks the aisle trying to sell his hard toffees for 25 cents while the engine noisily acts as our brakes through the downhill gradient as we descend into the green lowlands.

Eventually, the smog and hustle of San Salvador envelopes us and we arrive at a faded sign that hangs crooked. 'Bienvenidos a Oriente Terminal.'

We disembark. The smell of hot trash and gutters full of rubbish are a far cry from Pital's fresh mountain air and little cobbled street.

Gina can't find her son Alvaro and calls again. Amy and I follow her across a busy street where a cluster of vagrants have made an empty carpark their home.

"¡Hijo!" Gina cries, pointing at a guy sitting in a red, lowered Honda Civic.

Alvaro, a short, round-faced guy, introduces himself and bundles us into the car before pulling out onto the highway. The bouncing clang of the undercarriage reverberates under us as the car drags itself through the minefield of potholes. Rain begins to dot the windscreen as we drive back to Santa Tecla.

I think back to the dilapidated van at Flores airport as I stare at Alvaro's glued in air bag hatch and the tangle of wires hanging from the empty hole where the stereo once lived.

WHISTLE STOP TOUR

"Necesito carro." Gina thinks out loud.

She needs to borrow a car. After the trip to Las Pilas, she now has a thirst to show me more of El Salvador.

I decide not to ask about the plan she has for the day, happy to be getting out of the house.

We meet with Pamela, the broad-set grey-haired lady who had silenced the disruptive class I was teaching. Now outside school hours, her demeanour is far less scary. The three of us take a bus north and find ourselves once again in the town of Lourdes. Squeezing ourselves along the aisle and out of the rear folding door, we come face to face with another MS13 gang mural outside.

"Aqui estamos," she says. We are here.

Crossing the traffic-choked road, two pear-shaped women gabble to each other in the entrance to a vast, mall carpark with broken light poles.

"El carrito esta allá." Gina points across the near empty carpark to her son Alvaro's red Honda. I think back to the hole in it's dashboard where a radio once lived.

Some shop front windows advertise package holidays, while others display cosmetics and clothing in the building we enter. It could be any mall in the United States. A smell of fried chicken is wafted along with the air conditioning's freezing current. The bank we enter is deathly quiet. Patrons wait patiently in their seats holding tickets stating their number in line. Heads turn when the armed security guard asks me to remove my hat.

Gina skips the line and explains she needs to speak to her son, who is busy scurrying to and fro behind the tellers. Dressed smartly in a shirt, tie and glasses, he wears an ID security card around his neck.

Before taking the car keys, she lectures him in front of the amused staff for not visiting her enough.

Alvaro's 'Hondita', as Gina calls it, is excessively low and without a doubt illegally modified.

I squash in the back while Pamela and Gina get comfy up front. Our combined weight literally puts the giant exhaust on the ground. The springs are most certainly chopped.

Pamela turns the key and the vehicle starts with an almighty burp. As she over-revs the already decibel-breaking engine, I notice the speed dial needle is broken. With a deep sinister gurgle, the car crawls out of the car park, leaking valuable engine pressure through a giant hole in the exhaust pipe, and converges in with the bumper-to-bumper traffic. Pamela, unable to merge fully across to the onramp, performs a complete circle through the town that brings us back to where we started twenty minutes earlier. Looking outside from my small quarter-pane of glass, I realise these two old ladies in this crazy lowered car must look ridiculous.

"Necesitamos comprar un llanta nueva." Gina informs us we need to get a new tyre as we successfully slip onto the highway on our second attempt. I had noticed the pizza cutter wheel when we'd jumped in but had overlooked it, more concerned with the state of the rest of the vehicle.

We finally escape the traffic and hit the open road. Untamed jungle and open fields whizz by as we bounce along the potholed highway.

"¡Allá!" Gina yells, pointing at a tyre shop at the side of the road.

Pamela slams on the brakes, sending us into a fishtail of red dust only inches from the large upright tractor tyre advertising the garage in the hard shoulder. With the arse end of the car sticking out into the fast traffic lane, I worry we'll get rear-ended, but the women are already out and talking to the tyre shop guys.

A giant semi-truck appears as it speeds towards the car. I frantically shoehorn myself past the passenger seat that won't push fully forward, escaping just as the truck almost swipes the back of the car. It honks its air horn as it passes.

The father and son duo, in dire need of a hot soapy wash, smirk at me as I join the ladies. Their garage is a shack fashioned from planks.

"No tengo," the father informs us. He has no tyres in our size. He lifts his filthy baseball cap and rubs his head.

Our next stop is a gas station where we're handed complementary Styrofoam cups of coffee by an attendant. He fills the tank staring at us curiously, unable to hide his expression of bewilderment. I don't blame him, knowing how bizarre this badly modified car containing such a band of misfits must look.

No sooner does the road become pothole free and smooth, we get stuck behind a smoky bus. A cloud of thick black exhaust forces us to roll the windows up, turning the inside of the car into an oven. Pamela thankfully decides not to try to overtake it on the treacherous road. I catch glimpses of volcano peaks through holes in the black smoke engulfing us and finally, levelling out in the hilltops, the bus pulls over.

"¡Bravooo!" the women shout, tooting the bus as we pass.

"Mal hombre, es asqueroso," Pamela says. Disgusting man.

Two giant steel gates hang off square concrete pillars. The uniformed security guard holding a pump-action shotgun is not impressed by the grade 5 maths teacher's skid that stops a metre away from him. He's standing in a small doorway that opens within the gate, and he flicks us away with his hand like we shouldn't be here. Pamela fires up the Hondita again and pulls in across the road, a distance we could have just as easily walked. She disappears into a smartly painted villa where more security guards walk among the trimmed hedges of its manicured gardens. She returns with permission to enter the gate opposite and tosses her head in disgust at the security guard as he lets us in.

Inside, giant sheds with silos attached to them are connected by rusty pipes that hang from wire overhead. Pamela proudly shows off the coffee farm that has been in her family for generations. Huge drying vats and massive sieves, filters and husking machines spill out a myriad of different coloured coffee beans as we follow her out to the rear of the farm where vast toasting tiers are covered in beans, drying in the sun. Forested coffee slopes and volcano peaks surround us.

Pamela hands me two small cotton sacks to fill with whatever beans I like the most. I scoop my hand into each pile; the smell is intoxicating. I gratefully collect one with a rich chocolatey aroma and another with a spicy tobacco scent.

"¡Vamos a Juayua!" she says, "Muy bonito." And with that we are back on the road.

*

The small pueblo of Juayua is very quaint. Founded in 1577, the town's central plaza faces the white church of Santa Lucia with a terracotta cross on its façade. The church is famous for a large colonial-era statue of the Cristo Negro, or 'Black Christ', which hangs dominantly behind the altar. There is no history of the statue to state why it's in a place where there were very few people of African origin. Back outside, a portly man masquerading as Elvis sings badly into a microphone. His white nylon flares, frilly collared shirt and sequinned belt get Pamela and Gina giggling, but we have no time to lose as I'm hurried back to the car.

Next stop is a small town called Ataco, and another famous for its coffee. Scraping over speed bumps, we somehow arrive with the exhaust still attached.

Loud music blasts from a bandstand in a plaza draped in red flowers and tarp roofs of market stalls shade an alfresco dining area where we eat our little tacos. A train of stray dogs snakes through the legs of the white plastic furniture in hope of a scrap or two.

"Vamos a Apaneca," Gina says. "Vamos a ver Maria." Now we're going to see Maria in Apaneca.

And again we are back in the Hondita.

Kids on neglected BMX bikes stare at the car like it's a spaceship as it shakes its way through the mist on the cobbled streets of Apaneca. The street names and house numbers are not required as Gina steers us through the thick blanket of fog via landmarks that only she seems to know. Left at the faded yellow house with the old roof. They've all got old roofs. Right at the house with the satellite dish and keep going until you see the black dog at the corner.

As we pull up, the family are already standing outside to greet us.

The Father 'Don Adam', his son and the husband and mother of Maria from the school are delighted to see us.

From inside, green wooden shutters stretch from floor to ceiling and give a wide view onto the cobbled street. The place is like a preserved National Trust house from a time long forgot. Photos and oil paintings of family members of the past hang on the walls and a drinks cabinet stands proud in the corner, its black walnut wood grain a beautiful, streaked pattern of chocolatey lines. More ornate cabinets are adorned with gold virgin Marys and picture frames of Jesus, but I'm brought back to the present when their teenage son wanders in wearing a pair of giant headphones and bopping his head. Stepping through another doorway, I'm thrown back in time once more as two native women grind maize into masa in large mortar and pestles in a small hay barn. The white flour they are producing is being mixed with water by another woman and patted into discs.

Maria's dad, Jorge, wears a pencil-thin moustache and a pin-striped dress shirt that hangs off his skinny frame. He leads us out from the barn and across a concrete yard area where tropical plants sprout vivaciously from wooden cask pots. Two white chickens peck at the ground undisturbed by our presence while two small dogs desperately try to hump each other.

Don Adam laughs at them. "Babosas." He cackles at their persistence and the fact they are both females.

The acrid smell of his distillery fills the air of a small wooden shed.

He grabs a bucket and heads back to the lounge and peels off a cloth draped over its top.

"Casi listo," he says, sniffing the liquid: almost ready.

Maria hands us four cups while he scoops out the dark red liquid before sharing it through a sieve. The taste is sharp but not unpleasant. Yucca and tamales are served over conversation with Don Adam. I mention I trained as a wood machinist as I admire the walnut cabinet. He tells me he was a carpenter but later became a border customs officer.

"Si, pero trabajo peligroso." He tells me of its dangers.

The gangs and drug smuggling ultimately ended in him leaving his job after stopping a truck full of cheese wheels filled with cocaine. Being the chief of the drug bust, he faced the ultimatum of either leaving his job or his family being assassinated by the gang. He relays his story as if he's telling me what he ate for lunch.

Once again, we are hurried along and exchange hugs before being bundled back into the Hondita.

Descending in the car back down through the green slopes, I feel so much gratitude being accepted into these family scenarios. We whizz past a lookout point that views a string of volcano peaks.

"Whoa!" I blurt out. "¡Por favor!"

Pamela skids into the dirt and performs a five-point turn on a blind corner. I'm helpless in the rear seat and pray as we manoeuvre through the 180-degree turn. I think back to the tyre shop and that semi-truck that almost rear-ended us this morning. Making it back to the viewpoint in one piece, the four majestic volcano peaks of Santa Ana, Coatepeque, Izalco and Apaneca are carpeted in deep green coffee plantations and stand proudly like keepers of the land. We soak up their grandeur for a few minutes.

"¡OK, vamos!" Gina shatters the peace and I'm bundled back into the Hondita.

Arriving back in Lourdes, the car slips down a street behind a wall smeared in gang graffiti.

"¿A donde va?" I ask the women worriedly.

"Todo bien," Gina says, sensing my nerves.

"Es area diferente a las maras." She senses my concerns, assuring me we are not going into the gang barrio.

We drive through a heavily guarded gate and into a half-built subdivision of small prefab houses. Across the high barbed-wire fence a sea of roofs weighted down by old tyres and bricks are a sure sign of a gang neighbourhood. We swing into a driveway back on the safe side and Gina's shirtless son Alvaro answers the door.

"¡Poner ropa!" Gina is more concerned about her son being shirtless than the gangland across the fence.

8
TECLEÑO

SHISHA

Gina invites me to the art museum in the city. She knows what an exhausting day I've had.

San Salvador is the last place I want to go after a long day in school, especially in a noisy bus but she is insistent and I'm too tired to argue.

We disembark outside a large sandstone building next to San Salvador's Sheraton hotel.

The cool interior calms my racing brain. White marble floors are so highly polished I can see my face in them, while sculptures and art chronicling the country's turbulent history are well-appointed throughout the building. She shows me a painting of vibrant red flowers by an artist that taught his style to the people of La Palma in Chalatenango where we had visited. In another room a Mexican exhibit, 'Pablo Infantile', shows works utilising bright rainbow coloured fur fabrics featuring a life-sized, masked and nude statue of a man on horseback drawing his bow.

The gallery exhausts our interest, leaving us satisfied but thirsty. We take a seat at a Turkish-themed café at the Sheraton Hotel next door. A rude waiter brings us a pot of spiced apple tea, while his colleagues watch us from inside. Gina decides to antagonise them, upset by their behaviour. Grabbing the hose of the large glass shisha pipe on our table, she pretends to smoke from it while I take her photo. The waiters immediately rush out and without saying a word, confiscate the pipe like we are naughty children.

"Babosos," Gina mutters as they take the pipe inside.

I leave a pile of the smallest loose change from my pocket for them to count.

MAGIC SOUP

"Voy a cocinar huevos en omelette, ¿Quieres?" Amy whisks eggs in the kitchen. She offers to cook an omelette.

She uses a whole box of eggs and serves something resembling a rolled-up yellow carpet with bits of tomato in it. No sooner has she eaten, she's off to work again. I eat the leftovers from the pan and retire early.

At 4am I wake in a hot sweat.

My stomach is cramping like nothing I've ever experienced. I lie in bed in agony until 6am and barely have the energy to call Jacob. I tell him I won't be at school today. He asks that I bring my books in for Angel to use in class. He's not listening to the story.

"If you want them, you'll have to come here, and bring some Panadol," I tell him.

"No puedo hombre," he replies. I swear I hear him laugh.

"Estoy muy ocupado," he says. Too busy!

I hang up on him and pass out again. When I next wake, it's mid-afternoon, I'm freezing cold and lying in a pool of my own sweat. The pressure in my head feels like someone is standing on it, pressing it into the pillow. No one is home and I crawl to the toilet and violently vomit, wincing with the intense pain of the stomach cramps. The thought of dengue fever briefly crosses my mind, but I pass out again in a pool of sweat. The night is plagued by hallucinogenic dreams. At 5am, I'm still weak, void of any food or water and still unable to leave the house.

I try calling Gina and Amy, but neither answers. I leave a message, hoping they'll come to the rescue.

Dragging myself to the kitchen, I prop myself up against the bench and boil rice in a pot of the untreated tap water. Managing to keep it down, I return to bed.

The next time I wake, Gina is standing over me holding a steaming black plastic bag of 'Sopa de pata' from the markets.

"Aiii, pobrecitoooo. Amy no puede cocinar, Darren." She was worried sick when she got my message. She says Amy poisoned me with the omelette.

"Toma, toma niño." Chunks of tripe, yuca and bananas float in the bowl of orange soup she spoon-feeds me. The magic soup works miracles and nourishes me instantly. With belly full and head at ease, I sleep like a log.

TAZUMAL

Manilo, Amy's uncle, is taking ages in the bathroom.

My stomach is still weak after Amy's poison omelette and I simply can't hold out any longer.

And so begins the day.

With no other option and pants down, I squat over an open plastic shopping bag in the corner of my room.

Manilo, none the wiser of what's happening in the next room, sings a love ballad while he showers.

I wait for him to leave before depositing the bag and its contents in the toilet.

I hope for the best as it flushes away.

Swinging in the hammock, Titi sniffs around in the heat for scraps while Zim the cat attempts to escape, throwing herself at the wall and doing backflips as she chases flies.

With ten days to go in El Salvador, I'm really struggling to keep myself occupied. Furthermore, I think Gina can sense it too and is now mollycoddling me to the point of annoyance. I know she means well but I don't like being spoon fed.

Gina's nephew José owns a silver Honda Integra that puts her son Alvaro's shabbier 'Hondita' to shame. Newer and shinier, this vehicle has a speedometer that still works and also a radio.

I am not sure how I find myself in yet another road adventure, but Gina has a knack for dragging me along, and this time I'm in the backseat with her, while her sister Noreen sits up front with her son, José.

The potholed Pan Americana highway has its usual share of hazards today. Joggers run alongside the fast lane in bright trainers and a group of teens spray graffiti murals on a dangerous left-hand curve median barrier.

We enter the town of Chalchuapa where, just on the outskirts, grazing long-horned cows share the highway's hard shoulder with lines of semi-trucks. Noreen asks a man for directions.

"¡Hombre! Los templos Tazumal."

"Cien metros por alla." The old man points further up the road.

We find ourselves back among countryside. We've seen no signposts directing the way to our destination. Matter of fact, we've seen no signposts directing us anywhere.

José makes a U-turn and veers right off the highway back in town. The street is crowded. Stray dogs wander aimlessly in front of our car while faded, shanty storefronts poke out into the traffic. I feel eyes staring at our shiny silver Honda and kind of wish we were in Alvaro's car, attracting less attention. Noreen tries her luck again with an old lady standing next to an 18th Street gang mural.

I'm beginning to wonder if we should be here. The old lady points at a dented green sign up ahead but a lattice of power cables hanging across the street make it hard to see: 'TAZUMAL 800m'.

We pull into a dirt lay-by that apparently is the home of 'Tazumal', a pre-Colombian Maya complex dating back to the eighth century AD.

Archaeologist Stanley Boggs excavated and supervised its dubious restoration project during the 1940s and 50s, encasing the damaged areas of the pyramid in tons of Portland cement. This unwittingly created sleek monuments that looked too perfect to be real and in 2004 on the pyramid's south face, one of his sloping concrete walls loosened in the rain, slipped off, and lay in a heap of rubble. El Salvador's small group of professional archaeologists saw this as an opportunity. To them, the collapse of the 60-foot-wide flank corrected overnight what many had long viewed as a hideous mistake. This prompted all the concrete that had wrapped the pyramid for nearly sixty years to be removed and the site brought under full-scale excavation to see what secrets lay inside.

These scars are all too apparent as we walk around the site, the poorly trowelled plasterwork covering these magnificent structures exposing, in hindsight, a very bad decision. Barbed wire cordons off certain areas and the occasional mini tornado of crisp packets and ice cream wrappers twirl in the trapped internal corners of the structures. The information cards are either stolen or torn.

I can't believe this huge part of the country's Indigenous history has been, in the first instance, butchered by a careless American and, secondly, not been given the care and attention that it now needs to preserve its history.

I walk its perimeter pondering its uncertain future and return to the car.

A string of stalls outside sell plastic trinkets, Mayan doll balloons and an assortment of food. We choose a stall selling 'Yuca Pepesca', a mix of mushed yuca and tiny silver fish wrapped in a banana leaf. Our picnic table is on the verge of collapse but conveniently shaded by a glade of prickly bush trees decorated in decades of collected crisp and sweet wrappers.

I look down at the fish mush in the leaf.

It reminds me of how my day began.

BLOWOUT

Returning from our trip to the temples, we pass a long, corrugated iron fence, smattered with MS13 graffiti and gang tags. I breathe a sigh of relief that we're in a moving car in such a volatile area but that relief is short-lived when José miscalculates a set of railroad tracks and pops a tyre with a loud bang.

"No importa, hay llanteria muy cerca." Noreen speaks of a tyre shop nearby.

There is a worrying tone to her voice.

As José pulls over to check the wheel, I fear for us, now in gang-occupied territory.

José states the obvious, saying it's not a good place to be changing a wheel. We continue on, driving slowly on the flat tyre avoiding the potholes in the highway. I'm not sure what's scarier; being close to a gang neighbourhood or a head on with a semi-truck.

Bumping into the dirt lay-by of a tyre shop, we see a greasy fat guy in filthy overalls leaning on a crudely sprayed yellow upright tractor tyre dug into the ground.

"¿Que paso?" he grunts, before answering his own question. "¿Las vías?" he says, clearly already surmising the problem with the train tracks.

Noreen wipes her brow as a huge semi thunders past.

Twenty minutes later, the tyre is fixed. We haven't been run over, kidnapped or robbed, and make a hasty exit from an area we really shouldn't be in.

SANTA ANA

Gina and her sister Noreen squawk directions from the back seat that make absolutely no sense. José, Noreen's son, ignores them, concentrating on getting us safely to Santa Ana.

I am once again being whisked through the Salvadoran countryside on another weekend jaunt.

We follow a long road under endless billboards that hang above us. The town's main plaza, is bounded on three sides by buildings of mid-last-century architecture. The fourth is predictably home to the city's large white cathedral. Leaves from the plaza are collectively blown to a set of steps at the base of a theatre painted in a magnificent minty green shade. Its façade, comprised of seven arches, is elegantly decorated in white cornice trim. At the opposite end to the cathedral, another two-storey, stately building has a portico entrance in the centre of a frontage of five arches. The plaza is a place that evokes history as I stand surrounded by its architecture, a stark contrast to the sun-bleached back streets where the wooden batons of mud brick walls are exposed.

At José's grandma's house, we are greeted by a muscular man wearing thick lensed glasses and a small boy holding a tortoise.

"Hola, Manuel." José greets him, asking of his grandma.

"A la iglesia." She's at the church.

We are welcomed into the lounge area, a comfortable and simply furnished space with linoleum floor, dining table, a two-seater couch and many framed family photos hung on the walls.

The small boy pushes the tortoise around like a toy car.

I can't bear to watch as the helpless creature's back legs are splayed out from the downward force of the boy's motion. I wander out into the yard area to escape. Moments later, Gina appears and asks me if I'm OK. I mention the tortoise to which she takes me back inside before putting the little animal up out of arms reach.

The family join us for the return walk to the car. A golden evening sets over pastel shades of blue, yellow and green walls. Two drunks sit on the sidewalk and eyeball us as we pass. We meet Grandma on a side street much to the joy of José and buy ice creams on the plaza before bidding them farewell.

Sleepy Santa Ana, a town like so many others here in El Salvador, always in the news for its gang crime.

But again, I see none.

SOLITUDE

A busty waitress in a tight blue t-shirt carries a tray of Bocaditas and a couple of rums to our table. Lively Latin music blares from speakers in the rafters.

Manilo's favorite bar in Santa Tecla is constructed of rough sawn logs. We could be in Texas, but we are in El Salvador.

"¡Se empieza!" he points at the TV on the wall playing the football game about to start.

I appreciate his efforts of including me when he can. He senses the solitude I'm feeling now that school holidays have arrived, but he, Gina and Amy won't be around much for the following week. The game ends and signifies my last evening for a while with company.

The minutes tick by each day in a blur of frustrating boredom. After the last six weeks of being part of the daily goings-on with the family, I am alone in the house, now empty of life. Amy's dog Titi is also feeling the abandonment and becomes very clingy, snoring like a chainsaw outside my door every night. Having this time alone takes me deep into myself. Although the original 2009 trip awakened my senses to a whole new world, it was only a matter of a few years back in New Zealand before I began to feel lost again. With little sense of purpose and a string of shallow, short-lived relationships, I was still missing something vital in my quest to being happy. These factors have all led to me being here.

Passing on knowledge and gaining an insight into the lives of the students and the homestay family have filled gaps in my life that pushed me to keep travelling but a foreign place is a lonely place without a travel companion or company.

I try to keep busy, exhausting all my books and wandering into the deserted town a few times daily for stimulation. I try to be more like German Jan – a man I met on that previous trip. Jan was always up for anything: fearless, affable and approachable, too.

I head aimlessly into town once more, ducking a window frame that is blocking the path. It's smothered in epoxy, and has been tied to a fence to dry in the sun. A man holding a gluey paintbrush laughs and performs a bob and weave with his fists up. Normally I'd find this funny but my mood is low. I continue on. Parked on a side road near the plaza, a vendor stands proudly next to his blue pickup truck that he is using as a market stall. The vehicle, draped with underwear and logo t-shirts has seen better days. Its panels are creased, and one side of its rear tray looks like it's been in a collision with a freight train. Completely ripped away from the cab, it reveals the whole rear wheel and axle. Written off and scrapped elsewhere, but perfectly road worthy by Salvadoran standards. The man fires up the engine and crawls down the kerb a little to let another pickup truck park up behind him. Inside the cab I spot Dayanara, one of my younger pupils reading a worn-out comic book.

This scene hits me hard.

Sometimes I gain a glimpse of my students' lives — seeing them and their parents in the markets, when I go there in the afternoons with Gina. But apart from here and there, I don't usually encounter them — and what they do outside the classroom is not something I think of when I'm teaching. This scene brings the day-to-day struggle of these families into perspective. I continue on, not wanting to bother her or her father.

Brooms, tools and other homewares hang outside the 'Ferreteria' hardware store where I'd failed to get my printing done a few weeks ago. I feel far more confident wandering these streets now than I did then. Stooping under a shovel, coils of rope and the fencing wire that hang in the doorway, I enter the grotto and muddle my way through purchasing tape, Blu Tack, balloons and drawing pins. My idea is to display the class paintings on a wall at school during the holidays to surprise them on their return. The man serving me pushes his fingers under his little flat cap every time I ask for the items I need, as if they are things he's never heard of. He is so thin and his hair so wiry, if he stood still for too long he could be easily mistaken for a rake.

The school cleaner slides back the little hatch in the entrance doorway and lets me in, but not before making me explain three times why I want to enter. Standing on a chair in the empty classroom, I survey the space. It feels strange without the kids. I go about hanging the pictures and blowing up balloons.

I reflect on Central America and the little I know and see of it. Towns and villages consisting of no more than what was left when the scavenging Spanish conquerors had finished with them. Then only to be pillaged repeatedly by dictators of more recent times, leaving economies on their knees and stripped to the skeleton.

The week crawls to a close and Gina, her son Alvaro and Amy return from their holidays. I'm so happy to see them once again. It's been a long and torturous week of solitude

They whisk me away in Alvaro's 'Hondita' towards San Salvador.

"Voy a pagar." I point to a man with a $3 parking sign.

"Muy caro." Gina complains of the price he's charging.

I insist, eager to leave the standstill traffic. Alvaro happily swerves the car out of the traffic and down into the private driveway of the man holding the sign.

Now on foot, we arrive at our destination – the 'Feria'. Fairground stalls overflow with crowds and long queues for the rides snake their way slowly forwards. Smiling women wear mini parasol hats, shading themselves from the extreme heat as they rummage in the pockets of their pinnies for tickets and change.

Taking a break from the rides, we are swept into an indoor market area where, bizarrely, out of all the exciting rollercoasters and rides the fair has to offer, the largest crowd of the day is gathered. At the front of the crowd is a man pitching his product into a microphone and demonstrating a utensil that completely juices a lime, leaving only the seeds and pulp inside. The crowd he's attracted is huge. They are clearly fascinated by the show, and they wait patiently to buy his breakthrough gizmo.

PERMANENT

Fifty six shallow graves of dismembered adolescents have been discovered on the edge of Santa Tecla. Another gruesome headline story I'm reading in the newspaper that after my pleasant experience here is hard to believe.

"¡Hijo de Padre! ¡Hijo de Santo!" Once again I'm startled from the daily news by the driver of a small truck bellowing bible verses into a megaphone and struggling to keep the vehicle in a straight line.

To me, this signals Santa Tecla springing to life once more.

The national holiday week is officially over and I'm excited about starting school again. More so that my solitude is over. The week of being alone has driven me mad.

I arrive early at school and am greeted with hugs at the entrance by Daniella and Marisol, two tiny girls from the youngest class. They return to their skipping game and I to the staffroom with my cakes.

Being back among everyone lifts my spirits. Entering the classroom, I'm excited to see the girls' reaction to the display I've made of their pictures but they have all peeled and wilted from the Blu tack and are heaped in a pile on the floor. The balloons have suffered a similar death and are all wrinkled and deflated from the heat. The girls help me to clear up the mess, grabbing their artwork to take home later. My feature wall was a failure.

Writing on the board, I hear sniggers and giggles behind me. I ask them what's so funny. They erupt in laughter.

"¡Teeechuur!" one of them says, smiling. "¡Esa pluma es permanente!"

Although they've watched me cover the board in labelled drawings, they failed to tell me that the pen that I've been using is not in fact a whiteboard pen, but a red permanent marker.

This ensures the whole of recess is spent cleaning the board with a bottle of turps and a rag. Incredibly, a few of the girls insist on helping.

IMMERSED

I wake to the sound of tinkering in the kitchen. It's 5am and Gina is boiling 100 eggs in a giant pot. She tells me they are for the food kitchen run by volunteers every Sunday in San Salvador. Inviting me along, I politely decline and go back to bed.

Later she calls, this time to meet her at Pamela's house for lunch.

A huge German shepherd is held back on its leash by one of her sons as we enter. The beast is after blood and gnashes at us as she drags it foaming at the mouth into the backyard and slides the door shut. Pamela insists one serving is not enough of her bean soup. Something I wholeheartedly agree with. She proudly ladles more into my empty bowl, still reminiscing about our trip to her family's coffee farm. I remember her terrible driving and smile. Amy joins us briefly before heading to the 'Galerias Escalon' mall to buy a pet thermometer, so I tag along.

The bus pulls into a spotless slip lane. I look across the road to where a patchwork fence of corrugated iron lines the roadside. Behind it are a sea of satellite dishes, jutting out of rooftops weighted down by tyres. Amy sees me looking.

"Emey essey." 'M S' she says, pursing her lips in the direction of the sketchy neighbourhood.

The thin iron fence separates us and the shiny mall of Lacoste, Benetton and Ralph Lauren stores from an MS13 gang barrio.

I stare over the fence at the rooftops for a second. I wonder what channels the satellite dishes are playing.

A girl with pink hair hands us each a free soda from an ice box as we enter the mall. This is a far cry from the desperation only a mile or two away on the streets of Santa Tecla. Buying the thermometer, we don't last long browsing around the designer stores and their depressingly sterile environments. Amy is stunned by the prices. The stiff floor staff follow us with watchful, suspicious eyes, hastening our exit.

Back at the house, Amy plonks the cat in my arms and tells me to hold her tight before ramming the thermometer up the poor thing's arse. The cat wriggles and strains, emitting blood-curdling noises but I manage to keep a tight grip.

Titi, knowing what's about to happen, bolts.

I manage to coax her from under a bed but she runs around the yard until I catch her in a corner and secure her in a headlock. Amy shoves the tube up her bum and she wriggles and twists, but I keep hold of her tight, not wanting her teeth to lock onto my arm. I let her go as Amy pulls the stick out. Poor Titi sits down in the yard with a look of violation on her face.

"¿Donde esta Manilo?" Gina asks me if I've seen her brother recently.

All I've heard of him over the last week are his late-night drunken arrivals at the house, a high-decibel snoring and aggressive sleep talking that I can hear through my thin walls. I decide to keep all this from her.

The following morning he's home when I wake and spins a story about being robbed in the plaza by a guy who held a gun to his chest and ran off with his wallet and phone. Something about the way he's relaying his story just doesn't ring true. It seems all too elaborate an answer. He asks to borrow $2.50 from me so he can go and use the phone booth. $2.50 seems a very high price for a phone call.

Prepping dinner later on, I find an empty box of matches that Manilo has not replaced after masking his stink when using the bathroom. I need to buy more if I'm going to eat. Heading out in the drizzly dark streets, I find a dimly lit store that's about to close. Customers hurriedly scuttle around grabbing what they need while I find ten boxes of matches for 33 cents.

As I make my way home, I see Manilo steadying himself outside a small bar with a beer in his hand.

"Heeey Darreeen!" he slurs, wanting me to join him.

His eyes are rolling in their sockets, void of anyone at the controls, and the corners of his mouth are crusted with little white frothy bits of saliva. I escape his drunken clutches and continue home.

I strike a match in the kitchen but the nib fires off and hits the wall. I try again and again with the same results as the faulty heads ping off across the room in different directions like missiles, leaving me with burn holes in my clothes and Titi yelping when she gets stung on the belly.

225

I'm woken by a crash in the dark courtyard. It sounds like Manilo's arguing with someone outside my window. Who is he bringing home this time of night? Slightly terrified by the commotion, I push in my ear plugs to muffle the blasting sound of his TV through the night.

Amy is shocked over coffee in the morning when I tell her how much the matches cost. I thought they were a bargain but she disagrees.

"¡Los ladrones!" she squeals. Thieves!

"No te pagan mas que 25c." Her anger that I've been robbed of 8 cents seems a little excessive.

She leaves for work, giving me the perfect alone time with Manilo to confront him again about the 'robbery'.

"Me mentiste," I say, calling him a liar.

He looks shocked, as if he knows what's coming. I mention him spending the money I gave him at the bar and not on the phone call he claimed he needed to make. His face drops and he knows he has to come up with something I'll believe. He confesses he did actually lose his wallet while drunk and the robbery was a lie. Embarrassed, he hurries off to work.

I mention to Gina over lunch that it might be better if I move to Pamela's.

"¿Por que?" she exclaims, clearly upset.

I explain about Manilo's behaviour, the robbery story and the unsettling nights being kept awake by his drunken state. Now Amy is mostly working night shifts, I'm alone in the house with him. She's ashamed of what I'm telling her, as if the family's name is being tarnished. Pulling her phone out, she calls him.

"No! no!" I tell her. "¡No importa!" I try to dispel what I've just told her but it's too late.

"¡No ven a la casa! ¡Me avergüenzo de ti! ¡¡BOLO BAYUNCO!!" She sternly shouts down the phone at Manilo, calling him a foolish drunk and telling him not to come back to the house.

THE MOUSE

I tread my way through the streets for my last day of school, reminiscing about my time here and the fond memories this tiny part of the world has given me. I feel bad about getting Manilo in trouble with Gina. I pass the Army barracks where the soldiers stare at me like usual.

Santa Tecla. It's a place that two months ago I never knew existed.

Rough, raspy voices call out in the market. The metal rim of a hand drawn flatbed cart scratches its way along the street, splintered, worn and pulled by a tired looking man in ragged clothing.

The teachers trap me and insist we get a group photo before classes. Moving through the morning, I continue with the same subjects, drawing my pictures on the board, making sure I'm using a whiteboard marker. I draw a belt, a coat, a pair of earrings, a hat and so forth while the girls try to guess the English names as I write the Spanish next to them.

Suddenly, the class is filled with screams of hysteria as they jump on their desks, frantically staring at the floor.

"¡Raton! ¡Raton!" they cry, screaming louder and louder.

Scared for its life and scurrying across the floor between the chairs, schoolbags and desk legs, a small mouse dashes around trying to find an escape route.

The scene unravelling before me is from a Roald Dahl book.

"¡Aiiiiii! ¡Aiiiii!" the girls shriek as their eyes follow the furry little critter desperately weaving its way underneath them.

Finding the door, it flies out into the schoolyard like a firework, closely followed by the now excited girls, no longer on their desks and eager to see where it goes. It tumbles down a couple of steps into the ball court, before righting itself and making a dash towards the 9th grade girls who stop their volleyball game as it approaches them at top speed. As it runs through the middle of them, Juan, their teacher, attempts to clear a way for the mouse, but without an ounce of hesitation, one of the girls raises her foot and brings it down with such a force on top of the thing that it explodes in a splat of blood and guts on the concrete.

"¡Eeewwwwwwww!" the girls shriek.

"¡OK!" Lola bellows after hearing the commotion, now standing outside her office. "¡El espectaculo ha terminado!" She tells them the show is over.

The sound of her voice silences the girls instantly and sends them in single file back into their respective rooms.

The volleyball game continues on another court while the janitor casually scrapes the remains of the mouse up with a shovel and tosses it into a rubbish bin.

I spare a thought for that little mouse. It started it's day in the bottom of a girl's bag nibbling on a mouldy sandwich with absolutely no idea that it would be its last.

A WELL-VERSED RITUAL

It seems like only yesterday I'd entered this school for the first time. I am sitting on the couch outside the staff room.

The transparent girl Angel sits in the adjacent couch and stares into space. I haven't seen anything of her in the previous few weeks.

Probably not a bad thing.

She's also leaving this week so the ceremony will be for the both of us. I briefly wonder if she's enjoyed anything about her time here. I decide not to ask of her 'internet boyfriend'.

Slowly, class by class, the girls fill the courtyard in preparation for the ceremony. Rows and rows of little faces are all excited to be a part of this. I can tell they've done it many times, but they still treat it like their first.

Lola addresses the school and explains that we are teaching to help them gain good English skills in the modern world where it will be so important. She stresses they should all be very grateful that we've taken the time to visit El Salvador to help them. She starts with Angel by handing her diploma and shaking her hand. The girls give a big cheer and applause.

Before she can finish introducing me, the girls turn into deranged animals, cheering, shouting and banging on rubbish bins filling every inch of the school with a deafening noise. This brings tears to my eyes, a lump in my throat and emotions I'm unable to hide. To be so connected with such a place, to be welcomed and cheered by people who were strangers only some months back, I'm humbled and proud of myself for doing this. The Brass band girls proudly march around the courtyard playing their instruments.

Next, the younger girls break into a dance while a song plays from the stereo.

And then, one by one, they pass me thank you letters delivered with hugs and kisses.

The time has come for my speech. I'm thankful of the constant Spanish I've had to speak for the last two months. I stand in front of this crowd of three hundred, unable to hold back my tears.

I finish my speech and am rushed by the girls, who almost push me off my feet.

Poor little Angel is swamped and knocked to the floor in the commotion.

ADIOS EL SALVADOR

The late August lights of 2013 San Salvador twinkle deep in the valley below. A strip of restaurants high up on a ridge in the Plane de los Renderos district teeter on the edge of the mountain where Gina, Lola and the family have brought me.

The cold night air hurries us inside a restaurant where a group of break-dancers flip and spin on a rolled-out strip of lino. Two huge stacks of pupusas ooze cheese and are shared out on our table with a couple bottles of Coke. I sense Gina's low mood and give her a hug. She knows I'll be gone tomorrow but doesn't let the way she's feeling dampen the mood. A band step up to the small stage, pick up their instruments and are joined by a girl who erupts into song, captivating her audience.

I drift away to her voice, thinking about the last two months and what a huge impact they've had on me. The love, warmth and generosity I've been shown from a country that I almost didn't come to out of fear. The students and all their chaos at the beginning, to then shine with appreciation, patience and interest in our classes together.

I'm being sent on my way with a full heart.

Back in Santa Tecla, Lola hugs me and says goodbye. Tears stream down our faces as she shuts the car door and walks up her driveway.

The tears and farewells continue as one by one, the family wish me well. Gina, Amy, Manilo, Noreen, José and Alvaro have all been such a huge part in how comfortable I've felt here. I go to bed with teary eyes.

The 2am alarm rings and a taxi takes Gina and I to the Tica bus station in San Salvador.

Pulling up, we hug for what seems like a lifetime.

This saintly woman has touched my life like no other. She has been my guide, made me laugh and cared for me like one of her own. I never thought it possible to match the unconditional love I felt during my first trip, but she has surpassed it by light years.

We pull away from each other, both weeping.

Sliding back into the taxi, she waves from the back window as it disappears around a corner at the end of the street.

9
NICARAGUA

Volcán Telica's active crater, Nicaragua.

EL AMATILLO

The overnight Tica bus slowly fills with passengers on a dark empty street in San Salvador. I take no notice of them. I'm lost in the memories of the last two months I've spent in this country.

El Salvador has left me with a full heart. I'm leaving with a sense of belonging to somewhere I never knew just a few months ago.

Santa Tecla's safety amidst the invisible violence of the country was something I never expected. A place where a precious quality of community life still thrives.

Most of my life has been engaged in a kind of forward momentum that comes with First World living. And while some of that offers rewards that I've benefitted from, there's also the unavoidable effect of such comfortable living: the desperate need for more. More money, more time, more things. In my world, parents are too busy for their bored, neglected children who spend their days hunched over tablet screens. The elderly are neglected or forgotten in their lonely flats and retirement homes, no longer useful and discarded like broken household appliances. It's not a world with a sense of real community, but what I've just been a part of for the last month or so was.

A young woman is in the seat next to me, passed out with her head resting on the window. I close my eyes and settle into a deep sleep. A bump in the road jolts me awake. I've been asleep for five hours. The girl next to me is now also awake.

I introduce myself, shaking her small hand.

"Me llamo Lesbia." Lesbia's smile reveals a gold tooth.

The girl has long, dyed blonde hair and a round face with blue contact lenses. I think back to Lucky on the little bus in the Guatemalan jungle and how long ago that seems. Lesbia is also travelling to León, where she will then catch a ride to a smaller village on the outskirts.

"Se llama Maria del Virgen de Alta." She proudly tells me the name of her village.

"¿Quieres?" I offer her some seeds.

She looks at me like I'm offering her rabbit droppings.

"Que ricas." I tell her they're good.

She nervously lets me pour a few into her hand and nibbles at them like she's chewing on grass clippings. She's been studying in San Salvador for four weeks to upgrade her nursing qualifications and works full time at the hospital in León. I tell her about living in the house in the San Sebastián neighbourhood of León back in 2009. She knows the area and seems surprised I'm familiar with it. I offer her a piece of chocolate. With far less hesitation, she gobbles it down.

"Vamos a pasar en la routa." She says we'll pass her village before we get to León.

I drift off again until a hand on my shoulder wakes me. The bus co-driver has border forms for us to fill out before we hit our first checkpoint.

The 'El Amatillo' border with Honduras is a gruelling hour of searches and passport checks but we're allowed off to stretch our legs. A couple of soldiers sit in the back of a police pickup truck.

"Buenas. ¿Como estamos?" I greet them happily.

They wryly smile back but say nothing. I get back on the bus, feeling it's the safer option. The soldiers board the bus but are not the slightest bit interested in me or my belongings. The locals however are hassled and questioned. Lesbia follows them with her suitcase and a tall man wearing a navy-blue business suit and tie is also taken outside.

Lesbia returns unscathed. The suited man never re-boards.

Dawn breaks and the bus pulls into a scorched dirt carpark where it idles in a line of semi-trucks. This is Guasaule – the Honduras / Nicaraguan border.

A squat but grandiose building, reminiscent of the Somoza era, sprouts grass tufts from cracks in its walls and a corroded roof gutter hangs precariously above two smashed windows. We are led single file through a warehouse holding area. Shrink-wrapped pallets of food are stacked ceiling-high behind locked, wire fences and wild dogs roam freely, sniffing us as we wait in line. Behind the fences, a 1980s Dodge van, a motorcycle, a life-sized statue of an Afghan hound and various industrial machines are blanketed in a thick layer of dust. It all looks like it's been in here for a very long time, perhaps denied clearance and forgotten about.

The line shuffles slowly.

A wriggling pile of stray pups snuggle in a loading bay that reeks of urine. We fend off children in rags who fight over handling our luggage. At the exit, our passports are handed back to us by the co-driver. Two gold-toothed women lean against a pole. They both balance baskets atop their heads; one is wearing fake Nikes, the other broken sandals.

They call me over.

"¡Señor Chele!"

"¿Quiere bebida guapo?" They cheekily ask me if I want to buy a drink.

I buy one from each of them to avoid argument. The restrooms don't disappoint. Rusty bolts that once secured the toilet seats to the bowls litter the floor while a spray of what looks like blood covers a broken mirror.

The bus continues south toward León, briefly stopping at Chinandega, a dusty little town and gateway to the northwest beach towns of Nicaragua.

"¡Aqui esta!" Lesbia points out the window at a giant statue of the Virgin Mary in a pale blue shawl.

Above the figure's head is a sign that reads 'Maria del Virgen de Alta'. The statue sits proudly on a grassy centre divider between the entrance and exit roads to her village. It seems strange the bus can't just stop here quickly to let her off. I try to imagine the life she leads here, commuting into León every day on a jam-packed chicken bus.

Before long, a familiar sight appears, a sight that was pitch black and deserted the last time I left León. The 'Puma' gas station-cum-bus terminal and its hum of taxi drivers, market stalls and minivans hasn't changed a bit. Women deftly slice green mango with wooden handled knives before salting and tying them in little plastic bags. Others sell sodas from ice boxes. This whole scene reignites my memories of Nicaragua. It feels comfortably familiar.

Lesbia disappears forever into the crowd.

FAMILIAS FAMILIA

A chatty Nicaraguan taxi driver takes me from the international bus terminal / gas station to León. He's interested in where I've come from. He's never been to El Salvador and tells me he probably never will.

On the outskirts of the town, I'm hit with a strong wave of nostalgia. The car rattles through the cobblestone streets, the buildings either side evoking ever stronger memories of last time.

"¡Hola, muchacho!" I'm greeted by a familiar voice before I can pull my backpack from the rear seat.

Hugo, my former teacher from 2009, is standing on the pavement. By his side is a slim, older lady with grey, streaked hair.

"Hola, Darío, soy Grizelda."

This is Hugo's ex-wife. I've not previously met her. She gives me a hug.

I'm a little confused as to the situation with her. Hugo has spoken of his ex-wife 'Griz' before but I was unaware they still lived together.

I follow them inside.

"Aqui es tu cuarto." Hugo leads me into my bedroom.

The thin plywood walls are painted in a pale-yellow shade and the mattress sinks when I sit on it. Griz cooks some lunch while Hugo and I reminisce at the dining table. Plates of chicken, rice, beans and tortilla are laid out.

"Gracias." I thank Griz, realising that apart from the bag of seeds and chocolate I shared with Lesbia on the bus, I haven't eaten today.

I tread familiar steps into town to draw some money. I feel confident in León's streets. I think back to how wary I was in Santa Tecla. As I enter the main bank, the security guard stops me.

"Quitar." He points at my cap. I remove it and join the line of people waiting. The bank teller's face changes from worry to relief when I speak in Spanish.

"Quinietos dólares por fa." I ask her for $500.

She looks startled at the amount but takes my card and continues with the withdrawal process. "Esta tarjeta esta bloqueado. Lo siento." Her words are not what I want to hear.

My card has been blocked. I ask her to check again, which she does with the same outcome. Frantic, I thank her and leave to find a pay phone. I have 50 cordoba in change from the last trip and jingle it nervously through my fingers in my pocket, waiting on the street for the man in front to finish his call. My mind starts to race. How am I going to get by without any money?

My bank informs me it's been blocked because someone has tried to use it in Nicaragua.

No shit. That's me.

Clearing up the issue, I'm back at the bank with the same teller.

"Vamos a tratar otra vez." I ask her to try again, smiling.

She hands me $500 US with a look like she wants to marry me. I stuff it in my pocket and head to the corner where all the money changers hang out.

On the way I see Raymond, the artisan I'd hung out with a little in 2009. His jewellery work has improved, his limp not so much. I tell him I'll return to have a beer with him later. A gesture I'm sure that will haunt him until my promise is fulfilled.

Pocketed fisherman's vests are in abundance at 'Cambio corner.' The money changers and I exchange currencies and I go in search of the school's new location.

"¡Buenas Darren! ¡Dar un buena acogida!" I'm greeted by Roberto, sitting in the new school reception behind his old desk.

I don't understand what he's said. He likes using phrases he knows I won't understand.

"Welcome back!" he laughs, glad I'm taking a few refresher lessons.

His wife introduces herself to me. "Hola, Darío, soy Guadalupe. ¿Me recuerdas?" She asks if I remember her.

Back in the town, Raymond tracks me down. I buy us a beer and a plate of chicken. He tells me his jewellery is doing well while he strips his chicken bones dry. He does the same with the bones on my plate, gnawing and picking every last slither of meat.

VOLCÁN TELICA

I arrive at the 'Quetzal trekkers' tour office in León at 05:30 sharp. Four French backpackers and two Swiss gay guys in very short matching pastel pink shorts are also taking the hike. Mary, an American girl wearing striped baggy cotton pants and matching headband serves us a meagre breakfast of fried plátano and egg. Our lead guide is a French guy called Matt.

Matt tells us he's been working with the tour company for eight months. "Mary is learning to be a guide, so she's helping me on this trek with you guys." He prompts her through the safety briefing while stuffing the backpacks with supplies and gear.

Our first port of call is the markets, a colourful hustle of chaos. Taxis and horse-drawn carts battle for space and a tangled mass of stalls sell everything from underwear to exotic fruits. Matt barters with various stall owners for our food. He has a good rapport with the vendors, picking through their produce while cracking jokes and laughing with them.

The excess weight is added to our already laden packs and a noisy chicken bus transports us into the lowlands. We depart at the side of the highway and start our hike passing through a head high trench cut into the charred dirt. A herd of oxen block our path, moving to the side when Matt prods them with a stick. Climbing slowly through lush green landscapes, we gain better views of our volcano peak in the distance. The iridescent blue and green feathers of the majestic Guardabarranco birds shine as they flit through the trees while we plod under the hot sun. We stop and collect firewood, strapping as much as we can carry to our backpacks.

"Here, look," Matt says, pointing at a tree trunk.

Just above head height and blanketing the entire circumference of the trunk are thousands of bright green finger-sized worms. I presume their red heads signify danger and Matt clarifies this.

"Gusanos," he says. "Muy toxico." Very poisonous.

The Swiss boys shriek like schoolgirls.

"They all stick together like that to stay warm."

Matt offloads his pack and calls a water break. I stare at the worms for a while, wondering why they need to stay warm in this intense heat.

"Are you guys hungry?" Matt pokes a hole into the soft trunk of another tree.

The group watches in horror as a flurry of tiny red ants crawl up his hand. Before the insects can reach his forearm, he licks them off and chews them up.

"They taste like carrots," he says. A few escape across his face. The group continue to stare on in horror.

I follow his lead and plunge my hand into the tree and lick it clean. "Yeah, carrots." I offer up the remaining ants scurrying on my arm to the group but they decline.

At the edge of the treeline, he stops us again. A banana spider has spun its web across the track. As big as an outstretched hand, the long spindly, striped legs and large bright yellow abdomen are certainly warning signs to stay away, but Matt navigates the web to another tree with a stick without disturbing it. A narrow path cuts its way through shoulder-high grassy plains with views of the smoking volcano. I stick with Matt as we climb higher and change terrain, picking our way over the rocks and scree.

"I was working for STA travel in the US," he says. "But they are closing up over there so this tour guide opportunity is a bit of fun before I go home to France."

He's an interesting guy and we chat some more as we make our way through the jungle.

I also make conversation with the Swiss guys, a friendly couple who've been travelling for quite some time.

"Za ferryboat from Managua to za Corn islands waz za highlight of za trip so far." They speak at exactly the same time. "Very off za grid in parts."

Their seven-day boat ride, travelling southeast across Nicaragua and out into the Atlantic, sounds incredible, but the conversation quickly dries as all of our energy is put to the last brutal hour of the hike.

We climb vertically over giant rocks in the insufferable heat as I focus on simply putting one foot after the other now dripping with sweat. I use both my hands as the incline steepens. When we reach the top, I'm both exhausted and elated. I find it hard to catch my breath, but am rewarded by the views back across the lowlands. Deep valleys of green farmland divided by hedgerows fill the view below as we traverse around the edge of the enormous blown out crater with a plume of smoke twirling from its bowels. The sulphur fumes are strong and the crater's circumference shows just how massively momentous the eruption must have been.

"OK, we will set our camp over there." Matt points to a cluster of palm trees on the other side of a large flooded, flat plateau where a lone ox drinks at the water's edge.

As we walk around the floodplain, the crater is reflected in its glassy surface, rippled slightly only by the ox's snout dipping in. The group pitches the tents quickly, except for Mary who struggles and asks for a hand. Watching her muddling through the setup, I'm glad we're not up here with only her as our guide. We stack firewood at the pit, before heading up to the crater.

Brown pits of lava bubble and spit 120 metres below in the 700-metre-wide hole. We lie on our stomachs peering over the edge until we can no longer bear the fumes and head down to the camp where Matt cooks up a rice, tuna and tomato dish over the fire.

The French group have not made an effort to join the rest of us and eat separately near their tent. I join Matt and Mary around the fire and share conversation until night falls.

Thousands of green frogs croak all around us as we make our way back up to the crater and resume our earlier position. The two pits of red molten lava glow, spit and bubble in the bottom. The ground rumbles and shudders beneath as we sleep through the pitch black of night.

We are woken by Matt and Mary who shake our tents at dawn. While the sun creeps up over the horizon, we eat breakfast and drink coffee. Hues of pink light up the land below.

"The farmers made these cuts in the land to herd their cattle." Matt leads us through a wide gouge in the earth on our descent. The shade of a giant tree with overhanging branches serves as a rest stop. Setting my pack down, I notice the floor is covered in rotting fruit being eaten by butterflies.

"Mangos! As many as you can eat!" Matt points up into the tree.

Looking up, I see the branches hang heavy with juicy mangos. I sit down on a log as one falls directly into my lap. Splitting it open with my knife, I relish its taste. I think back to little Maycol on Meanguera Island and the mango tree that we threw sticks into.

I linger to frantically stuff my pack with the fruit, then eventually set off to catch up to the group. After a few minutes' pacing through a field of tall yellow maize, I discover there is still no sign of them. I continue on until up ahead, two of the French group are sat on a rock, also unsure of where they are.

"Where do we go?" they ask me.

Now you want to talk to me, I think to myself.

I'm as lost as they are, but we continue to follow the path through the maize. Suddenly a dog leaps up from a nearby tree and lunges at us. It jerks back as the rope it's attached to chokes it.

"We would've heard it when the others passed by," I tell the French guys. They stare at me. "We must be going the wrong way," I say.

A farmer comes into view across the field of maize and I call out, asking him the way. My Spanish proves good and he points to his left and yells a few directions.

It's not long before we see Mary pacing towards us looking distraught. She apologises and leads us through the tall maize field reuniting us with the others. Matt apologises before we all carry on. Farmers work their fields to either side as we trudge to the tiny village of San Jacinto, passing some 'bubbling hot pools' that the village prides itself on. These 'pools' are merely some farting holes in a flat piece of rock.

A black-and-white-striped, rising barrier arm crosses the road, where two lazy looking men in hammocks pay us no attention. Matt approaches them and pays the fee for our hike before leading us to the village comedor.

The scantly furnished, red and ramshackle restaurant serves up cold cokes, chicken and beans while skeletal dogs scrounge around under the tables. I gingerly enter the toilet, having a fairly good idea of what I'm about to walk into. I just wish I only needed a pee. Slathered in red paint, the main door to the bathroom is hanging on one hinge with a lock fashioned from a wire coat hanger looped around a catch. Inside, the urinal and toilet are undivided.

The moment I squat over the bowl, a scruffy fat man bursts in. "¿Puedo orinar?" He asks if he can take a piss, but he has his dick out before I have a chance to answer.

Leaning his hand on the wall next to me and fire hosing the urinal, he tries to make conversation while I squat with stage fright.

XIOMARA

The bus ride back from Nicaragua's Telica volcano is a quiet one. The group is clearly exhausted from the last couple of days hiking. I know I am.

A full house awaits me back in León. Hugo's son Roberto is in town with his wife and children. Grizelda passes me hurriedly as I head to my room and quickly goes about scooping up toys, nappies and blankets, throwing them in a buggy and wheeling it all out the door.

When I reappear after a shower, I discover they've all left. Grizelda's been too busy with family to prep dinner, so Hugo and I go in search of rum. Families rock in their chairs on the pavement enjoying the cooler evening air.

On the way, we bump into a friend of his.

"¡Xiomara!"

He greets her and introduces us. Illuminated by the orange glow of the streetlights, the pretty girl's blue eyes pierce through me like Cupid's arrow. She joins us while children kick footballs and play chase on the sidewalks. Hugo chats to the girl in an obvious effort to match-make us.

Our next introduction is 'Don Pechote', a large, sweaty and out-of-breath friend of Hugo. His belly pushes the bottom of his Hawaiian shirt out so it hangs uncomfortably forward. In one hand he clutches a bottle of rum. Hugo makes light banter while Xiomara and I smile sheepishly at each other. Hugo points at the bottle of rum Don Pechote is clutching, eager to buy his own.

We enter the little store and peruse the selection of cheap 'pocket rocket' bottles and arm ourselves accordingly. The neighbourhood is a cacophony of chatter as we return home. People wander the evening streets, searching for stimulation while birds in the trees recount their day to each other. Xiomara leaves us but we agree to meet at a café tomorrow. We continue on before meeting another man on the sidewalk, this time with a lazy eye and dressed in a pink suit. Hugo asks of his mother.

"Se murio ayer." He tells us she died yesterday.

I feel sad as we continue but Hugo contradicts what the man has said. "El es borracho." Hugo says he's a drunk and adds that he saw his mother a couple of hours ago at the market.

The following day I find Xiomara sat at a table in the café. We drink ice-cold Cokes over some light conversation and the crazy characters of Hugo's barrio that we encountered last night. Her demeanour is pleasant and the conversation easy.

"¿Quieres ir un hospedaje?" She suggests we find a hotel room.

Slightly shocked at her bluntness, I freeze for a second.

But only a second.

We go in search of a room. As we walk, my phone rings. It's Hugo.

"¿Se hace el transacción?" He asks about the 'transaction'. It seems a weird term to use but I think nothing of it.

"OK, amigo. Ciao." He chuckles and hangs up.

Hotel Casa Viejita is situated near the markets. Xiomara says we can get a room for 200 cordoba an hour. The old woman at reception fires me a look of disgust as I pay up front. She unlocks a door behind the reception desk. Simply furnished, it has a bed, a small TV and a shower.

Xiomara wows me again as she strips naked, her curvaceous firm body prompts me to do the same. I am standing in my birthday suit, when a hard knock raps at the door. I throw on my shorts and open it slightly, but it's shoved ajar and a flying toilet roll bounces off my head followed by two threadbare towels. The old woman clearly disapproves of our intentions.

The whole scene feels awkward. Even more so when she takes a phone call midway and keeps asking me if I've finished yet. If she'd stop talking on her phone and get into the moment a bit, I may well be able to do that.

It was her idea after all. I feel strange as I take a shower. The whole situation doesn't feel right.

I could have squeezed more emotion from a sheet of cardboard with a face drawn on it.

Back in the room, I find that she's gone. I instinctively check for my wallet and find the 600 cordoba that was in there is gone too. I hurry outside, still pulling my t-shirt on, but of course there's no sign of her. Violated and with ego bruised, I laugh to myself as I walk home.

The novelty gringo fell for that scam, hook line and sinker.

SANDINISTA

Hugo can't stop laughing when I relay the dodgy hotel experience with Xiomara to him.

"¡Como caballo muerto!" *Like a dead horse!* He slaps his thigh laughing when I recount the experience and the toilet roll bouncing off my head.

I'm late for lunch and his wife Grizelda is a little annoyed. She tells me it may be a little cold. If only she knew about Hugo's set up with Xiomara, she'd be mortified.

I apologise, explaining I'd lost track of time. After lunch, I ride the bus out to the coast.

It's apparent that nothing has changed in four years. The half-laid-out subdivision destined to be a hotel complex is still an empty lot, and the storm-battered remains of the beach-side buildings still sit emptily in limbo. The fierce waves crash into the reclaimed front yards that sprout miniature jungles. I grab a drink at 'Barco de oro' situated on the cove that sits back from the beach on the inlet. Sand flats hold deep sections of trapped tidal water and fishermen wait for the return of the tide to sail out. I sit for a while watching daily life before moving to the hostel / bar that almost washed away while we slept back in 2009. Now re-established according to its new shoreline, I watch giant pelicans swoop across the waves, diving for food, while fishermen roll their boats on logs down the sand to the water. Well-versed in this daily operation, two of them grab the back log as it spits out the rear, running with it to the front to continue the movement. They shout, laugh and joke performing this Roman task before loading up their lobster pots and navigating the ferocious waves.

Back in León, Hugo and I spend the evening with more rum and war stories. He talks of endless months of rain in the highland forests near Matagalpa and knife fights with the enemy rebels in the pitch black of night.

"No visto nada, solo las sonidos." He says they couldn't see what or who they were stabbing and slashing at. "Just the sounds of the blades swishing past your ears and the groans when the knives went in."

"¡Sheeeah! ¡Sheeeah!" He swipes his arm in the air like he's holding a knife.

His recollections of the mornings after these incidents are just as horrific. He describes the bodies of the dead literally stripped of their skin and flesh by white ants, a vicious species that have since been eradicated by agricultural pesticides. They now only survive in the Amazon.

MALENA

A heat haze hangs over the quiet León street where I'm residing with Hugo and Grizelda. The quiet is not to last as we are forced outside while a fumigation team pump toxic smoke into each house as they pass with noisy air blowers. Hugo tells me it's a government anti-Dengue fever measure. He wants me to meet his friend Karina for coffee. I tell him I do not want a repeat of the Xiomara day. I have no further interest in his matchmaking.

We escape the smoke and head into town.

León's very weathered cathedral is midway through a huge restoration project. The street stall vendors that once overflowed around the edges of the plaza are no longer permitted to do so and the rubbish that was so prevalent in 2009 has all but gone. Seeing these streets so clean is impressive. León has come a long way in four years.

We meet Karina outside a cute little café. Short, athletic and with a gap between her two front teeth, she's obsessed with the soccer playing on the TV. We sit down and drink a pitcher of iced hibiscus flower tea, a fuchsia-coloured, sweet drink that does a fine job of cooling us down in the morning heat.

"Patty es muy religioso, Darren." Hugo warns me of my new teacher's strong religious beliefs as we sip our drinks in the cool of the café lounge. He chuckles as he tells me, patting me on the back and wishing me good luck.

Roberto welcomes me into the language school, its layout similar to the last location with desks placed around the edge of an open courtyard under awnings.

"Buenas, Darren. Soy Patty," my new teacher greets me.

Short in stature with her hair tied up in a bun and a pair of stylish spectacles perched on her nose, she guides me to my table. We begin with conversation to ascertain where my weaknesses lie, but after two months of mostly talking with 8-year-olds in class, my head is a jumbled mess.

I take my break outside the 'El Calvario' church that I frequented back on my first trip here. The memories flood back as I sit on the same crumbling concrete yellow bench, staring at the cold drinks and cakes in the glass case of the food stand. I sit in thoughtful silence with a cooling drink.

Patty fries my brain for the last hour of school with the subjunctive verb group.

Back at the house, a woman's voice is wailing out at a high volume from next door. We are able to hear it through the wall.

"¡Aiii! ¡Esa mujer!" Hugo grumbles. He says the woman is a drunk and stays up all night. She's incapable of caring for her baby, letting it cry day and night. I leave the chaos to visit old friends.

Nostalgia hits me walking the route that I'd taken daily a few years ago. Turning into a front yard opposite a clinic, the mobile phone company signs still hang off the porch advertising her SIM card sideline. Knocking the door, my nerves disappear as she greets me.

"¡Darío, Darío, Darío!" Malena hugs me tightly.

The lounge is exactly the same, the virgin Marys still in abundance and the dusty moped still unused and in the corner. She compliments me on my Spanish, laughing about my frustrations with it when I first moved in with her. She's been making good money in Miami, working in her brother's restaurant but is recovering from a fall she had there, caused by prescribed pills that affected her heart.

The mood lightens as she comments on the movie playing on the TV. "¿Darío, por que no hay hombres de plastico con la cara de Vin Diesel? ¡Es muy hombrrre!" In her infectious humour, she asks why inflatable male sex dolls don't have faces like Vin Diesel.

She's got a point.

Being with her reminds me of all the fun we've had. Out the back, she proudly shows me the construction work being done on the student accommodation rooms and how she's using all the Miami money to build more. I help her set up an air conditioning unit in one of the rooms and she stares at me stunned when I read the instructions to myself in English.

"Nunca te oí, Darío." She's never heard me speak English before. I guess I was so immersed last time, I never spoke it.

A familiar voice calls from inside.

"¡Malenita! ¡Venga!" The voice has a raspy bellow.

Raphael, Malena's ex, the rum-guzzling man that I'd shared so many bizarre moments with when last staying here, is chasing a rat across the floor with a block of wood.

Of course he is.

Where he or the rat appeared from is anyone's guess, but the show unfolding is amusing all the same. The daughter Malenita comes running down the stairs and into the kitchen as he splats the rat with the block of wood.

"¡Ewww!" the little girl shrieks as her father puts his foot on top of the block and presses down with all his weight.

The rat splits, oozing blood all over the floor. This is the second rodent in as many weeks that I've seen meet its maker in this manner.

"Hola, chele." He greets me with his foot still on the block.

I'm pretty sure the rat is dead.

"¿Como va?" Although his greeting seems familiar, I don't think he remembers me from last time.

Malenita grabs me by the wrist and takes me up to her room to help her with some English homework. I miss this family and the warmth. It feels so comfortable being here.

Malena makes me promise I'll visit again.

MANAGUA

The ripped orange vinyl seats of the micro bus are scalding to the touch. The children on board, seemingly flame-retardant, excitedly squirm around on them in shorts and t-shirts.

With only a few weeks in Nicaragua, I'm travelling south to stay on the twin coned volcanic island that sits in the middle of Lake Omatepe.

A skinny dog drags a pig's spine with the ribs still attached from a huge pile of rubbish outside Managua's UCA terminal. I navigate my way to find a taxi driver who will take me to the Roberto Huembes terminal on the other side of Nicaragua's capital city.

As my ride pulls away, a gold-toothed man leans through the window and tells me the taxi isn't licensed.

"¡Vayase Hombre!" the driver shouts at him, shooing him away.

I ask the driver to stop.

"Calmase. Todo bien, chele, es bromista." He tells me that the guy was just joking.

The joke isn't funny. I'm shitting myself enough being in this city I've heard so many horror stories about. I don't appreciate strangers joking about me being in a dodgy taxi. The short cut he takes through a poverty-stricken neighbourhood has me on edge.

Huembes terminal is psychotic. I'm immediately mobbed by touts that push and pull me trying to get me onto their respective buses.

"¡Directo! ¡Directo!" Two drag me to a red and white chicken bus and shove me on.

I meet 'Manny', a middle-aged, fat Mexican guy with shiny white hair. He reminds me of Elton John. He swipes away on his tablet wrapped in a fake Louis Vuitton cover, seemingly not bothered about flashing it off on the bus while throwing gay insinuations around to anyone who wants to listen. Friendly and hilarious, he's a harmless man and a very likeable character. His company ensures an otherwise dull bus ride to be entertaining although his advances during it are a little unnerving.

As the bus unloads, he asks if I like plantain.

I know exactly what he's getting at and laugh awkwardly, as do the other passengers around us.

He climbs into a taxi trike like the Queen, still swiping away on his tablet, and waves goodbye.

VOLCÁN MADERAS

The words 'El Ferry Che Guevara' adorn the side of a small wooden ferry that creaks along the shore of Lake Nicaragua, the white letters dripping down the side of the boat's blue hull.

On board, mismatched car seats are crudely bolted down, and a chest freezer slides around the slippery floor, chained to a roof support pole. The crew of the vessel don't hide the beer cans they swig from as the ferry miserably groans its way across the vast lake towards the twin coned island of Omatepe, where taxi drivers hover on a wharf, watching the boat approach. I pick a 4x4 van, telling its long-haired driver my destination.

The man appears a little unhinged but seems friendly and introduces himself as Norvin. He tells me it's $20 for the hour drive over to Volcán Maderas, stressing that the local bus takes twice as long. I take his word for it and jump in.

He curses a police car that passes us in the opposite direction before saying I should give him $30 to secure a deposit for the return trip. The road cuts through dense jungle while he tells me about the freshwater sharks in the lake that swim up the Río San Juan from the Atlantic.

"Uno se mato mi madre." *One ate my mother*. He says it void of emotion.

The van tackles a rough track that leads to the 'Finca Magdalena' coffee farm on the slopes of the volcano. The farm overlooks a magnificent view of the giant Volcán Concepción and its cloud ringed peak. Blue jays, butterflies, exotic flowers and pigs cohabit the well-kept gardens. I pay my $6 for the two nights and watch a lightning storm around the cone's peak. The light show is intense, but the rain forces me off the deck and into bed while it continues through the night.

At breakfast I meet two German girls who are going hiking and decide to join them. Our guide Mateo arrives, fully prepared in the typical Nicaraguan attire: flip flops, board shorts and a Quiksilver rash shirt. I'm not sure if he's taking us hiking or surfing.

The hike takes us up through a humid cloud forest where beaming light shafts cut through the canopy of cacao trees hanging with pods.

White-faced monkeys stare down curiously at us while Mateo stares at the girls.

"Mono de cara blanca," he says, averting his stare and pursing his lips, kissing at the curious primates above us.

We climb higher across slippery rocks through dense forest. Mateo tells us we are in a microclimate where plants and fauna use protection mechanisms to shelter from high winds. Thick moss carpets the floor and strange red roots covered in a slimy clear gel, grow in a downward direction from the tree trunks.

"How far eez eet?" one of the girls wheezes as we climb.

I too feel out of breath but stay quiet to conserve energy in the heat.

"Zis track is not as vell maintained as zee vons in Chermany," she continues.

I translate to Mateo. He smirks.

We cross a ridge and descend for fifteen minutes into a clearing where a shallow frog-inhabited lake fills the view. The lake is surrounded by high crater walls covered in thick forest. Blue butterflies flit in and out of orchids that grow around the lake's edge. We relax in our surroundings, regaining our breath before descending through coffee and banana plantations.

"¡Mira! Shhhh!" Mateo stops us, pointing out a small snake wrapped around a tree branch.

Its black and brown markings make it hard to see.

"Es boa," he says. 'Boa constrictor.'

The girls grab each other, looking terrified.

"¡Tranquilo!" Mateo giggles, amused by the girls' reaction.

Tired after the day's walking, the coffee farm is a sight for sore eyes and tired feet. In our group of just four, we've seen and heard more on the trail than we would on a usual tour.

Sat in the common area, the girls waste no time in slopping cream on their insect bites.

I ask Mateo if just the two of us can do a similar walk tomorrow.

MATEO

A white, candy-floss ring of cloud encircles the pointed cone of Volcán Concepción. Wildlife sings loudly across its jungle covered slopes and across Lake Nicaragua. My first day on Omatepe Island has been magical.

The setting sun casts an orange sheet of warmth across the islands giving way to an umbrella of twinkling stars. I fall asleep in this place that time seems to have forgot, isolated in the middle of central America's largest lake.

Four separate travellers eat breakfast at four separate tables with eyes glued to their laptops while a rowdy British group command the largest table and talk loudly. One of them shuffles over to the desk in his flip flops, with his shorts hanging off his arse, and hands over his cup.

"CAV A TOP UP?" he says to the lady standing near the coffee pots in the kitchen.

Not even a please. His arrogance enrages me.

The audacity that she'll even understand what he's saying makes me embarrassed to be from the same country as him.

I avoid them all, swinging in my hammock until my guide Mateo arrives.

"Hola, amigo." He greets me, wearing the same clothes as yesterday's trek we did with the German girls.

"¿Vamos?"

He doesn't have to say it twice.

We follow a trail out the back of the farm and around Volcán Maderas in the opposite direction to yesterday. We pass through more cacao forest and reach a clearing.

"Mira." He points at the rocks embedded in the ground.

Looking closer, I can see carved patterns in them.

"Petroglifos," he says.

He pulls out a weed pipe with a Father Christmas face on it and stuffs half a pre smoked joint in the bowl.

I wander through the rocks in disbelief. Carvings of figures and animals, scratched into the stones over 10,000 years ago, surround me. I linger a while, thinking of the civilisations that would have passed through here.

Mateo passes me the little pipe for a puff.

Pushing on further, we cross rice and plátano fields, every so often catching a glimpse of a terracotta-tiled roof through the treeline. Dogs bark from their yards, desperate to know who or what is out here in the jungle. Butterflies, in a splendour of red and yellow, flutter around almost as if they are guarding us. Mateo carelessly pushes back a spider web with a stick. I think back to one I got tangled in on the way to the Mirador toilet shed.

Stepping across a stream, he stops. "Jaiba." He points down at the water's edge where a land crab snips its pincers at us.

The brown shelled creature is bigger than my outstretched hand and camouflaged against the similar tones of the earth. I carefully step over it, feeling glad he saw it.

"Las pipas," Mateo says. We listen to a faint rumbling sound that becomes nearer as we walk.

He brushes a few leaves away with his foot before tapping a PVC pipe that runs along the ground.

"Agua," he says.

The pipes tap off the waterfall to supply the houses in the area, much like the waterfall in Coroico, Bolivia that Dan and I had hiked to a few years back. I think back to those coca growers who stared down at us from the terraces.

The spray from the cascade of water cools me instantly. The waterfall has created a plunge pool surrounded by square shaped rocks. I take full advantage and dive into its refreshing and invigorating depths. Mateo merely wets his feet and splashes his face.

Arriving back at the finca, ever changing clouds sweep across the cone of Concepción evoking the odd lightning storm around its peak.

As night falls, the sky gradually changes colour while the lightning's forked veins light up the sky.

A young Austrian couple join me to watch the show. In their early 20s, they are dressed from head to toe in gym gear apart from the guy's bare and hairy chest. Bursting with excitement, they probe me for information about León and its surrounding volcanoes. I'm happy to share some scraps of information with them, but the guy butts in mid-sentence and proceeds to tell me in excruciating detail about his week in San Juan del Sur. A popular beach resort town. The highlight of the place being a 'tractor and trailer bar crawl' that loops the beach, delivering passengers to its many waterfront bars.

"We got the coolest free t-shirts!" the girl squarks.

I return to the light show in the sky.

Norvin, the driver of the 4x4 van, is not answering his phone about my pick-up in the morning. I swing in my hammock, fearing the worst. It's not the first time I've fallen for a scam. I search my guidebook for another mode of transport if he doesn't show tomorrow.

It seems a three-hour bus ride back to the ferry is the only alternative.

NORVIN

I wake at the coffee farm with both feet numb and swollen.

It seems the mosquitos have savaged my ankles and blocked the circulation of blood to my feet.

I massage them, squeezing out as much pus from the bites as possible until the feeling slowly returns to my toes.

Much to my relief, Norvin, the taxi van driver who had picked me up a few days ago and coerced me into paying a deposit for the return trip to the ferry, finally calls. "Amigo, se murió mi teléfono. Lo siento, amigo." His phone was dead last night, it seems; he'll pick me up soon.

I'm relieved he stuck to his word and that I won't be riding the local bus for three hours.

"¡Amigo, vamos!" he shouts, turning the 4x4 van around on the track outside the finca a few minutes later.

It's sad to be leaving the farm and its wonderful view, but I'm happy that Norvin has proved to be trustworthy. He skids out into the road and soon we catch up to a girl riding a motorbike in only swim shorts and a bra. I can see a nasty scar on her head and back.

"¡Es mi prima!" He says she's his cousin and the scars are from an accident involving the bike.

"¡Mira!" he says, looking in the rear-view mirror. A police motorcycle flies past us and pulls her over up ahead.

"¡Aiii, otra vez! ¡Puta policía!" he shouts, hitting the roof of the van with his fist as we whizz past them. Fucking cops again.

A BUS NORTH

"Nos vemos, amigo. Que le vaya muy bien." Norvin wishes me well.

Although only meeting a couple of locals here on Omatepe Island, they've made me wish I could stay longer.

'El ferry Che Guevara' is practically empty. Ten passengers make it hardly worth using the fuel. A kids' programme marred with interference, screens from an old TV hung on a wall with wire while the old vessel drags itself across the lake to the mainland. Back on land, the taxi skids to a stop at a very long line of cluttered market stalls in the transport hub town of Rivas. The driver tells me the terminal is a short walk from here and points through a tunnel of market vendors.

Idling in Bay 2 is a fire engine red chicken bus with chrome trimmings. The sign above the windscreen reads 'Managua non-expresso'.

Non express, I think to myself, knowing how many stops it will make. In no rush to be anywhere, I jump aboard.

The guy seated behind me keeps pulling himself up and peering over me in my seat. It's slightly unnerving, especially as he's not saying anything. I buy a bag of sweets from an aisle vendor and hand him a few. He sits down and starts sucking them loudly. They seem to get him off my case.

The route skirts past Volcán Masaya and gives a good view of the steaming crater and the cross on top. I think back to Volcán Telica and how we peered into the bubbling pit of lava.

A well-groomed man boards and begins seating people who have also joined at the same stop. I find this strange at first, but then realise his efforts are to gain listeners for his 'on board sermon' that unfolds. Making himself comfortable and in full view of the passengers, he stands in the aisle at the front of the bus and begins preaching abrasively about his twenty-three years in prison and drilling god's law into us.

I put my head back and pretend to be asleep.

The giant bus lines up at a small gas station in Managua waiting to refuel while the passengers alight and scatter. Across the road, Huembes terminal is a mess. The taxi touts stand like poised coyotes before a kill. I confidently stand my ground, speaking in Spanish and haggle them down 50 cordoba. I feel liberated knowing the language.

At UCA, a factory line of microbuses leans painfully on their maxed-out shock absorbers and one by one are filled up and sent on their way. I rest easy as I travel north towards León. I've faced my fears and safely navigated the place I have purposely avoided on other solo trips. The mean streets of Managua.

LA GRITERIA

My brain shifts up a gear in my morning Spanish lesson. I feel comfortable here in the León school I originally learnt the language in those few years ago. I briefly think back to my first lessons here with Hugo. I've come a long way since then. Patty, my new teacher, explains some new forms of conjugation I never knew existed and I leave a little smarter than I arrived. I meet with Hugo for another afternoon of madness.

'La Griteria', roughly translated, means 'The Yelling' and celebrates León's long history.

Judging by the town's streets now bursting at the seams, it's certainly a celebration not to be missed.

The festival is very popular with the people of León because it makes fun of the period of colonisation and is a joyous way of forgetting the brutal past inflicted by the Spanish.

The park is full, the plaza is full, in fact, everywhere is full. People have travelled from all over the department of León to be here. Nuns' veils are scattered throughout the sea of heads in the crowd.

Inside the cathedral some kind of ceremony is played out for an intimate private affair, while at its main entrance, a heaving crowd waits for the archbishop's speech. Two studded, giant, wooden, arched doors are opened, revealing him and his entourage. The moment his speech finishes, airhorns blast and fireworks are set off. The bells of the cathedral are rung violently while four traditional 'Gigantonas' – giant puppet costumes – spin around to the sound of the bells, while 'El Enano Cabezon' – the big-headed dwarf – bobs around beneath them. This bizarre-looking figure and its paper-mache head is worn by a small child in a suit, while the 'Gigantonas' are giant plait-haired dolls, wearing black puritan hats and frilled costumes stretched over wooden frames.

Air bombs and fireworks continue to explode in the sky, their ember red remains falling on the crowd that seem not in the slightest bit bothered about catching on fire.

Just when it can't get any crazier, three men with wooden boxes loaded with fireworks and strapped to their backs run around while rockets scream out horizontally from them and into the crowds. Streaks of light fly through the air in all directions.

These are the 'Toros Encuetados' – the surveying bulls.

I escape the mayhem in fear of losing an eye.

EL HOYO

They drag splintered planks of wood up to the edge of Cerro Negro's yellow-streaked sulphurous crater before scraping slowly back down the outside of its loose scoria cone. These fluorescent-green-boiler-suit-wearing adventure seekers are known as 'Volcano boarders'. I'm sure the view of Nicaragua below is stunning, but the suits, along with the effort needed to get any speed from the old planks during the descent, ensures it is something I will not be partaking in.

I'll be hiking to the mountain behind it – the one with a giant sinkhole in its side: 'El Hoyo' – The Hole.

At 5am the Quetzal trekkers office is a hive of activity. The French guide Matt has since moved on. A large group are gearing up for their boarding experience, a few others for the hike to El Hoyo. A shirtless guy introduces himself as Jim and shakes my hand from the hammock he swings in. Jim's arms are tattooed with assorted mountain bike parts, a pedal crank on his chest and a handle grip on his left bicep. A thin man called Phil and an American girl Ginny are our guides. Ginny approaches me to introduce herself, but she trips on a bag strap, sending her flying.

A loud Australian guy called Warren who we come to know as 'Wazza' comments at her stumble. "Waheey! She's had one too many!" he laughs.

We are told to take equal amounts from a communal pile of old tramping gear in the middle of the room and stuff it into the 40-litre backpacks Ginny hands out. Eight litres of water, a couple of sleeping bags and some assorted cooking items go into mine, as well as a tent.

"I got all our food, guys!" Ginny is very enthusiastic. She ushers us into the old school bus waiting outside.

We alight at a ranger station perched between Cerro Negro and the Las Pilas complex. Ginny and Phil check our packs and set the pace as we tread the black scoria track towards Cerro Negro.

This particular cone of the Las Pilas complex is said to be one of the youngest volcanoes in the world and first erupted from a quiet cornfield in 1850. It's been having growth spurts ever since.

At a fork in the road, Phil and his 'Volcano boarders' bear right while Ginny and our group head left towards the lush green slopes of Las Pilas. Being one of the easiest of Nicaragua's big hikes, apart from its completely shadeless three-hour climb, it attracts the most people due to the fact that every tour outfit in the country has it on their itinerary.

Two Spanish girls joining the hike remind me of the gay Swiss couple on the Telica hike. They wear matching identical Nike rain jackets in a lemon shade, tangerine orange wispy running shorts and brand-new Nike trainers. Possibly not the best choice for the razor-sharp volcanic gravel. Bike fanatic Jim won't shut up about being able to string his bloody hammock up somewhere and the loud Australian, Wazza, is arguing about something with his wife Dayna. Already it seems like they've only left Australia so they can complain about everything. They remind me of many travellers I've previously met.

We hike for an hour or so before reaching the base of Las Pilas, passing through scantly wooded areas where the round and rock-hard jicaro fruit grow from thick trunks.

"*Maaaaayte*." Wazza baas like a sheep. "Ya can't eet 'em and they're hard as fuck."

Nobody in the group replies.

Our lunch area is riddled with hidden mini-sinkholes that would swallow us if not for Ginny pointing them out. She lays out tortillas, boiled eggs, tomatoes and some fruit on a ground sheet.

"No meat, aye?" Shayne points out the obvious, to which no one replies.

Hammock Jim was already in his strung-up sling before Ginny had the food laid out. He waits, staring at us to congratulate him.

Nobody in the group speaks.

Beginning the steep ascent up the park's second most active peak, the Spanish girls are already complaining about their shoes being ripped and have since ditched their sweat drenched matching jackets.

The trail winds through old forests and craters where butterflies outnumber us and noisy gangs of white-throated magpie-jays squawk above. How regal they look as they proudly parade their curved crests of feathers that rise up from their heads. The water breaks become more frequent, and our pace slows to a crawl.

As if out of nowhere and to our left through the trees, the wonder we have come to see appears.

The almost perfectly round sinkhole looks like a giant portal to the centre of the earth. We all stop in our tracks and stare at the magnificent sight.

"Keep moving, guys!" Ginny calls back at us,

"Alright, maayte, we jus wanna have alook addit. Blardy Shelia don't warnna stop, does she," Wazza barks back, looking for affirmation.

"We've got all the time in the world to stare at it once we're at camp." Ginny counters Wazza's negativity with a cheerful reply.

The tents are pitched on a grassy plateau where a few trees grow at the edge. Ginny collects and stacks sticks in a circular rock-walled fire pit.

I head over to the Spanish girls who look like they are having a bit of trouble with their tent.

"Vee are fine, sankyou." The one not tangled in guy ropes is clearly lying as she helps unravel her friend.

Jim is desperately trying to figure out a way of suspending his hammock between the only two trees up here which are, much to the group's amusement, just slightly too far apart.

"Does anyone have para cord or rope?"

Nobody in the group replies.

His look of defeat is priceless, and I'm relieved that our view this evening will not be filled with him and his bike shop of tattoos swaying in his precious hammock.

"Strings too blardy short, maayte." Wazza adds his unwanted and obvious input to Jim's dilemma.

With camp set up, we climb up to the hole and lie over its sides, peering in.

"Blardy steeenks, dunnit!" Here he is again, old mate Wazza.

I've had it! I creep behind him and push him with all my might into the boiling hot hole, watching his hairy farmer legs disappear forever. A cartoony plunge into the fiery abyss. Of course, I don't do that, but I feel the group is all wishing somebody would. Possibly even Dayna, his wife.

Ginny cooks up a huge pot of curry over the fire as light dims the view below. The lake-filled crater of Asososca dominates while Lake Managua sits motionless like a giant puddle with the cone of Volcán Momotombo poking up from its middle. The evening closes under a blanket of stars.

Ginny is up at the crack of dawn shaking our tents for the sunrise as the fading colours of last night happen again in reverse.

Breakfast is followed by a camp pack-up a lot speedier than yesterday's set-up, and we trudge down through the farmland before arriving at Volcán Asososca and its crater lake. Howler monkeys call out across the water from the jungle that wraps around it. Jim, Wazza, Dayna and I swim in the water. Phil, Ginny and the Spanish girls dip their feet.

Back out at the side of the road a bus pulls in.

"We're gonna go to La Paz Centro for some food, guys!" Ginny is happy she's guided the trip without a hiccup.

We enter the outskirts of the small town of La Paz Centro, a place I remember visiting with Dan, Eva, Carlos and the kids back in 2009 to visit Eva's 104-year-old great-grandma. I briefly wonder if she's still alive as we eat our chicken rice and beans.

"That dunny steenks, maayte!" Not wanting us to forget him just yet, Wazza returns from the toilet waving his hand past his nose.

GISSELLE

I feel the need to escape for a night and Hugo suggests a little port town called Corinto about an hour north of León on Nicaragua's northwest coast.

"¿Que busca, chele?" A fat man selling cold cans of drink at the León terminal asks me what I'm looking for.

"El micro a Chinandega," I answer.

He begrudgingly points to the bus I need, frowning that I haven't bought a drink.

The packed bus rumbles north for a half-hour to Chinandega's terminal where a man is stood screaming. "¡Corinto!" He shoves people into another microbus.

I join them and get pushed up into the mess, miraculously finding a seat while expertly buying a Coke from a woman outside who hands it through the window. An old lady sat next to me makes quesillos in banana leaves to sell on the tiny bus. The heat is intensified by the smell of the cheese that fills them along with more sweaty passengers who squeeze on. I watch them disentangle themselves to get off – this is truly a skill that can only by perfected by years of practice.

The Corinto 'terminal' is merely a concrete shelter in a dirt carpark. A clutter of undernourished boys in branded t-shirts wait on taxi trikes to transport people into the village. Before I reach them, they are all swiftly commandeered, leaving me alone in unfamiliar surroundings and unsure of which direction to walk in. Not wanting to look lost, I straighten up and follow the route that the trike taxis took. Walking in a no mans land along the side of a deserted road for 15 minutes, I finally reach civilisation where people stare at me in bewilderment. A large grand building appears on the opposite side of the road, the pink and blue colours of its façade divided horizontally by a white marble strip with the words 'Teatro municipal de Corinto' in gold across it. The theatre strikes a vast contrast with the run-down abodes that surround it.

An older man on a trike squeaks past me.

"¿A dónde?" he asks.

I give the address of a hotel and he tells me to hop in. The guy is an interesting sort. He wears a Bob Marley t-shirt and his trike is painted in the colours of the Rasta flag. I learn that he lived in Florida for twenty-three years after he left Nicaragua during the revolution where he was a Contra soldier fighting for the Honduran sect backed by Somoza and the US. I imagine Hugo's dislike for this man who would have once been his enemy at war. He tells me all manner of things in our short ride.

Squeaking down narrow streets that are similar to León's, the trike stops outside a building with brown bars across its windows and a door opening masked by a mosquito net.

"¡Aqui esta!" he says "¡Hotel Tortuguita!"

The paint is new and it's the tidiest looking place on the street. A short girl appears in the doorway. She is beautiful. Dressed in a denim mini skirt and a tight striped t-shirt, she flicks her blonde highlighted hair away from her face, revealing two beautiful brown eyes like deep liquid pools. Rattling off something to the trike man through her smile, she beckons me to come in.

"Me llamo Gisselle. Bienvenidos." She welcomes me with a smile.

The foyer is a wooden panelled living room complete with reception desk, couch and TV area. The floor tiles are so shiny I can see my reflection. Gisselle shows me to my room where I merely dump my bag, and follow her back to the foyer lounge, making myself comfortable on the couch next to her. I spend the afternoon backstroking in her beautiful liquid eyes while she watches back-to-back telenovelas.

As the evening darkens, rain sets in and the dogs of the neighbourhood start to howl. Moments after retiring to my room, there is a knock at the door. It's Gisselle, who has locked up for the night and is keen to keep chatting. I invite her in and we talk about this and that until one thing leads to another and we spend the next few hours cuddling and giggling.

Downstairs in the foyer the following morning, Gisselle has arranged for her friend to watch the reception so she can show me her little town. The desperate streets crumble and flake paint in the breeze from the Pacific. Two seafood restaurants near the main plaza have seen better days.

Days when they served the cruise liner ships that have since re routed and stop off elsewhere.

In the centre of the plaza stands a bizarre two storey-high town clock, set in a giant red cricket ball balanced on top of a structure resembling a power pylon. A trike guy pulls alongside us sucking through his teeth to get our attention.

"¿Que haces aqui?" He asks what we are doing here.

I tell him we are exploring, sparking a lengthy conversation. He tells me the tourists from the cruise ships don't speak much and it's nice to chat with a foreigner. I imagine the old American couples in pastel-coloured swishy shell suits from the cruise ships, looking in horror at the neglected buildings and fearful of these shifty men riding their trikes.

Gisselle, insistent on holding my hand, leads me into a tiny indoor fish market buzzing with flies, telling me we can grab breakfast. The foul stench and grease-stained walls are not exactly what I'd had in mind but when a whole grilled fish, gallo pinto, chorizo, scrambled eggs and an iridescent purple cactus juice is placed in front of me, I momentarily forget the smell. Gisselle smiles, eagerly awaiting me to try the feast she's ordered.

"Pitaya." She points at the juice and waves a few flies from her food.

Back at hotel Tortuguita, we share a kiss and exchange numbers. I catch a taxi from the hotel door all the way to Chinandega. Dogs jump out of our way as the driver speedily skirts through tiny villages en route.

I drink a Coke and think about this mysterious girl I've met as the bus returns me to León. Those eyes, that infectious giggle. A kid in front throws up on his t-shirt. His mother, obviously well versed in this, swiftly rips the shirt from his torso, mops up the puke around his mouth and rolls it up, stuffing it in a plastic bag.

As the little bus continues south along the Pan Americana highway with the waft of vomit swirling through its interior, I 'm reminded of the pink bus in the Bolivian mountains and the almost exact same scenario.

MATAGALPA

A blue pickup truck rolls through León's terminal, its rear tray full of giant squealing pigs caked in dried mud while the usual barrage of buses and taxis jostle for space. I'm almost run over twice in the chaos as we walk over to our bus, already bursting at the seams. Like a pile of iron filings being drawn by a magnet, impatient passengers surge towards the door, blocking it as they jam themselves in.

"Idiotas," Hugo mumbles.

A few days ago, he raised my hopes with a promise of visiting his daughter 'Blanca' in the northern highlands of Matagalpa – but then he dashed them a day later, telling me he couldn't afford it. The excuse he gave was without conviction, but the price of our travel and food for the weekend wasn't going to break my bank, so I agreed to shout him.

And here we are, with pre-booked seats. I'm delighted and settle in for the ride. It's only when the bus pulls onto the road that I realise our seat is directly over the rear wheel arch.

"¡Ai mierda!" Hugo curses, as he squeezes in with his knees up around his ears.

A woman sits down in the seat across the aisle. She's holding a huge birthday cake. How she thinks it's going to be in one piece after two hours in this death trap, I have no idea. If it doesn't get squashed, it's sure to melt in this inferno.

We part the sea of microbuses, rickshaws and dogs, scraping out onto the highway. A breeze flowing through the top windows takes little edge off the heat. The passengers smirk at a foreign traveller wiggling his hips to the Reggaeton blasting from the speakers. Hugo mercilessly laughs out loud.

The northern mountains are reminiscent of Ecuador. Women scrub soapy piles of brightly striped clothes on flat rocks and hang them to dry on barbed-wire fences along the roadside. The green carpet of forest behind them reminds me of Hugo's stories of wartime Nicaragua. A time he's clearly not thinking about right now as he plays 'snake' on his little mobile phone.

"¡Hijo de puta!" He curses as he dies over and over again.

Dusk falls as the bus pulls into Matagalpa terminal and the lady opposite's cake has miraculously survived the ordeal. I wait alongside a row of closed roller doors while Hugo takes a leak under a 'No urinating' sign.

"¡Bienvenidos a Matagalpa!" he laughs, looking over his shoulder and pissing against the wall.

A stream of taxis ignores us as we try to flag them down, but eventually we are whisked to the other side of the city.

"¡Aqui esta!" Hugo chirps.

We pull up outside what looks like a bright red Chinese-themed restaurant.

"¡La casa de China!" he laughs.

An oriental-style pitched roof shelters six families in separate rooms. Wet laundry hangs over the railings of the first-floor balcony that looks down over a large central ground floor hall.

A stray dog with a skin rash and a one-eyed cat called Shakira wander around the space.

"Eso gato es la policía," Hugo says, laughing. The police cat.

"Es mio," says a stocky man appearing through a doorway wearing a cop uniform.

He passes me a cup with brown lumps in it, explaining it's 'Chica', a fermented sugar water and pineapple skin drink. A muscly young man hugs Hugo and introduces himself as Brayan, Blanca's boyfriend. I'd already met him at Hugo's in León when I returned from the Telica volcano trek, but he doesn't remember. He lays out a schedule of his plans for our weekend like he's conducting an interview. I learn that he's 26 years old, a devout Christian and an unemployed agriculture diploma holder. His pride for Matagalpa shines as he reads through our schedule.

Within 15 minutes of arriving at the Chinese house, Brayan borrows a motorbike from the yard and we whizz without helmets up through the steep, wet and dimly illuminated streets to the hospital. A grid of orange streetlights twinkle below us across the valley. Brayan stops and pulls a wrapped sandwich from the helmet box.

"Es comida por mi amor." He disappears to deliver the sandwich to Blanca, who is working the hospital night shift.

I stare out across the grid of lights, happy to be in such unfamiliar surroundings. Brayan returns and takes me on a quick tour of the town, stopping in Plaza Morazán where a group of young men and women congregate and laugh among themselves.

"Prostitutas." He clearly disapproves of the group. I'm unsure why.

It seems Brayan is overly occupied by how to impress me for the next two days. He insists I take his bed, leaving him to sleep on a foam mattress on the floor. I graciously accept. I guess he would probably sleep in Blanca's bed if Hugo wasn't here.

Glorious sunshine and the sound of a gardener's machete wake me. The communal area is in full swing when I enter. Blanca and Brayan brew a pot of coffee. Hugo continues to play 'snake' on his phone.

The four of us take a walk along a caramel brown river that runs through the middle of town.

The river is lined with tin-roofed houses on either side, their brick walls oozing crusted drips of dried cement.

We arrive at an uncared park with a rusty climbing frame, the swings long since snapped off and never replaced. Brayan points to a dozen cages containing animals.

"Es un Parque Zoologico chiquito," he says proudly.

We've arrived at the local 'mini zoo'.

A man shovels animal droppings into a small cart behind him. The animals sit lifeless in their cages. A couple of old monkeys, an owl and a pack of foxes look at us with sad eyes. A crocodile lies motionless in a crumbling concrete paddling pool. It could be dead. The sight upsets me. These animals would probably not survive if they were freed.

At the edge of a muddy football field, the roofs of tiny adobe houses are weighed down with old tyres. Hugo tells me that similar ones exist on the hillsides, built illegally on farming land.

I sense that Brayan is a little ashamed and would rather keep these particular facets of his cherished town hidden.

"OK, we go the best place in Matagalpa," he tries his English. "¡El Museo de café!"

The large sign on the green door tells us the coffee museum is closed. Brayan is deflated, Blanca is tired, Hugo laughs.

Back at La Casa de China, a thin stick of a man in a sheepskin jacket and wellington boots introduces himself as José Luís. He shakes my hand in his bony fingers. Brayan persuades him to drive us to a lookout point. Leaning proudly against his rusty Nissan pickup truck, he tells us he can take us for five dollars but will need a battery for the engine. I look at the truck and suppress a laugh: the wing mirrors are hanging off and it has a flat tyre.

The cop agrees to lend us his battery and they connect it with some wire pulled from the fence, while Brayan and I change the flat with a spare wheel that we find in the tall grass. José Luís tips the remainder of an old gas can that may or may not contain gasoline into the tank, and seals the open hole with a rag.

Everybody cheers when the engine fires to life – their elation a good indication the truck hasn't been driven in years. The old Nissan miraculously delivers us to a dirt track at the top of a steep hill where the sun beats down on a manicured area of hedgerows looking at the view of the city below.

I can see how much pleasure Hugo is getting out of spending some quality time with his daughter. It was worth the trip just for that.

The city sprawls up the valleys in all directions from a blinding white cathedral that commands the centre of the view. We sit for a while and watch rain clouds move in.

"¡Vamos!" Brayan herds everyone back to the pickup truck.

Within minutes, the steep cobbled streets are now running rivers of water and I fear we'll be swept in the current or worse still, the old Nissan's brakes give out. Somehow José Luís delivers us back home safely, where the unfit relic rolls to a stop in the tall grass of the garden.

AROMAS

Tinny music blares out from the rafters of Matagalpa's indoor markets. The morning chill of the northern highlands of Nicaragua is a far cry from the inferno-like heat of León.

"Es tia mía." Brayan introduces his auntie, a heavy-set woman wrapped in a woollen shawl.

Stood behind stacks of carrots, nuts and little pyramids of red berries, his auntie beams a smile of gold teeth. The whole of Brayan's family seems to work here under the same roof. His uncle wiggles a wispy moustache on his top lip as we arrive at his stall. He sends us on our way with a bag of hot sugary donuts.

Back out in the street, hocks of meat, animal parts and pig heads hang outside stores as we walk under a chaotic mess of overhead signs. Brayan diverts left down an alley where we are immediately hit with a mouth-watering smell.

"Ah, huele maravilloso," he says, sniffing the rich aroma lingering in the air.

"Los mejores en Nicaragua."

According to him, the best Nacatamales in the country are found right here in this alley, a cherished dish of corn masa, lard, vegetables and a little egg-shaped chilli, all tied up in banana leaf.

A crudely painted sign hangs next to the door Brayan knocks in the dead-end lane.

'Nacatamal – se vende'

An old woman opens the door letting out a deliciously rich waft of warm, flavoursome steam.

"Solo los dos," she says: two left.

It's only 8.30am.

Unravelling the large banana leaves back at La Casa de China, we find a doughy mix of pork rump, orange juice, potatoes and onions. We tuck into them greedily, finishing them in record time.

Not satisfied with his guide services, Brayan borrows a motorbike for a trip to a place called 'Apante'. The bike grinds up through steeper streets than we've yet attempted. The old Nissan wouldn't have stood a chance up these. Cobbled lanes of tin shacks climb further up the hillside. I lean forward to stay on. I'm literally sitting on his shoulders.

The road turns to dirt and ends at the edge of a green forest.

"OK, vamos." He locks the bike and takes the lead, disappearing into the trees.

Spiders and butterflies I haven't seen before are pointed out and named as we walk. We reach a bridge constructed of bamboo poles shaken to pieces by the rushing river that slides dangerously close underneath it. Parts of it have been crudely tied back together with twine and wire but it's far from a convincing job.

"¿Podemos pasar?" I'm curious if we'll be able to cross.

"¡Si hombre!" he shouts back, smiling, already halfway across it on his hands and knees.

The Jimmy Cavalier jeans I bought for a song in the flashy mall in San Salvador were the worst choice of attire for this jaunt and, now saturated, are almost impossible to move in, and leak dark indigo on to my shoes. I dread to think how stained my legs will be when I take them off tonight. I crawl slowly across the slippery bridge spanning the river.

As we near the top, I hear a rustling in the bushes. Suddenly a girl runs out from behind a tree and tosses a bloody tampon over her shoulder. Brayan pretends not to see. The poor startled girl is ruining his efforts to impress me.

We reach a wooden viewing deck that provides views of the town below but the startled girl and her family have occupied it to bursting.

"¿Cómo llegan?" I'm curious to how this not-so-healthy-looking bunch got up here.

"Hay una routa mas fácil." *Now he tells me there is an easier route to reach the top.*

The next morning is damp and cold, but Brayan's keen that before our return to León this evening, we visit the house where Carlos Fonseca died. The site is an interesting look into the Sandinistas' founding member and a man who essentially changed the country. Hugo shows an especially deep interest in the tiny abode and the leader of the liberating army he fought for.

We meet an old poet friend of Brayan splayed out on a park bench. The man is wider than he is tall, and his breath is putrid.

"¡Ugghh!" Hugo waves his hand across his mouth when the fat man isn't looking.

"¡El hallotosis! ¡Que terrible!" He pinches his nose as we walk to the terminal.

Brayan is sad as we say our farewells. He has made my time here a fascinating experience. I cannot express my gratitude enough.

Boarding the bus, Hugo pinches his nose again.

"¡Huele a meado!"

An ending to a remarkable day: the bus stinks of piss.

CORINTO

I'm back at the León terminal waiting for a bus only a day after returning from my trip with Hugo to the Matagalpa highlands.

Gisselle has invited me back to Corinto.

A spherical woman pushes an old black cauldron disguised as a BBQ on wheels. Along its side reads 'Cosas de Horno' in drippy white letters. Her 'Things of the Oven' cart isn't attracting much attention, nor her desperate screams that try to sell the tired looking meat hanging over its sides.

Swallowing my shoulder with a flabby armpit, a lady squeezes in next to me on the micro bus. Her pit locks me in place like a Venus fly trap and goes about dissolving my shoulder with its vinegary venom during the hour it takes to travel to Chinandega.

At the Corinto bus stand, I catch a trike to Gisselle's with a young man called Antonio. He takes an interest in my tattoos and rolls his sleeve up, proudly showing me a little smudgy lion.

We squeak up outside the hotel. Gisselle is in the doorway with a beaming smile. Dressed in a pair of black leggings and a frilled black top, she looks amazing. Inside, a telenovela plays in the background while she fixes her hair. A child propels himself across the tiled floor on an old skateboard.

We take flight to a fish restaurant.

Once a hot spot enjoyed by the cruise ship passengers of years gone by, the restaurant is void of all customers today. Peeling walls and crumbling concrete bannisters eroded by the salt waves stand in stark contrast to the white cotton tables cloths laid with silver cutlery. From our balcony table, a blue canopy of sky hovers over a cluster of islands where palm trees sprout. Gisselle chooses the cow's tongue and I take a local fish in garlic called covina. Giant pelicans fly by and dive for fish between small fishing boats that bob in the water and off in the distance, the silhouette of a large cargo ship waits patiently for clearance to port.

Hand in hand, I'm guided through the streets of the shantytown. She grabs a beach cruiser bike from outside a random house. She says it's hers, telling me someone borrowed it a week ago and never returned it. I'm lost in the slow pace of this little town. I'm lost in her onyx eyes.

It feels a world away from the world I know. Dogs wander the dirt lanes, cohabiting them with the taxi trikes that squeak by. I imagine myself living here and having a family with a girl like Gisselle. Maybe I could work at the port and sustain this life I'm daydreaming about. She snaps me from my thoughts, reminding me I'll need to catch the last bus and hails a trike. We kiss and promise to stay in touch.

I wonder if I'll ever see her again.

I daydream about my new imaginary life in Corinto as the trike squeaks its way to the bus.

Back in Chinandega, rows of women swat flies from mangos in wicker baskets. The micro bus is hot, cramped and accompanied by a sweaty guy playing a shit game on his little phone at full volume.

I sit next to him and the techno tune for a frustrating forty minutes as he repeatedly dies at exactly the same stage over and over again.

ZOO

Dirty micro buses splash through the rain and mud at León's terminal. A group of leather-jacketed men purse their lips like they are about to blow trumpets, crowing calls of destinations. They're a happy bunch, firing cheeky comments to passers-by and play-fighting with each other. A mud-splattered taxi slides around in the slushy lot before coming to a halt. Eva waves and calms her excited girls as we meet. We're off to the zoo – a special outing Eva and I have planned for her daughters, Florencia and Dani. Eva, the teacher who first taught me Spanish while staying in Nicaragua in 2009 – and who subsequently became a romantic interest at that time – is someone I still have a special connection with, even if now only platonically.

We carefully navigate our way over to the bus through the brown slush. From the shore of Lake Managua, we're rewarded with wide views of the volcanic cones of Momotombo and Momotombito as the bus heads south.

In Managua's frenetic terminal, I hold the girls' hands as we walk the rows of taxis and microbuses. People are extremely helpful as we search for our bus, guiding us directly to it. Being with the children disarms any would-be opportunists. A blue-eyed, curly-haired boy with a cheeky quip secures us seats and collects our fare.

Two hours later, we push ourselves out at the zoo. The entrance is at the end of a long road flanked by tall white kerbs holding overgrown planters. I buy jocote fruit; Eva laughs that I purchase a whole bag. (She failed to tell me the sour green berries are for cooking only.)

"¡Típico chele, jaja!" I find a bin and toss the bag away.

A giant stuffed crocodile called Roco lies on a rotting plinth beside a war-torn ticket booth. With patches of scales missing from years of rubbing and poking hands, the poor thing is a sad sight. The girls shy away, petrified, when I put my hand out to take them closer. I pay 20 cordoba each for Eva and the girls and the 100 'Extranjero' fee for myself.

If there was ever a reason to put an end to animals in captivity, then look no further than the animals in this zoo. Two old Guardabarranco birds sit motionless on their perch – so old, their tail feathers have fully grown.

"¡Muy gordos!" Florencia points at their fat bellies.

A white and yellow Indian python squirms its long body against the dirty glass of a small fish tank, and an old primate sits slumped at the bottom of a tree in his enclosure chewing a bamboo stick and looking demented. A gum disease has spread to his cheek, exposing his jaw and the inside of his mouth reminding me of the living road kill dog in the Salvadoran mountains. A sign on his cage reads 'Pipo the Ape'. Ushering the girls on, we move to the guinea pigs, otters and stoats that roam in a less restricted area. The girls spend the most time here, fascinated by the not so familiar animals.

We have our own chaos to tend to. Dani pisses herself instead of asking to use the toilet.

This enrages Eva, who scolds the child as she cries standing in her pink, urine-stained sweatpants in the middle of the zoo. Eva refuses to change her in the bathrooms, with their doorless cubicles and two half-smashed urinals hanging on the wall. It seems Dani will be wearing her piss-soaked pants while we continue.

Thousands of butterflies fill the air amidst a sea of tropical flowers in the netted 'Mariposario' enclosure. Florencia, so excited by this before entering, now cowers behind her mum, scared of the harmless creatures. Dani sobs quietly, still drenched in her own urine. In a small shop outside, Eva lays the child down on her back, bagging the pissy pants and fashioning a skirt from a towel in her bag. Dani is mortified at her new nappy she's been forced to wear. Poor kid.

A blue and white chicken bus pulls up. We add to its overloaded cargo.

Back in a wet and muddy UCA terminal in Managua, we are squeezed out of the doors like pastry through rollers. Exchanging hugs, I'm glad the farewell is not as upsetting as I'd imagined. We're exhausted from our day at the zoo and the girls are excited about seeing their grandma.

Eva and I part gracefully – and platonically.

If ever there was a day that even slightly swayed my thoughts on having my own children, this could have been it.

OUTBOUND

Hugo wakes with me at 03:15 to say his farewells. It seems so soon after my arrival here. It is a dark Nicaraguan night, late September 2013. It feels like my farewell with Gina and El Salvador was only a few days ago.

The last three months have drawn a lot of the introvert out of me. It's given me an even greater understanding of this part of the world and its people, Hugo being one of them. I will miss his company and the laughter we've shared.

We hold a strong embrace for a moment, both knowing it could be years before we see each other again. Carlos the Spanish school's preferred taxi driver pulls up in his dented Hyundai outside. The last time I saw him was a couple of years ago when he picked me up at Managua airport. I'm amazed he remembers me.

The night is dark and wet as motorbikes fly past in the opposite direction with no headlights. He asks me about my adventures over the past few months while we speed through the rain.

A dark shape scurries along the pavement up ahead, illuminated as it runs under each streetlight.

"¿Que es?" I ask him.

"Rata," he says casually. "Muy grande." A giant rat, the size of a piglet.

Before we reach it, it darts into the undergrowth.

The rain pelts down outside, cutting through our full beams that light up the dark highway and then another shape, this time in the middle of the road.

As we get closer, it looks like it could be a discarded rubbish bag, maybe a pile of clothes.

Carlos guides the Hyundai straight over the top of it, ensuring it passes between the wheels, untouched.

"Boa," he says, again very casually.

"A fucking Boa constrictor!" I shout. He laughs at my outburst.

Soon we are among the corrugated and deserted outskirts of Managua airport and finally the drop off point. Pulling my bag from the boot of the taxi, he shakes my hand, wishes me well and jumps back into his car. I amble along the glass frontage of the airport. The lights are on, but it seems nobody is home and I almost bang into the automatic sliding doors when they don't open.

I look back to see the rear lights of Carlos' taxi disappearing into the night.

I'm alone. It's 5am and I feel a little uneasy. A nerve-racking fifteen minutes pass until a minivan pulls up and unloads a young national football team in matching blue and white tracksuits. At the same time, the doors make a clicking sound and slide open.

Soon the airport is busy with a variety of people from different walks of life. Businessmen line up to check in suitcases alongside backpackers and families going on holiday.

The crowds are far more orderly than the bus station chaos I'm used to. The armed airport security guards see to that.

Check in is an easy process. I think about Dan and our agonising Mexico City airport experience a few years ago.

Day breaks through the boarding gate windows, revealing a control tower surrounded by coconut trees.

A row of retired planes with grass growing around their wheels sit lifeless at the side of the runway. Their proximity to landing and departing planes would most certainly be a safety hazard in other countries. Clearly no problem here.

I imagine an airport official merely shrugging and saying that phrase I've heard so often. "No hay problema, es normal."

I cross the potholed runway and climb the stairs into the aircraft. It seems like only yesterday I was walking across the tarmac in the evening heat in Santa Elena, Guatemala. So much has happened since then: the jungle, the school, the mountains. New friends.

I find my seat and settle in. The plane waits for a half-hour due to 'computer problems'.

We take off with a bump and fly north. I look down on a thin silver vein coursing its way through a carpet of dense green wilderness.

A river winding its way through the Honduran jungle.

'El Hoyo' campsite, Nicaragua.

EPILOGUE

"So ya'll live in Nuuuu Zeeelayand. Ya'll born in Engayland and ya'll arriving from Nicaragua?" The passport officer speaks in a southern drawl. The buxom lady of African American descent smiles suspiciously at me.

The arrival back after a long stay in Latin America is always strange. We have just disembarked from the plane in Atlanta, Georgia, and I'm not sure how to respond.

"Ya'll wawna explain that to me?"

I'm uncertain what there is to really explain, but I give her a little more information about my trip. It seems to satisfy her suspicions; she waves me on through.

Atlanta airport is the busiest I've ever experienced. A constant rush of people come at me from all directions, their wheelie luggage bags nipping at my ankles like handbag dogs. I escape the chaos, ducking into a fast-food counter and order up fries and a soda. I think back to the thimble of mash potato at Guatemala airport and how long ago that now seems. News networks force their stories through the television screens while patrons stuff burgers into their mouths. I eat the food slowly until my plane is boarding and make a dash for the gate at the last minute, walking straight on.

In the seat next to me is a heavy framed rapper with gold teeth. His red and orange camouflage shorts are big enough to fit three or four humans inside and sag halfway down his legs. The red theme continues with his XXXXL t-shirt, basketball boots and boxers, that, due to the saggy shorts, are literally on full show.

On the top of his chubby right hand supported by the arm rest, a tattoo reads, 'If it ain't making money, it ain't worth doin.' He raps to himself for a while before fidgeting in his sleep the rest of the flight.

The sky mall magazine is full of useless things to buy but cures my boredom for ten minutes as I peruse the junk it advertises. A remote control for your remote control, a sail that attaches to a skateboard and a training manual to teach a cat to shit in a toilet. I turn on my in-seat TV to find everything is 'pay to watch' except the little 2D plane that crawls slowly across the world map towards Los Angeles. Wobbly ladies bash into each other like bumper cars at a fairground as they pass awkwardly in the aisle of the plane for their frequent toilet visits, and an old man in a trucker hat and dungarees shakes every head rest as he steadies himself en route to the toilet. His attire reminds me of 'Uncle Jesse' from the TV show *The Dukes of Hazzard*. Soon I'm drifting off to sleep, dreaming back to Saturday afternoons when I was a boy, eating fish and chips on the sofa with my little brother and watching that very same show.

I'm in a crowded schoolyard, surrounded by kids. Gina towers over me, dressed as a 'Gigantona' tearing open black plastic bags of steaming orange 'sopa de pata' soup. On a giant screen, Uncle Jesse's nephews, Bo and Luke Duke are being chased by a tribe of bloodthirsty Mayan warriors down a chalky jungle road. Giant rats appear out in front blocking their escape, but they avoid both the rodents and Mayans, as they jump the broken section of a wooden jungle bridge in their bright orange car.

The wheels of the 1969 Dodge Charger squeal as Bo, Luke and Uncle Jesse touch down.

Now I'm awake and we are on the runway at LAX. With eyes still closed, I recount my bizarre dream while the plane taxis to the gate. My mind is moving rapidly over the last three months. How quickly they've flashed by.

Opening my eyes, I'm shaken back to First World reality in an instant.

My face is inches from a clump of pubic hair that sprouts from the top of the rapper's red boxer shorts as he reaches into the overhead compartment above me.

ABOUT THE AUTHOR

Originally born in Berkshire in the UK, Darren Howman's passion for skateboarding sparked a travel bug at an early age, taking him far and wide across the globe. With this grew a descriptive, humorous and deeply observational outlook on people and everyday life.

Darren's first book *Perro Callejero* was published by Everytime Press in July 2020.

Now a citizen of Auckland, New Zealand, Darren manages the inner workings of film set infrastructure for international and local productions of all shapes and sizes.

Find more about Darren on Instagram at @daz_dot_com

Also from
EVERYTIME PRESS

everytimepress.com/everytime-press-catalogue/

Perro Callejero
by Darren Howman

ISBN: 978-1-925536-96-6 (paperback) / 978-1-925536-97-3 (eBook)

Nine months with only a backpack. Nine months to explore fourteen countries, some places welcoming, some inhospitable. Nine months of adventure, anxiety, connection, distance and encounters with the new unknown … all seen with fresh eyes and little expectation of what's to come next. Unusually honest, often hilarious and always heartfelt, *Perro Callejero* reveals two young lads unwittingly provoking danger, causing embarrassment, forging friendships, even making enemies. This is a raw adventure tale from the perspective of an everyman – not a seasoned traveller, not a polished chronicler. But a keen observer of human beings – both the heart and the folly.

Also from
EVERYTIME PRESS

everytimepress.com/everytime-press-catalogue/

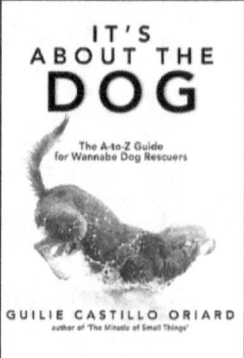
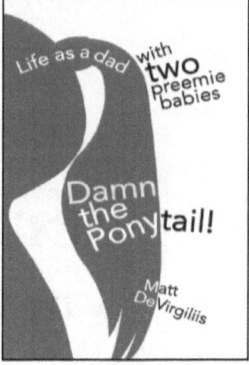

- Lenin's Asylum by A. A. Weiss
  ISBN: 978-1-925536-50-8 (paperback) / 978-1-925536-51-5 (eBook)
- Sydneyside Reflections by Mark Crimmins
  ISBN: 978-1-925536-07-2 (paperback) / 978-1-925536-08-9 (eBook)
- This Is Me, Being Brave by Len Kuntz
  ISBN: 978-1-922427-63-2 (paperback) / 978-1-922427-68-7 (eBook)
- All Roads Lead from Massilia by Philip Kobylarz
  ISBN: 978-1-925536-27-0 (paperback) / 978-1 925536-28-7 (eBook)
- It's About the Dog by Guilie Castillo Oriard
  ISBN: 978-1-925536-19-5 (paperback) / 978-1-925536-20-1 (eBook)
- Damn the Ponytail! by Matt DeVirgiliis
  ISBN: 978-1-922427-72-4 (paperback) / 978-1-922427-80-9 (eBook)

www.ingramcontent.com/pod-product-compliance
Lightning Source LLC
Chambersburg PA
CBHW032125160426
43197CB00008B/516